Memoirs of a Jewish Extremist

Memoirs of a Jewish Extremist

AN AMERICAN STORY

Yossi Klein Halevi

Little, Brown and Company
BOSTON   NEW YORK   TORONTO   LONDON

First Edition

Library of Congress Cataloging-in-Publication Data

Klein Halevi, Yossi.
    Memoirs of a Jewish extremist : an American story / Yossi Klein
Halevi.
        p.   cm.
    ISBN 0-316-49860-2
    1. Klein Halevi, Yossi. 2. Jews—United States—
Biography. 3. Children of Holocaust survivors—United States—
Biography. 4. Jewish radicals—United States—Biography.
I. Title.
E184.J5K54   1995
973'.04924'0092—dc20
    [B]   95-13589

10   9   8   7   6   5   4   3   2   1

HAD

Published simultaneously in Canada
by Little, Brown & Company (Canada) Limited

Printed in the United States of America

For my parents, and Chani

Contents

Author's Note

ALL THE EVENTS and characters in this book are real. Some of the characters' names, as well as some identifying traits, have been changed, especially those of former militants of the Jewish Defense League. Most now lead quiet and respectable lives — very different from their teenage years and the events described here.

Memoirs of a Jewish Extremist

One

Planet of the Jews

MY FATHER lived in a hole. The hole was four feet deep, six feet long, and eight feet wide — high enough only for crouching, but long enough to lie in.

Two men shared the hole with my father. While it was light, they played chess. The pieces were crudely carved bark, marked with distinguishing signs; the board was scratched onto the earth. At night the three men slipped through an opening on the side of the hole and went foraging: leaves for smoking, pinecones for chewing, water from a nearby stream. Sometimes an old forest keeper named Muresán, a Christian, brought raw potatoes.

When the Nazis invaded Transylvania and the Jews of my father's town, Nagy-Károly, were sent to the cattlecars, he didn't go. Instead, he fled to the forest, dug a hole, and lived in it until the end of the war. It was 1944, and he was twenty-five years old. After the war he returned to his town, found a Jewish wasteland, and made his way to America. He met my mother, who'd left Transylvania as a girl just before the war, in a basement grocery in Brooklyn, and married in 1952. A year later I was born.

"Tell me a story," I said to my father at bedtime.

"You remember, Yosseleh, how we buried ourselves in the bunker. I called that bunker our grave."

"You remember": My memory was to be an extension of his. The stories filled me before I could understand them. They were my starting point, which was their purpose: Growing up with his knowledge, I could learn to breathe in it.

The stories offered only essential details. Seasons stopped; scenery vanished. He wasn't a storyteller, and he wasn't reminiscing. He was a teacher, choosing each detail for its lesson. In those moments before I fell asleep, as he stroked my cheek and spoke of the war, was his first lesson: Confronting reality won't harm but protect you.

The lesson of the hole was that only individualists survive. When the Nazis came, Nagy-Károly's Jews assured each other that trying to escape would only make things worse. And so, my father said to me, don't listen to what "people" say. "People" are fools, victims. When they go left, go right; when they go to the cattlecars, go to the forest.

The most innocent details of our lives contained awesome lessons for survival. There was the Independence Lesson. My parents owned a wholesale candy business, a large, half-empty warehouse in a state of constant potential. Though often in debt and threatened by suppliers with a loss of credit, my father refused to shut down the business and work for someone else or even to take in a partner. There's nothing like being independent, he said to me solemnly — a warning "for the future." For the same reason, he'd insisted on becoming a wholesaler rather than a retailer. Wholesale offered independence: Instead of sitting in a store waiting for customers to come, you could plan, maneuver, scout out the city. Retail meant dependence, passivity; and passivity led to the cattlecars.

There was the Accordion Lesson. After the war, while waiting for an American visa, my father lived in Cuba. Since refugees couldn't find work there, for days at a time he ate only mangoes picked from trees. Once his landlady, an old woman who suffered from nausea, invited him to dinner, just to watch him eat: His fierce hunger, tempered by elegant table manners, stimulated her appetite. But when her nausea passed, he returned to the mango trees. None of his

friends ate any better — except the Accordionist. Hired to play horas at the affairs of rich Havana Jews, the Accordionist was paid with
buffets.

And so at age six I was given weekly accordion lessons, "for the
future." I wasn't expected to become a virtuoso, only a competent
entertainer. How good did one have to be for the Havana Hadassah?
But I wasn't even competent. My arms barely embraced the massive
box; its heaving folds seemed about to devour me.

My father persisted. He borrowed to pay for the lessons, increased
them to twice a week. When he was my age, he told me, his parents
had bought him a violin, but the boys called him "Gypsy" and he
stopped playing. Had he continued, he too could have eaten in Cuba.

He tried to teach my little sister Chani and me to nurture hunger
and gratitude, to take nothing for granted, least of all existence. But
we laughed when he tore paper napkins in two, followed us around
the house turning off lights, recycled tea bags until the water remained
colorless after lengthy steeping. Our laughter dismayed him; he wondered how his American children would ever become survivors.

The lessons in asceticism became more urgent after his first, near-
fatal heart attack. The doctors said his survival was a miracle, but it
was no surprise to me. The Houdini of the Holocaust, the man who
had emerged from his own grave, had done it again. His extraordinary willpower was now summoned for the war against his weak
heart. He adopted a diet so strict that even his cardiologist urged
him to be flexible.

Asceticism meant survival. Though he was almost flagrantly generous toward anyone who asked for his help, he rarely spent money
on himself. Buying a cup of coffee during his long rounds visiting
customers seemed to him indulgent. His greatest pleasure was to eat
hot red peppers, hiccuping loudly as tears filled his eyes; he enjoyed
performing minor operations on himself, removing ingrown toenails
with a glowing knife. Even the tricks he performed for me were
demonstrations of ascetic bravado, like waving his finger back and
forth through the flame of a Sabbath candle. The secret, he said,
was to move so quickly that there was no time to think about danger or pain. I practiced until I became as good as he was, entering
the fire without getting burned.

                    *   *   *

And yet however vital those lessons appeared, they were in fact tangential to my father's main teaching: to know the world without illusion. He made certain I learned the wisdom of the Jewish Exile: *Halakhah*, it is law, *Esav sone l'Ya'akov*, Esau the Goy hates Jacob the Jew. The Goy. Not merely one or another group, not even an entire nation, but the whole non-Jewish world. Every country had shut its doors to Europe's Jews. The earth had been so inhospitable that the only refuge my father could find was to burrow beneath it.

The most friendly goy might one day reveal the Nazi within. Even, said my father, a woman who had fallen in love with and married a Jew: "Everything will be all kissing and who knows what. Until the first fight. Then, all of a sudden, it is 'dirty Jew, filthy Jew.' And you say to yourself, 'Where did *this* come from? What happened?' "

Yet he himself had been saved by a goy. He'd entrusted his hiding place to Muresán, the forest keeper, and wasn't betrayed. And though he never said so, he obviously understood the contradiction at the heart of his most important lesson. When he'd tell me about Muresán, his voice became gently rhythmic, almost melodic: "There was a peasant, a simple man who couldn't read, who couldn't write, but was very good-hearted man." He never told me the names of the two Jews he hid with in the hole, but he made certain that I knew "Muresán," as if offering me a name to counter Esau.

In 1940, four years before the Nazis came, the pro-Nazi Hungarian fascists occupied Transylvania. In 1941 my father was drafted into the Hungarian army. "That was not an army like normal army; that was a labor brigade for the Jewish boys." The recruits were given shovels instead of guns; yellow stars were pinned to their sleeves.

One of the fascist officers took a liking to my father, drawn perhaps by his dignified intactness: He was handsome, slender but sturdy, with enormous self-confidence; his deep laughter was charismatic. The officer appointed him manager of the camp's kitchen, rescuing him from slave labor and assuring him of access to food. "That good man took care for me like his own son." In our family album there was even a photograph of the officer, wearing a large Iron Cross, symbol of Hungarian fascism. My father had carried that photo across the ocean, through all his postwar wanderings; I resented its intrusion into our home and couldn't understand his gratitude to a Hungarian Nazi goy.

As with Muresán, the presence of the officer in my father's stories was not merely disturbing but subversive. If there were two exceptions to his rule of gentile enmity, then perhaps there were others. And if that were so, how could a Jew be sufficiently wary and
know to sort enemies from friends? It was far safer to live without
exceptions. Muresán and the officer confused me; I tried to forget
them.

For my father, Jew-hatred was a given. His stories about Nagy-Károly
began with his childhood, when Christian boys taunted him to "Go
to Palestine!"; they ended with his return home just after the war,
when gentile neighbors greeted him without pleasure: You survived?

Still, you didn't question natural disasters, blame volcanoes for
periodically erupting; you learned to protect yourself. In his stories
non-Jews were almost irrelevant — a nameless, indifferent storm.
Gentile hatred wasn't extraordinary, only Jewish naïveté. And so he
directed his rage not against the Gentiles but against the Jews.

He didn't accuse the Jews of going like "sheep to slaughter." The
one time I asked him why Jews didn't fight back against the Nazis,
he laughed in an incredulous snort. "Fight back? With how? Your
bare hand?" Once the Nazis came, the greatest heroism possible was
to hide in a hole.

But why, he demanded, hadn't the Jews prepared *before* the Nazis
came? Why were the Jews taken by surprise? How was it possible
that when the Nazis reached Hungary in 1944, its Jews were as unsuspecting as Polish Jews had been in 1939? Hungary's Jews had had
five years of warning; all around them Jewish Europe was burning.
Yet they'd prepared no hiding places or arms caches or illegal boats
to the Land of Israel.

They didn't even try to verify the "rumors" of what was happening across the border. My father had met a Polish rabbi who
smuggled himself into Hungary under a wagonload of hay and who
told him about the camps in Poland. My father repeated the stories
to other Jews. Some pitied his gullibility, while others cursed him
for weakening Jewish morale; no one believed him. Instead, they told
him that this was the twentieth century and Jews weren't gathered
up in bonfires anymore, that they were Hungarian citizens and their
government would surely protect them. Desperate optimists, they

8 MEMOIRS OF A JEWISH EXTREMIST

doomed themselves with hope. And that was another crucial lesson: A Jew must always expect the worst.

My father was an emotional, even sentimental, man who cried easily and often. He wept when we gave him his annual birthday handkerchiefs, wept thinking of my sister as a bride. But when he spoke of the Jews of Nagy-Károly — most of whom, including his parents, had been taken away and gassed — he was dry-eyed. Before mourning must come judgment, lessons "for the future." Why had we been such perfect victims? No murderers had ever been more methodical than the Nazis, no victims more disorganized than the Jews. In my father's stories, Nagy-Károly was not a place but a symbol for all of European Jewry's failures, for every fatal illusion.

Of Nagy-Károly's eighteen thousand people, four thousand were Jews. My father's father, Josef Klein, was a self-made millionaire, one of the wealthiest men in Nagy-Károly and president of its Jewish community. He owned vineyards, wine cellars, warehouses of beer. He was my father's favorite example of Jewish naïveté: His wealth had deceived him into believing in security.

My father never described the luxurious home in which he grew up — a deliberate, contemptuous omission. After the war he returned to his family home and lived there, alone, for a time. But he kept nothing from it except his mother's broken timepiece and individual portraits of his parents, which a photographer later enlarged and tinted blue and which hung, framed, in my parents' bedroom: Josef, jowly, mustached and severe, and Hannah, smiling dreamlike in a pale blue wig. I was named for them both, Josef H., their names crammed into mine. I was my parents' firstborn; and should no children follow me, my grandparents would be assured a memorial.

Once a year in their honor, we lit *yartzeit* candles. The wax-filled glasses were placed on the rim of the bathroom sink, an uneasy intrusion of holiness into a place of impurity. On those nights when the candles burned, I tried to avoid the bathroom, afraid of encountering white forms floating in the blue light. After the wax melted away, we used the cups as drinking glasses.

The memorial candles were lit on the evening of *Shavuot*, festival of Sinai and revelation of the Torah, because that is when the trains from Nagy-Károly were said to have reached Auschwitz. We assumed my grandparents had been gassed immediately after arriv-

ing there, and their bodies burned later that night. My grandparents
had disappeared, leaving no proof that they ever lived or even that
they had died. All that remained of them was the lesson of their illusions. I resented being named for them, as though it were a curse.
I tried not to think about them and never called them "my grandparents," only "my father's parents." To be intimate with them was
to risk infection with their easy dying.

"And my parents should rest in peace could have been saved!" my
father repeated, not with grief but rage. The Land of Israel, though
ruled by the British, was accessible before the war, waiting for the
Jews. But instead of fleeing while there was still time, Nagy-Károly's
Jews trusted the solidity of Exile.

One of the most outspoken anti-Zionists happened to be the
Hasidic rabbi of Nagy-Károly, Reb Yoilish, who later moved to the
neighboring town of Satmar and became famous as the Satmar
Rebbe. Reb Yoilish's great enemy were the Zionists, whom he denounced on Shabbos — the Sabbath — from the pulpit in Nagy-
Károly's main synagogue. The Zionists were worse than anti-Semites,
he said, a greater danger because they would provoke God by their
mad attempt to hasten redemption. The Jews had been exiled from
the Land of Israel by divine decree; only the Messiah himself could
reverse it. And until his arrival, they were to remain dispersed among
the nations.

One day it was announced that the famous Tisbi Illés was coming to speak in town. Tisbi Illés was a journalist who wrote passionate
appeals urging Hungarian Jews to flee to the Land of Israel before
it was too late. Tisbi Illés's real identity was hidden; his name was
a Hungarian pseudonym meaning Elijah the Tishbite, the prophet
who will announce the coming of the Messiah. And so when Tisbi
Illés came to Nagy-Károly, the synagogue was filled with curious
Jews, my father, still a child, among them.

Everyone was stunned: Tisbi Illés turned out to be a Nagy-Károly
boy, son of one of Reb Yoilish's most prominent Hasidim. There is
no future for us here, said Tisbi Illés. No matter what we do, the
goyim will hate us. For our wealth, for our poverty; for our capitalists, for our revolutionaries; for being tribal separatists in Nagy-
Károly, for being pushy assimilationists in Budapest. There was only

one solution: Extract the Jews from Exile and return them to the Land of Israel.

For my father, Tisbi Illés was indeed a messianic messenger, appearing in a forlorn corner of Transylvania to save those Jews forgotten by everyone but their enemies. Inspired by Tisbi Illés, he joined the town's tiny B'nai Akiva group. B'nai Akiva was a Zionist movement, both Orthodox and socialist — faithful to the past and the future, contemptuous only of the Jewish present. After synagogue on Shabbos, my father took off his white shirt and replaced it with the light blue workshirt of the Zionist pioneers. On his sleeve was a blue-and-yellow patch: the Ten Commandments, a sickle, and a sheaf of wheat. In his workshirt he felt as if he were already in the Land of Israel, surrounded by empty hills covered with white rocks that, in the distance, looked like grazing sheep.

On the street he was now physically attacked not only by non-Jews but by Reb Yoilish's Hasidim. Josef Klein was ashamed and spoke with his son only when necessary. A few of the older B'nai Akiva boys emigrated to the Land of Israel; their fathers sat shivah in mourning for them, as if the boys had died. "Those handful boys who went then to Israel are all today alive. And those who sat for them shivah? They went to the gas chamber." And then, as though addressing a court, he concluded, "I blame our leaders, so-called leaders. Instead to warn, 'Escape with your lives!' — no, they kept us back, they didn't let us go to Israel. And do you know where is this Tisbi Illés today? One of the greatest scholars of the kabbalah at the Jerusalem university."

Finally, there was the story of the train. On Passover 1943 it was announced in the synagogue that a train carrying Slovakian Jews bound for "resettlement" to an unknown destination was passing through Nagy-Károly. "And so everybody went home, myself including, and gathered some food and clothe. At the station we saw there a train. That was not a passenger train, that was a train with wagons. For animal. Cattle."

Outstretched arms reached through the small barred window of each car, a transport of limbs. "Where are they taking you?" my father shouted into one window. "They told us to factories," someone inside shouted back. But there were old people, babies, in the train; were they also going to work in factories?

"And then we went home, and nobody thought to speak again about the train, as if it never happen. Nobody thought to say *tehilim*, a few words prayer, to ask that God should help those 'poor people' — poor people, we called them. No one made a move to save even himself. The Romanian border was only few mile away; we could easily run there. And so life was going on another year. And the next Passover — came the train for us."

Selfishness, naïveté, infighting, anti-Zionism: These were the sins of Nagy-Károly's Jews. But my father considered them guilty only so long as they could have saved themselves; once on the train to Auschwitz, they became *kedoshim*, holy martyrs, dying together in unity, a perfect Jewish death. My father even forgave his non-Zionist father. Every time he mentioned his father's name, even to condemn him, he appended it with a hurried "should rest in peace." Having vanished into the Six Million, Josef Klein achieved greatness. It seemed fitting that we lit memorial candles for my father's parents on a holiday that belonged to the whole Jewish people: There was nothing personal about their dying.

But just as Nagy-Károly's Jews were redeemed by death, the real criminals of my father's stories appeared: the American Jews, especially their leaders. They knew what was happening; why didn't they chain themselves to the White House, sit down in the streets of Washington, lose their minds with grief? "And what did they do, these leaders, so-called leaders, these nothings? Dance at bar mitzvahs? What did they *do!* Instead to be dined and wined in the White House while every day, every day, thousand more were burning."

The only time in his stories that his voice turned almost shrill was when he spoke of the American Jews. I felt the purity, the thrill of his rage. American Jews didn't try to save the relatives they'd left behind in Europe because they didn't want to draw attention to themselves with a noisy rescue campaign, jeopardize their assimilation into America. The six million American Jews had survived in place of the six million of Europe; we had burned so that they could move to Long Island. "We": of course, we. Though born in America, I was no American Jew. I would never assimilate, become a spectator to Jewish suffering.

The Holocaust, implied my father, had happened because of the failure of Jewish solidarity. And so, he said to me, you must cherish the Jewish people — this most unloved of peoples — compensate for all the hatred against it with a great, uncompromising love. Goyim hate someone just because he's a Jew? You love him just because he's a Jew. You don't like him as a person? Love him as a Jew.

My father's survivor friends had small ambitions, seeking comforts to dispel humiliating memories. But my father's ambition was to save the Jewish people. He wanted not just personal but group survival — as if, having died together in our millions, we had become physically transformed, no longer single beings but melded Jews. Not surprisingly, his most persistent grammatical error in English was confusing the singular with the plural.

The candy business often seemed like a pretext for him to spread his message of Jewish survival. On his weekly rounds to customers, he offered long commentaries on "politic" — politics, the latest Jewish news — and only toward the end of his visit would he inquire about an order. He didn't seem like a salesman at all, but rather a wandering preacher. His customers cherished him like a celebrity, this courtly man who wore a fedora tilted slightly over one eye and a folded handkerchief peeking from the breast pocket of his jacket, who alerted them to billing mistakes in their favor, and who spoke softly when not discussing the fate of the Jews.

His great fantasy was to be a Jewish leader, addressing vast audiences and demanding that Jews teach their children the lessons of the past. But that, of course, was impossible; he was just an immigrant with broken words.

And so he planned his revenge on the Holocaust through me. The real intent of his stories was to train me to become a leader, a savior, a new Tisbi Illés. I would teach the Jews how an entire people could be led to a singular death; teach them to be ever watchful, as obsessed with surviving as the goyim were with killing us; teach them to plan ahead, even in quiet times, intervals between holocausts; teach them, above all, to support each other, to be as powerful in our unity as our enemies were in theirs, united against the world in an embrace of love.

*   *   *

We lived on the border of Borough Park. Beyond our Brooklyn en-clave, populated mostly by Orthodox Holocaust survivors like my family, were Italians, Puerto Ricans, Scandinavians. They evoked no curiosity in us, only fear. We saw them all as members of the same ethnic group: Jew-haters. Goyim, we called them, a Hebrew word that literally means "the nations" but that we understood to mean the enemy. The more polite word we sometimes used was "non-Jews," defining them by who they were not.

The neighborhood ran west to east from Eighth to Eighteenth Avenue, north to south from Thirty-ninth to Sixtieth Street. Though invisible, those borders were inviolate: The Jewish streets abruptly ended, and a Jew crossed them at his own risk.

We lived on Fifty-first Street, between Seventeenth and Eighteenth Avenues. That placed us safely among the Jewish side streets; but Eighteenth Avenue, the eastern border, was just a few houses away. When I walked along Eighteenth Avenue, I would cross the street to avoid the Italian pizza shop on one corner, then cross back to avoid the candy store. Goyim with greased hair and leather jackets gathered there; and you never knew when they might grab your yarmulke and toss it among themselves like a Frisbee. I mapped out the stores into which I could flee, just in case: the Hasidic bar-bershop where they shaved boys' heads and left only sidelocks re-sembling sheep's ears, the *glatt* kosher butcher shop whose meat was slaughtered in an extra-kosher way.

Borough Park was symmetrical, as though preplanned: quiet streets of two-family brick homes with red stoops and gray, dignified apartment buildings; every two or three avenues was a commercial strip. But this ordered geography broke down at the borders. Suddenly there were factories with cracked windows, random lots, train tracks — chaos. Outside our borders, the sanity of the streets couldn't be trusted.

We lived in a sealed Jewish world. The restaurants and bakeries were kosher, the pizza shops sold knishes and felafel, bookstores of-fered only Judaica, furniture stores displayed bookcases built for large volumes of Talmuds, hardware stores sold plastic prefab sukkahs and

"Shabbos clocks" that automatically turned lights on and off (to circumvent the religious law against using electricity on the Sabbath). We were self-contained; all we wanted was to be left alone. We were like survivors of a nuclear war, in need of quarantine, except that we were protecting ourselves from humanity. We had been poisoned by a knowledge no outsider could understand; only in isolation could we nurse each other back to equilibrium. Had it been possible, we would have surrounded Borough Park with a moat.

Borough Park's Hasidim didn't read secular newspapers or watch TV; they didn't want to be reminded that "the world" existed. But we were a modern Orthodox family, meaning that non-Jewish culture — in limited doses — was permitted in our home. My mother was almost an American, one of the few Jews in Borough Park who wasn't a survivor; she offered me an opening to a reality not defined by Nazis or victims. She joined the Dr. Seuss book club and bought the *World Book Encyclopedia* on installment and took Chani and me to museums. Because she'd left Transylvania as a child, she spoke English without a European accent: Her *rs* didn't tremble, and her *ws* didn't harden into *vs* — an unburdened speech.

We watched the world from a distance. Television was safe: Goyim could appear and disappear, in precisely timed segments. My father loved westerns. One of the few boyhood memories he cherished was watching cowboy movies in Nagy-Károly's theater; when the movie ended, he and the other children would chant together in English, "Happy end!" That was a strange Nagy-Károly anecdote: Hasidim weren't harassing Zionists; goyim weren't harassing Jews. Only in westerns, with their lonely heroes defeating lawlessness, could my father return to a childhood that wasn't a prelude to the Holocaust.

My mother and sister took refuge in sitcoms. Donna Reed reassured them that the Holocaust was an aberration, that the world conformed to their basic goodness. They lay together watching TV in my parents' bedroom, sometimes laughing so hard they kicked the covers off the bed.

I was drawn to any TV program about history: the American Revolution, Napoleon's conquests, the War of the Roses. Here was a world where people died in normal wars and tragedy happened in manageable doses, where suffering could be mourned rather than resisted and compensated for. And I *liked* the goyim on television. They seemed decent, familiar, human: people like Ricky Ricardo, the hand-some husband on *I Love Lucy,* who reminded me of my father be-cause he too spoke an eccentric English and came from Cuba.

But aside from watching them on TV, goyim were as alien to me as they were to the Hasidic children. Naturally, I had no non-Jewish friends. An Italian family lived on our block. If I saw one of the Italians at a distance, I'd cross the street to avoid the awkwardness of saying hello. My parents and the Italians were cordial, but of course they never visited each other's homes. I wished the Italians would stop sabotaging our Jewish intactness and would move away.

Borough Park's interests were limited to its own borders, and leapt over the Christian neighborhoods to embrace other Jewish en-claves — as if the only civilized parts of the world were Jewish, the rest being inhabited by rabid creatures capable at any moment of unprovoked violence. "The world" existed only insofar as it affected Jews. If I read about a country I hadn't heard of before, I needed to know how many Jews lived there and whether they were in imme-diate or merely long-term danger. When I scanned a newspaper, I could instantly spot the words "Jew," "Nazi," "anti-Semite," as if they glowed on the page.

Whatever fears Jews once had about goyim before the war, what-ever fantasies of destruction they had conjured, were naive compared with what we, the survivors, knew. The Jews and "the world" could never coexist; at best we would endure each other from a distance. Some of our religious laws seemed meant not to bring us closer to God but to separate us from the goyim, and I accepted that es-trangement as self-evident.

I learned most of my father's survival lessons at best partially: I wasted food and toilet paper, kept lights burning in rooms after leav-ing them, was a failure on the accordion. But I did master his most crucial lesson: to see myself as a stranger in a hostile world, a mem-ber of a people related only formally to humanity — in effect, a sep-arate species.

We feared the goyim and wanted nothing to do with them; but we turned our hatred inward, toward the Jewish assimilationists, the traitors: the American Jews who were embarrassed to be "too" Jewish, who laughed when a Yiddish word was mentioned in a joke as if that

were itself the punch line, who turned an identity we'd been martyred for into vaudeville.

My father told me how some Jews in pre-Holocaust Europe had
tried to assimilate, imagining themselves Germans in Berlin and
Hungarians in Budapest. They called themselves "emancipated," as if
Jews could ever be freed from the burdens of history. Other Jews had
tried to become communists, members of no nation at all, of something nonexistent called "humanity." They'd cared more for the goyim,
said my father, than for their own people. His contempt was based on
simple logic: During the war, Jewishness had become the central —
the only — fact of a Jew's existence. And so if one could be killed for
being a Jew, then one simply had to live as a Jew. There was no joy
in that decision, but neither was there regret. To reject one's Jewishness made as much sense as to deny one's gender. The only alternative to accepting the basic dictates of fate was suicide; and that, implied my father, was precisely the meaning of assimilation.

Even if assimilation were possible, self-respect required Jews to
reject it. When my father spoke of Salk and Freud and Einstein, he
wasn't boasting of Jewish intelligence but presenting an indictment:
After everything we had done for "the world" — that foreign entity —
it repaid us with Auschwitz and Treblinka. *Now* the world was ready
to accept us? Now it was too late.

On Sunday afternoons Christian missionaries walked the streets of
Borough Park, trying to convert survivors. The missionaries distributed glossy pamphlets about Jews with names like Justin Benington
Goldblatt who'd become Christian. "Now I am a fulfilled Jew!" ex-
ulted Goldblatt.

In the spring two old missionaries wearing string ties would appear on the steps of a Borough Park bank. One of them held a giant American flag on a pole while the other made speeches. I joined
the hooting, laughing crowd that invariably surrounded the two shriv-
eled men; I spat at them and shouted, "Nazis!" I saw these pathetic
do-gooders as a threat to Jewish survival: Borough Park was all
that remained of Jewish Europe, and even this they wanted to take
from us.

What I knew about Christianity was that it worshiped a dead Jew.
The idea made me queasy: Christians seemed to be celebrating

Jewish death. Hasidic children called Jesus "Yoshke," a mocking name meant for a village idiot; some grown-ups called him the *Yimach Sh'moinik*, the one whose name should be blotted out, the traitorous Jew who'd brought disaster on his people. My father told me how Jews would hide in their homes on Christmas and Easter, anticipating pogroms. "One Jew is killed two thousand years ago and they can't forget it; but six million Jew they kill twenty years ago and for this nobody says even a word."

In the yeshiva, or religious school, I attended we got a children's magazine called *Olameinu*, Our World — an appropriate name, because nothing non-Jewish, extrasystemic, penetrated its pages; even the cartoons and crossword puzzles were Jewish. In one issue there was a cartoon story about a Jewish boy who is kidnapped by his Christian nurse; raised in a monastery, his past is slowly erased until he becomes an amnesiac. Finally, he is ordained a priest. Then one evening he happens to pass a synagogue. It is the night of Yom Kippur, and the cantor is chanting *Kol Nidre*, the prayer asking God's forgiveness for violated promises. The priest stops: The melody is familiar. He enters the synagogue. Naturally, he finds his parents among the congregants and triumphantly returns to Judaism.

Some Borough Park children said it was a *mitzvah*, a religious commandment, to spit when you passed a church. An alternative opinion held that it was forbidden to even walk within spitting distance of a church. There was a big church on one of the border streets near Eighteenth Avenue, and I'd cross the street rather than pass it. If I got too close, grasping hands might suddenly emerge from its massive doors and drag me into the basement, where priests would imprison me and force me to become a Christian.

My father told me about the notorious priest Cuza. One day, before the war, Cuza announced he was coming to Nagy-Károly to start a pogrom. Yossi Katz, a butcher's son and a "big boy," waited for Cuza at the train station. When Cuza appeared, Yossi Katz lifted the priest by his lapels and threw him back onto the train. Cuza never returned to Nagy-Károly.

I wanted to be a protector and an avenger like Yossi Katz. ("Katz Yossi," my father called him, placing the family name first, Hungarian-style: Where you came from was more important than who you were.) But instead of defending my community, I lived in

fear of the pogromists across Eighteenth Avenue: the Tough Doody
Bomb Gang. At any time, its members could swoop onto our street,
riding sleek bikes that seemed to glide just above the earth and shouting "Jee-ew!" as though the word itself were a jeer. To me, they weren't
mere bullies but storm troopers. Any anti-Semitic taunt or joke was
an unbearable reminder of Auschwitz. We were like people whose skin
had been stripped, without resistance to the mildest pressures.

When the Tough Doody Bomb boys appeared, we would scatter
into our homes, even if we outnumbered them, because Jewish children didn't know how to fight. In moments of rage I felt I could
single-handedly beat the entire gang. Just below my white arms, thin
as kindling wood, were muscles waiting to swell; sometimes I could
feel them stirring. But my body betrayed me. Objects were either too
solid, refusing to conform to my grip, or elusive, slipping from my
fingers. I grabbed randomly, without thinking — avoiding the physical, as if every day were Shabbos.

Once the Tough Doody Bomb boys chased me down my block. I
ran before their bikes as they shouted "Dirty Jew!" and I fled to the
top of my stoop. But instead of escaping into the house, I turned to
face them. "Dirty Christians!" I shouted. I stopped breathing and
braced for the massacre. But they just stared at me. Then they rode
away and never bothered me again.

3.

The first picture of the Holocaust that I saw was a cartoon in a comic
book. One frame in the *Classics Illustrated History of the Second
World War* showed a Jew sealed into a block of ice. Over him stood
a Nazi soldier with a stopwatch, measuring how long it took for a
human being to freeze.

Clearly, matters were far worse than my father had indicated; even
he hadn't told me about the experiments in the camps. But even
more compelling than the fact that Jews had been used as laboratory animals was the image of the dispassionate Nazi. He wasn't directly torturing his victim, merely watching him. I could more easily accept the existence of evil than the brutality of the spectator. To
be a good person meant acting in a manner opposite that of a Nazi,

as dedicated to saving as the Nazis were to destroying. After the Holocaust minimal decency required total selflessness.

For a long time that comic book image was the only confirmation I had of my father's stories. I constantly watched World War II on television, documentaries about great battles and Hollywood movies about the French resistance; but none mentioned the Jews. There were almost no films about the Holocaust, as if acknowledging that event would destroy the world's intactness.

Even in yeshiva, the conspiracy of silence persisted. My teachers spoke only about tragedies from the remote past, offering us euphemisms for the Holocaust. A woman named Hannah had refused to bow to a Greek idol and was forced to watch the execution, one by one, of her seven sons. Rabbi Tarphon was wrapped in an oil-soaked Torah scroll and set on fire, his soul rising to heaven with the burning letters. Rabbi Akiva's flesh was peeled by Roman soldiers with a giant metal comb; he died in ecstasy, having finally learned to love God with his entire will.

Most of my classmates carried the names of murdered grandfathers. But even they knew little about the war, because their parents refused to discuss it. Only occasionally would parents let the war slip out, usually as a rebuke to their children for some offense: "For *this* I survived Hitler?" Some of my friends didn't even know if their parents had been in a camp or in hiding. To me, that was like not knowing your parents' names.

The total public and even private silence made the Holocaust seem mythical. I didn't consider my father's stories literal accounts, but allegories. Perhaps his town had never existed; after all, he wasn't even certain of its name. Sometimes he called it Nagy-Károly; sometimes, Carei. When I asked him about the discrepancy — reluctantly, afraid to catch him in a lie — he said only that those were his town's Hungarian and Romanian names. But any town whose very name was contested had to lack solidity.

The Holocaust took the place in my mind that for other children God held, a presence at once awesome and intimate. The war formed my closest bond with my father: It was *our* war; we were the only members of our own secret society, initiates of historical mystery. And yet I couldn't discuss the war with him. Instead, he spoke and

I listened, waiting for him to tell me what I needed to know. Partly I was afraid to hurt him. And I was also ashamed: Our knowledge was so unbearable that no one else could even mention it.

Unlike my father, most of his friends had blue numbers on their forearms. But the numbers were concealed by suit jackets, even in summer. Still, sometimes their sleeves slipped up, and a few numbers became visible. I pretended to look away, peeking sideways.

Together with my friend Sandy, I tried to figure out how the rows of little blue numbers had been tattooed on the arm. Did someone draw them directly onto the skin? Or was there a machine that did it? There was no way of knowing, because none of the parents who'd survived the camps would speak. I felt vaguely ashamed that my father hadn't spent time in a camp and wished he'd been deported to Auschwitz like Sandy's parents — and then escaped to the hole. That way he could still have been a hero, one step ahead of all the passive Jews, while also sharing their knowledge.

I was far more ashamed of my mother. My friends were "children of survivors," whereas I was merely the child of *a* survivor. I felt incomplete, inauthentic. Ironically, my friends envied me for having at least one parent who wasn't traumatized, who was totally sane; they liked coming to my house because my mother's presence made it seem "American."

My mother's most prominent trait was sympathy. Her survivor friends, suffering from nameless ailments they diagnosed simply as "the war" and speaking in sentences that ended in sighs, confided to her secrets they could tell no one else. Though an outsider, she lived with a survivor and compensated with compassion for what she couldn't understand. Once she wrote an essay for a friend about the woman's experiences on a winter death march; the woman won an appearance on the *Queen for a Day* show, which awarded her with appliances for having the most pathetic story among the contestants.

My mother's face was fresh and lovely, her figure almost as slender as it had been as a teenager, when she'd come in second in the Miss Jewish American Beauty Pageant. Among her friends with heavy makeup and wigs and blue numbers on their arms, she was radiant. But my mother knew it was no coincidence that she, an almost American, an almost beauty queen, had found her home among the survivors. She had gotten out of Transylvania, she said, on the last boat — an exaggeration, by which she meant to say that she took nothing for granted.

But she lacked a survivor's resiliency. She found the merest pain unbearable. Her cheerfulness helped her appear energetic, but climbing a flight of stairs left her breathless. She was finicky as a child about food and could enjoy only her own or her friends' cooking. Eating the food of strangers was too intimate and made her queasy.

My father never mocked her weaknesses. Instead, they amused and even delighted him: Her fragile will and her kindliness were inseparable symptoms of tenderness.

But not for me. I had to resist my mother, become her very opposite. My father was the survivor, my mother the American — the nonsurvivor. Her decency and optimism threatened to undermine my father's grim lessons about "the world." If I wasn't careful, her influence could be fatal.

In 1961 the Holocaust suddenly appeared on TV. Adolf Eichmann, CEO of the Final Solution, had been kidnapped by Israeli agents in Argentina and flown back to Israel; his trial was broadcast live from Jerusalem. Chani and I watched the trial with our parents, sitting on their bed. Spectators in the courtroom bit their lips to suppress hysteria; witnesses wept and fainted. "Why are people so cruel?" my mother asked. "Why?" I wanted to shout at her, "Because that's how it is, all right?" Suffering was supposed to harden you, prepare you to become a savior, not make you squeamish. Once you began crying about these things, where would it end?

The defendant sat in his bulletproof glass cage, making notes. The wry turn of his mouth reminded me of an expression I sometimes saw on my father, as though an awful truth, long suspected, had suddenly been confirmed — a knowing look, without shock, that said: So this is how it is. In fact, Eichmann and my father seemed to share the same secrets, inhabiting a reality no one else could enter. Could it be — was my father one of them? What better disguise for a Nazi, after all, than becoming a survivor in Borough Park?

I didn't really believe my father was a war criminal, but neither could I be sure that he wasn't. I lived in a world of infinite grotesque possibilities. Reality had overtaken fantasy: The Dracula story seemed tame compared with what had actually happened to Jews in Transylvania.

My father's possible Nazi identity was merely one of the many speculations with which I tried to explain the strangeness of my life. Perhaps the Jews had come to earth on UFOs and were despised everywhere as aliens because that's what we literally were; one day we would return to our true home, the planet of the Jews, where everything would finally make sense.

At the time of the trial, I was eight and my sister, five; our parents would banish us from their bedroom whenever clips of the death camps appeared. But sometimes images filled the screen without warning and I saw the piled bodies, the upside-down faces with gaping mouths and empty eyes. The pictures were blurry and quickly passed, but they offered a kind of relief: The most important event of my life had really happened.

I told Sandy we had to kidnap Hitler. "He's alive," I said, "I know it." We had to hurry, though, because Hitler was already old. Sandy asked me what I would do once we caught him. "Put him in a cage," I said, "and drag him around Borough Park. And then scratch out his eyes."

Of course Hitler was alive. "In every generation a new enemy rises to destroy us," grimly warned the Passover Haggadah — not merely to defeat or enslave us but to wipe us out. Only the form changed, never the threat itself: a boundless hatred of Esau for Jacob, which not even Auschwitz could exhaust.

4.

Every Friday, as if to subvert the approaching peace of Shabbos, the *Jewish Press* arrived in the mail. More than just the voice of Brooklyn's Orthodox Jews, the *Jewish Press* was a cosmopolitan digest of disaster. It probed the world, looking for woe: In Russia Jews were sentenced to death for "economic crimes"; in Argentina a swastika was carved into a Jewish girl's breast; in Germany they vandalized Jewish cemeteries, trying to erase the memory of Jewish death.

The editorials, cartoons, letters to the editor, and blue-and-red headlines all merged into a single *"Gevalt!"* a great cry of alarm. Stories were said to continue on nonexistent pages or ended mid-sentence, as if some calamity had suddenly struck its author. The *Jewish Press* was a newspaper with a mission and had no time for the formalities of grammar; its typos were the stutter of an urgent messenger.

The *Jewish Press*'s implicit motto was, No threat can ever be exaggerated. Its editors preferred to risk ridicule for transforming the most minor anti-Semitic incidents into banner headlines rather than to repeat the Nazi-era mistake of understatement. One never knew which threat would turn into genocide: The Holocaust, after all, hadn't begun with Auschwitz but with smashed windows in Jewish shops. The Jews had been almost pathologically unprepared for the Final Solution; and now we, the survivors, would always be alert, searching for hidden warnings of apocalypse.

Each of the paper's columnists was expert in a different area of crisis. A rabbi appealed for funds to secretly circumcise Jews in Russia. A rabbi's wife warned that we were losing more Jews in Cleveland and Los Angeles than died in Auschwitz, a holocaust of assimilation. And the paper's associate editor, a rabbi named Meir Kahane, warned of the *physical* holocaust that was coming in America.

Only the *Jewish Press* dared speak of it. Dozens of local hate groups were said to be thriving, with good American names like the National States' Rights Party. There was even an American Nazi Party, whose leader was named George Lincoln Rockwell, an all-American führer. Rockwell had dozens of followers, probably as many as Hitler had started with in the Munich beer hall.

The hate groups obsessed me. I *needed* Rockwell. An American Nazi party made sense of my life, reconciled nightmare fantasies with a benign childhood. I lived in opposite worlds, Brooklyn and Nazi Europe; one of them would have to yield. My father's reality seemed so much more compelling than mine; the value of my life would be determined by how much of his experience it could hold.

Rockwell helped me transform America into a Holocaust landscape. The Nazis could come at any time; to turn even briefly from danger was to risk repeating the mistake of Nagy-Károly's Jews, blinded to the approaching end by the distractions of daily life.

I spied swastikas everywhere, death messages surfacing from some deep underground. They were scrawled in chalk on the sidewalk, traced in the dust of car windows, faintly scratched onto silver lamp-posts. To find them you had to look beneath the world's seeming order, possess a microscope-like Jewish vision that could penetrate surface solidity and reveal the teeming chaos.

The news worsened. Rockwell spoke on a California campus, and hundreds of students came — curious, not hostile. Even Hitler had probably never been invited to a college. And if *he* had taken over a cultured country like Germany, why not Rockwell in America? What happened once could — must — happen again.

And "it" had nearly happened here. In a used-book store I found a copy of *Under Cover*, written by an Armenian who had infiltrated America's pro-Nazi movements in the 1930s. The book, printed during the war on brittle, rationed paper, spoke of organizations like the America First Committee and the Christian Crusade, with a combined membership of millions. Only the war and the end of the Depression had saved American Jewry.

Some day, I decided, I would infiltrate the American Nazi Party and write a sequel to *Under Cover*. Though my nose was long ("Jewish"), my hair was very blond ("Aryan"). Indeed, our family doctor liked to call me "the little Nazi." My mother demanded that he stop, but I was secretly pleased: I could pass. When I got sick, I practiced swallowing aspirin without water, in preparation for the cyanide capsule I would take if captured.

In sixth grade I formed the Anti-Nazi Agency (ANA) and recruited my classmates, fellow children of survivors obsessed with Nazis. We printed leaflets on a handpress that produced barely visible pale blue letters, and taped them to lampposts all over Borough Park. OUTLAW NAZI HATE GROUPS NOW!! SHOULD DEMOCRACY GIVE RIGHTS TO THOSE BENT ON DESTROYING IT??? We decorated the leaflets with large swastikas, then drew careful Xs through each one. Just like on the holiday of Purim, when we wrote Haman's name on the soles of our shoes and then rubbed it out. Jewish logic: You pray that Haman's memory be blotted out, and thereby keep it alive.

Every Shabbos afternoon, the members of ANA would meet to plan strategy, a dozen boys in preknotted ties that clipped onto the starched collars of our white shirts. We would read aloud excerpts from the *Jewish Press*, then eat cookies. I felt the pain of our youth, our inadequacy before history, but took comfort knowing that in the Warsaw Ghetto children had instantly aged, becoming smugglers of weapons and food.

We went door-to-door in Borough Park with a petition to President Lyndon Johnson to ban hate groups. Some survivors refused to sign, suspicious of what we would do with their signatures. My father cautioned me: Petitioning a president is no small thing.

Incredibly, even he seemed blind to the imminent Nazi takeover. "America is different," he said.

But why? In the *Jewish Press* I read how America had turned back from its shores a Jewish refugee ship and hadn't bombed the train tracks leading to Auschwitz. I retaliated by refusing to join in my class's recitation of the "Pledge of Allegiance."

My father wasn't pleased. He loved America. He would invariably end his bedtime stories to me as a child by saying, "And then I came to this great country, America, and met Mommy, should live and be well, the most wonderful woman you could want." America was inseparable from my mother: Both had offered him refuge.

My father's love for America, I thought, was a classic case of Jewish self-delusion, of refusing to perceive the world as it was: a place as hostile to Jews as Pluto was to humans. I wanted total consistency, without exceptions: no good goyim like Muresán, no good countries like America. My father had known a life before the Holocaust, knew that reality didn't always conform to one's abstract judgments. But I'd learned of the Holocaust almost from the moment I became conscious, and its absolute distinctions between good and evil left no room for subtleties.

We gathered a few hundred signatures for our anti-Nazi petition and mailed it to the White House. Months passed, without response. I wrote an irate letter to the White House; an aide replied, claiming he had no record of our petition. Why don't you try writing the president again, he suggested. But we'd spent *weeks* collecting signatures, a last-minute cry of warning by hundreds of survivors to an unsuspecting America!

We had given democracy a chance. In ANA we discussed acquiring sewer maps of Borough Park, for the time when we would have to go literally underground.

Two

Invisible Homeland

SHABBOS morning, my father's hand on mine, we walked to the synagogue of the survivors. We moved slowly, almost drowsily, as if incapable of hurrying on Shabbos. Sometimes we passed non-Jews washing their cars, and I sensed their distaste as we walked by in our suits and fedoras — the elegant Jews parading.

"When you're older you'll know what it means, a Shabbos," my father said to me. "Even if there is no God, I wouldn't give it up, not for all the money."

We lived from Shabbos to Shabbos. Beginning sundown Friday until sundown Saturday, the family withdrew into itself. My parents closed the business and wouldn't answer the phone. We didn't watch TV or ride in the all-purpose business-and-family van; even touching money was forbidden. Shabbos was the only time my father slept without nightmares. The outside world was suspended, neutralized. No harm could come to us on Shabbos.

On nearly every street were *shtiebls*, one-room Hasidic synagogues, located in basements or on the ground floor of private homes. The Yiddish signs read, "Munkács," "Lelev," "Bopov," "Sanz," entire towns in Europe condensed to a room. Though we weren't Hasidic, we too prayed in a *shtiebl* — the Nyirbator, named for a town in Hungary. We went there because most of its few dozen congregants were from my father's town, or nearby.

The Nyirbator was a converted storefront. Its windows had been replaced by brick, and only toward the very top, well above the heads of passersby, did glass slits remain. The Nyirbator fortified itself against even an accidental glimpse of a passing goy, a reminder of menace.

One entered from the street through a steel door, without steps, directly into the fluorescent-lit room. Along the empty white walls were joined tables, flanked by wooden benches without backs. The men around the tables were clean-shaven, the front brims of their black fedoras turned down; businessmen, they weren't expected to go into "the world" wearing beards and Hasidic hats with upturned brims.

Throughout the service, they discussed business and politics; their prayer books were usually opened to the wrong page. They took turns leaving the tables to pace the room, absentmindedly stroking the white braided fringes of their prayer shawls, sighing loudly, and calling out a random phrase from the prayers, like amnesiacs recalling fragments of their past. One man circulated with smelling salts, to revive those resting their heads on the table. Sometimes he would sneak his little jar under the noses of the children and laugh when we recoiled. Other men crept up and tickled our ears with the fringes of their prayer shawls, then looked away, feigning innocence.

The Nyirbator was a synagogue of men without faith. God had nothing to do with their Judaism: They were preserving the rituals of the *kedoshim*, the martyrs who had died in the Holocaust. If the prayers were holy, it was only because the *kedoshim* had said them. The men of the Nyirbator expected neither divine reward for repeating those prayers nor punishment for neglecting them. To forget the prayers, to be severed from the *kedoshim*, was itself the punishment.

My father said to me, "Do you think any of these people here were religious after the war? *None* of us believed. There was nothing, absolute nothing."

In 1945, just after the war, my father returned to Nagy-Károly from the forest and there met his fellow survivors drifting back from the camps. They were a "handful children," as he put it, meaning youth in their teens and twenties; older people didn't survive. Until the Nazis had invaded Nagy-Károly a year before, most of the "children" had been Hasidic; they'd been wrenched from their sheltered homes and introduced to the world at Auschwitz. In the months after the war, they spent their days gambling and drinking whiskey from large glasses, "just so to forget." Gradually, as they moved to America, married, and had children, they'd drifted into Borough Park's Hasidic community, trying to reinhabit their prewar innocence.

My father returned to Judaism only grudgingly: My mother, a rabbi's daughter, made that her precondition for marriage. "What you believe is your business," she'd said to him, "but we will have a proper Jewish home." For love, he assumed the role of Orthodox husband and father. He insisted I follow the most minute customs, "so you should know" — know how to function as an Orthodox Jew. He never spoke to me about God, except as irony. Echoing my mother, he said to me, "I don't care what you believe, as long as you live a Jewish life."

And yet his ambivalence was subversive: I couldn't pretend loyalty to an intact religious tradition. I knew that Borough Park was a mere fragment of a dead world. I was raised with my father's memory and had no nostalgia for the past. I despised the self-destructiveness of European Jewry; how could I enter its religious life?

I began to cheat on the prayers, skipping words and then entire sections. At first I cheated only to keep up with the remarkable speed of the Nyirbator service. But then I skipped even when I prayed at home. My prayer book became spotted with blanks, as though the pages were corroding.

Toward the end of services my father and I washed the hands of the Nyirbator's *cohanim*, descendants of the priests who serviced the destroyed Temple in Jerusalem. My father and I were Levites, members of the tribe that had played music in the Temple and assisted *cohanim* in their purification.

The Nyirbator *cohanim* gathered at a sink outside the bathroom.

The adult Levites filled a large brass cup with water. My fingers reached for a space on the crowded brim, as we tilted the cup to pour water over the waiting hands of the *cohanim*. Then the *cohanim*, in stockinged feet, stepped before the Torah ark and chanted, their palms spread toward the congregants in blessing, their heads covered with black-and-white-striped prayer shawls.

My father drew me close and spread his prayer shawl over our heads. I closed my eyes to prevent an accidental glimpse of the *cohanim*; the Nyirbator children claimed that if you saw the *cohanim* during their blessing, you'd go blind.

Once I peeked. Terrified, I saw headless bodies, black-striped humps slowly swaying, their outstretched fingers grasping. My father laid his hand on my shoulder, and I knew that if I watched the *cohanim* from under his prayer shawl, I'd be safe. Still, for days afterward, I shut my eyes and then quickly opened them, to see if the darkness lingered.

Once a year, on the holiday of Simchat Torah, celebrating the completion of the weekly Torah readings, we danced. I joined the line of men winding around the packed little room, closed my eyes, and entrusted myself to the safety of the circle. I placed my hands on the waist of the man before me, while the man behind me lay his hands on my shoulders. *Vitaher libenu*, we sang, over and over like a chant: Purify our hearts, God, to serve you, to serve you, to serve you with truth. The men's faces were strained with memory; they danced not from joy but because this is what their martyred parents would have wanted them to do. *Vesamahta bihagekha*, we sang in a sad tune: Rejoice in your holiday and only be happy. Despite everything, the Jews were still singing, still trying to approximate joy. *Ashreinu ma tov chelkeinu!* How blessed we are, how good is our lot, how pleasant our fate.

For the Hasidic survivors, all good had preceded the abyss; any new idea or practice was tainted by Auschwitz. The customs and melodies and clothing styles of Europe were venerated as much as a written law in the Torah — equally inviolate, as if received by divine revelation. Having been practiced by the holy martyrs, the rituals entered timelessness. Borough Park was trying to erase history, undo its chronology by pretending that European Orthodoxy was a changeless stream extending from the very origins of the Jewish people until the Holocaust. Abraham and Moses wore black felt hats; King David spoke Yiddish. Were a biblical figure to resurrect, he would feel at home only inside a *shtiebl*. In Europe Jews had dreamed of returning to the Land of Israel; in Borough Park they now longed for Hungary and Poland.

The Hasidim raised their children to see themselves as a seamless continuity of Europe. And so they grew up imagining the Holocaust as a distant, mythic event, like the destruction of the Jerusalem Temple two thousand years ago. Jewish Europe wasn't destroyed, merely transplanted and reduced to twenty blocks in Brooklyn.

Though my family followed the same religious calendar and observed most of the same laws as the Hasidim, we inhabited different realities. They lived before 1939; we lived after it.

My father insisted that the Holocaust be the starting point of a Jewish identity. A Jew's first responsibility was to "know the world" and learn the lessons of the Holocaust: vigilance, unity, power. By teaching their children only about prewar Jewish life rather than the event that destroyed it, Hasidim were dooming their children to a fateful ignorance, raising innocents in a hostile world. And if *survivors* produced stupid children, what hope was there for the rest of the Jews?

Alone among his friends, my father sent his children to modern Orthodox, rather than Hasidic, yeshivas. The children in the Nyirbator studied mostly Torah; "English" — by which they meant all subjects not specifically Jewish — was added to their curriculum only because the goyishe authorities demanded it. In my yeshiva the day was evenly divided between religious and general studies. We didn't learn religious subjects in Yiddish but in modern Hebrew and even in English. In the Hasidic yeshivas, rabbis taught that the secular State of Israel was a desecration; our rabbis called it "the first flowering of redemption." Our yarmulkes weren't large and black like Hasidic head-covering but knit from colored woolen swirls and attached to our hair with bobby pins; the Hasidic boys called them "Pepsi-Cola bottle caps," to mock their small size.

My father sabotaged dinners with friends, berating them for sending their children to Hasidic yeshivas, where they learned fairy tales

instead of historical truth. My mother would kick him under the
table, trying to stop his tirade. "What did I say?" he'd ask, deceptively innocent. He remained in Borough Park what he had been in
Nagy-Károly: a rebel among the Hasidim.

The Holocaust should have convulsed the world; but it seemed
to have changed nothing, not even the survivors themselves. Borough
Park's premise was that an entire civilization could be shattered and
its pieces fall back into exactly the same places. My father resisted
the return to a mythic past: Something drastically new must emerge
from our brokenness.

The most galling symbol of the Jews' refusal to learn from history
was the astonishing rise of my father's old Nagy-Károly nemesis, Reb
Yoilish, renowned as the Satmar Rebbe. A tiny man with white ear-
locks that resembled long candlewicks, Reb Yoilish had survived the
death camps and was venerated by thousands of Hasidim as a holy
man. He studied Torah through the night, taking brief naps while
sitting upright in his chair. His blessings to followers were said to
ensure recovery from illness and success in business. Though he
lived in nearby Williamsburg, his influence in Borough Park was decisive. Small Hasidic sects were drawn into the powerful orbit of the
Satmar movement, which called itself *Malchus Satmar*, the kingdom
of Satmar, as though it were a separate people.

Reb Yoilish remained an unrepentant anti-Zionist. My father considered him a literal murderer, one of the principle "misleaders" who
had discouraged Europe's Jews from escaping to the Land of Israel
before the war. And yet for Reb Yoilish, the murderers were Zionists
like my father — for hadn't Reb Yoilish warned that the Zionist apos-
tasy would be punished by God?

Reb Yoilish continued his anti-Zionist campaign, except this time
not in remote Nagy-Károly but in the middle of New York, in full
view of the media. His Hasidim picketed the Israeli consulate in
Manhattan with misspelled English signs, and pasted stickers in the
subways that read, "Zionism and Judaism: Oh no! They can never
be united!" They painted swastikas on the facades of synagogues that
dared to display the Israeli flag; they broke into one Borough Park
synagogue and tore up prayer books that contained a blessing for the
State of Israel. *Soinim*, my father said in Yiddish. Enemies.

Reb Yoilish's Hasidim called him a *"godol,"* a giant of Torah scholarship and piety; my father called him "a nobody." One of his favorite jokes was to make crude changes in Reb Yoilish's last name —"Teitelshmuck" instead of "Teitelbaum." Returning from a trip to his Manhattan customers, he'd drive through Williamsburg and fill his van with Satmar hitchhikers. Throughout the drive, he shouted at his stunned passengers about the crimes of Reb Yoilish. Then, as they neared Borough Park, he half-turned toward them and in a calm, even cheerful, voice asked, "So who goes where?"

2.

Jews lived in Borough Park only formally; in reality, we inhabited invisible landscapes. The ultra-Orthodox returned to pre-Holocaust Europe, while my family spiritually emigrated to Israel.

On our kitchen wall hung a bronze plate engraved with the image of Herzl, bearded and bareheaded, the Zionist rebbe. Even more than the TV in our home, this is what distinguished us from the ultra-Orthodox: We lived for the future, not the past. The existence of a Jewish state — able to rescue endangered Jews in forgotten corners — meant that the world was not exactly the same place it had been before 1939, that Jewish reality could never be the same again. That is why my father was a Zionist and why the Hasidim were not.

Israel's "embassy" in Borough Park was the Yemenite pizza and felafel shop. During school recess, when student monitors made sure no one left the yard, I waited by a side gate for its guard to get distracted, then slipped out and ran crouched behind parked cars until I reached the pizza shop. It was owned by dark-skinned Yemenite Jews, whose abrupt Hebrew made each word sound incomplete, abandoned. They were *yordim*, failed Israelis; but I saw them as emissaries dispensing a taste of Israel to our Brooklyn exile: fried brown balls of mashed chickpeas in round pocket breads stuffed with salad and sauerkraut and covered with watery tahini and an optional fiery sauce of crushed chilies, which I ate as a Zionist initiation. On the walls hung Israeli tourism posters, whose intense blue skies were extensions of the sea, unlike Brooklyn's pale, distant sky. Deserts ended in beaches, mountains shadowed the lowest point on earth, Hasidim prayed in Jerusalem, and motorcyclists rode in Tel Aviv. Israel contained every opposite, a huge embrace.

My father's brother, Yitzchak, lived in the town of Tiberias, on the shore of the Sea of Galilee. In the early 1940s Uncle Yitzchak had been sent to the Ukrainian front by the pro-Nazi Hungarian army, to lay mines in the cross fire; captured by the Russians, he spent the rest of the war as an enemy prisoner in Siberia. After his release, he emigrated to Israel in the late forties. Every year he sent us gifts for another holiday: a silver box to store the *etrog*, the perfumed yellow citron blessed on Sukkot, a gold-embroidered book of Psalms so small it could be hidden in one's palm, a Hanukkah menorah that played the mournful tune of the Israeli national anthem. These were displayed in our living room breakfront, especially sacred because they were from Israel.

The only noncandy items my father sold in his business were Israeli. There were fat memorial *yartzeit* candles, flat tins of gefilte fish, jars of plums that leaked and stained the floor purple. Though his Manhattan customers argued that they couldn't sell *yartzeit* candles and gefilte fish in their fancy shops, my father insisted it was their Jewish duty and offered increasingly larger discounts until he sold the last of the goods at a loss.

Why hadn't he gone to Israel after the war? In a rare moment of weakness he'd placed his own interests before the Jewish people's: "I was tired, war was in Israel, I wanted only quiet and peace."

I would undo his mistake. With my friends from ANA I planned *aliyah*, the Hebrew word for immigration to Israel meaning "ascent": One didn't merely immigrate but rose up to the Land. We would build a kibbutz in the Negev desert; there I would toughen, taking on the desert's leanness. We dug holes and uprooted weeds in an empty lot, preparing to become pioneers.

But could Israel survive until I was old enough to move there? It was a tiny country of refugees surrounded by enemies and the sea; half its land was desert, its pinched center contracted to a mere eight miles between Jordan and the Mediterranean; its borders were so jagged they seemed to have been drawn by an arthritic hand.

The *Jewish Press* constantly reevaluated Israel's fate, alternately trembling and gloating. SYRIA DIVERTS JORDAN RIVER — Israel would turn into desert and wither. ARAB SPY RING UNMASKED — Israel was impenetrable. NAZI SCIENTISTS BUILD DEATH MISSILES IN EGYPT —

Israel would become a nuclear gas chamber. ISRAEL DOWNS SYRIAN PLANE — Who were they kidding to even challenge us?

I often pictured my father's death, as a convulsion of the heart; but Israel's death was unimaginable to me. In my fear for Israel's tenuousness, it was as though I belonged to my parents' generation and hadn't been born with the Jewish state a reality.

I marched with my friends through Borough Park's streets singing pre-state Zionist songs: "We will build our homeland/that is our generation's command, the command of all the generations!" When Hasidim passed, I shouted the words, as if reliving my father's childhood struggle against Reb Yoilish. In my seeming rebellion against Borough Park, I was in fact vindicating its most cherished assumption: that American-born children could be raised to mimic their parents' European lives.

3.

On Israel's Independence Day, Melvin Pickholtz wore his Betar uniform to class: navy blue shirt with breast pockets and epaulets, and a light blue tie. On his upper sleeve was a yellow patch with a map of biblical Israel, including all of Jordan, the borders sharp and generous.

Betar was the youth movement of right-wing Revisionist Zionism, of Menachem Begin and Ze'ev Jabotinsky, the fighting Jews. Though I wasn't quite sure what Betar was about, I wanted to wear its uniform, which gave even Melvin, a scrawny boy, a certain stature.

Our sixth-grade class was filled with boys who wore their plaid shirts buttoned at the neck and polyester pants belted above their stomachs, and whose mothers came at recess to bring them snacks; but even among those boys, Melvin was pathetic. He moved his little body noiselessly, afraid to offend with his presence, eyes to the floor, spying sideways. He accepted his role as an underling, the downtrodden Jew: When a teacher asked for a volunteer to get coffee or chalk, Melvin, without speaking or raising his hand, stood and shuffled out the door.

Melvin was a Betari, a member of Betar, because his father had been a Betari in Poland before the war. Every summer Mr. Pickholtz sent Melvin to Camp Betar in the Catskills. Melvin said the camp had a firing range and staged night maneuvers. Obviously, the rigorous training hadn't helped him; but I was hopeful that if I went to Camp Betar, it might transform me into a tough Jew.

Becoming tough was urgent for me. I lived in a neighborhood of victims, easy targets. A single thug could push his way through crowds of Shabbos strollers, shout that "Hitler didn't get enough of you," and walk away unscathed. The Holocaust should have changed us genetically, made us dangerous, untouchable; instead, we remained the same harmless Jews.

One Sunday Melvin and I took a bus to Betar's Brooklyn headquarters, in the Italian neighborhood of Bensonhurst. We were two boys in yarmulkes surrounded by Gentiles; we sat near the driver, for protection, then walked quickly through the enemy streets.

Betar headquarters was in a basement — appropriate, because the room was a virtual shrine to Revisionist Zionism's underground movements of the 1940s, the anti-British Irgun and even more extreme Stern Group. On the walls were the earnest young faces of underground fighters hanged by the British; the books on the shelves, with titles like *Triumph on the Gallows*, told their half-forgotten stories. The official heroes of Israel were left-wing Labor Zionists like Ben-Gurion and Moshe Dayan — not Revisionists, who were widely despised as extremists.

Perhaps two dozen young people gathered for the weekly Sunday meeting in the basement headquarters, which was called in Hebrew the *maoz*, or stronghold. The meeting began with the singing of the Betar hymn, urging young Jews to "sacrifice blood and soul" for their people, to "die or to conquer the mountain." The hymn predicted that a new generation, "proud, generous, and fierce," would arise from among the powerless ghetto Jews — Jews, I thought, like Melvin and me. Despite its major key, the melody sounded elegiac, partly because it was sung slowly but more so because it had been sung by Betarim in pre-Holocaust Europe. We stood at attention, hands at our sides, an honor guard for the young Irgunists hanged because of their ferocity and for European Jews murdered because they weren't sufficiently fierce.

Then came a briefing by the group's senior leader, a young man with white braids through his epaulets and known as *mefaked ha'maoz,* commander of the stronghold. Betarim, he announced, had thrown water balloons at anti-Israel demonstrators and attacked neo-Nazis in a Manhattan bar. I was thrilled. The mainstream Zionist youth groups taught Israeli folk dancing, but here was a group fighting the enemies of the Jews. Instantly the basement fortress felt like home.

I began coming regularly to Betar headquarters. There I learned Revisionism's alternative Zionist history and assumed its bitter grudges.

According to Revisionism, the revered leaders of Labor Zionism were actually traitors who abandoned European Jewry to the Nazis. Only one Zionist leader had tried to save the Jews: Betar's founder, Ze'ev Jabotinsky. Throughout the 1930s he traveled in Eastern Europe, repeating his cry, "A fire is burning!" He demanded the immediate evacuation of European Jewry to the Land of Israel and the establishment of a Jewish state, despite British and Arab opposition. And he pleaded with Europe's Jews: Don't be the only people in this world — you, the most hated of peoples — who can't handle weapons.

The Labor pioneers, who dominated the Zionist movement, denounced Jabotinsky as an alarmist, a madman, a fascist. They opposed his rescue plan as not only impractical but undesirable. Their priority was creating a socialist Jewish state; only after its founding would the Jewish masses be encouraged to come. Otherwise, their experiment would be overwhelmed by refugees, and the Land of Israel transformed into just another mundane country.

Jabotinsky, the antimessianist, despised Jewish fantasies. Zionism was meant to restore Jews to reality, teach them how to survive, not indulge their *luftmensch* utopianism. Labor dreamed of integrating the future Jewish state into a new world of socialist brotherhood; while Revisionism saw the state as refuge from an unredeemed world's hostility. Labor wanted to turn Jews into farmers and workers; Revisionism, into soldiers.

In 1940, the Holocaust begun, Jabotinsky died in New York of heart failure, defeated by the catastrophe he couldn't prevent. Even as evidence of the Holocaust gathered, Labor leaders failed to organize a rescue campaign. Instead, they continued to build their model socialist society.

In Betar's version of Zionist history, I found the context for my father's insistence that the Jews were partly responsible for their own destruction. But even he had underestimated the extent of our self-betrayal. Except for the Revisionists, the entire Jewish leadership — religious and secular, Zionist and anti-Zionist — had led us to Auschwitz.

Incredibly, despite their vindication, the Revisionists remained Zionism's pariahs. In my home, too, the heroes were Ben-Gurion and Chaim Weizmann, not Jabotinsky and Begin. Betar initiated me into a secret history that not even my father knew; and that knowledge allowed me to assert myself, by being more Zionist, more extreme than he was.

He tried to temper my rage. He conceded that Labor leaders had failed as rescuers but insisted they weren't traitors. It was indeed ludicrous to accuse Israel's founders of willful apathy: Their relatives also died in the Holocaust. Still, it was precisely Betar's judgmentalness that appealed to me. The Holocaust had been so unequivocal that it demanded equally absolute indictments. I wasn't satisfied with villifying entire nations — the murderous Germans, the collaborationist Hungarians and Ukrainians and Lithuanians, the British and American bystanders. Like Reb Yoilish blaming the Zionists for the Holocaust and my father blaming Reb Yoilish, I too needed internal enemies.

Other ideological and historical disputes, besides the Holocaust, divided Revisionists and Laborites: capitalism versus socialism, anti-British terrorism versus political moderation. But those seemed to me secondary issues. I became a right-wing Zionist because I believed that only the Revisionists, those hard realists, could be trusted to lead us in this world. Even if the Messiah came and nations beat their swords into ploughshares, wrote one Revisionist poet, Jews would cling to their weapons, permanently watchful.

I lived with Jews in Borough Park who were trying to resurrect European Jewry. By becoming a Betari and joining the one group that had tried to stop the Holocaust, I would, in a sense, be joining Borough Park's retroactive rescue mission. Among Jews dressed in black fedoras and gabardines, I too would wear a uniform borrowed from prewar Europe — not the uniform of the victims but of the would-be saviors.

Becoming a Betari wasn't like joining other Zionist youth movements. Those groups merely expected members to attend meetings; but to be worthy of wearing the Betar uniform required a lengthy probationary period, an immersion in Revisionist history and ideology. I devoured the Betar reading list, obscure books with angry titles like *Perfidy* and *Woman of Violence*, and became an amateur expert in Revisionist arcana.

For all its activism, the movement's true passion was the past. Betar resembled a secret society devoted to memory, transmitting a history forgotten or distorted by the rest of the Jews.

The other Zionists were celebrating Israel's happy ending of Jewish history; but for us, the state had come too late. Our symbols of militancy evoked mourning, not triumphalism. We paraded military-style and sang songs about the blood of the Macabees flowing in our veins; yet we knew those rites weren't meant for Brooklyn Jews in the sixties but for Polish and Latvian Jews in the thirties, to invigorate them with the will to live.

Even our emblem — the map of biblical Israel, including Jordan — was a symbol of loss. Jabotinsky had demanded maximalist borders for the future Zionist state, to accommodate Europe's Jews; but few Betarim believed anymore that we would ever conquer Jordan. Instead, we kept that map as an empty space of mourning, for all the Jews who would never fill it.

Ironically, the Revisionists, who glorified Jewish power, were themselves politically powerless. The Labor Zionists controlled the state that, we insisted, the Irgun had liberated. And so we settled into a permanent, grieving opposition, without hope of affecting the future, with hope only of rescuing the past from amnesia.

We lived in that past. We mimicked the ideal Betari, whom Jabotinsky had envisioned as a kind of Jewish knight: soft-spoken but strong, courteous but inflexible, sacrificing personal ambition to serve his people. An exemplar of *hadar,* majesty. Remember that you are sons of biblical kings, Jabotinsky exhorted Eastern Europe's ghetto Jews, trying to fill them with a spirit of resistance. I wanted to be an exemplar of *hadar*, unafraid of pain or death: like Shlomo ben-Yosef, an Irgunist hanged by the British, who on the morning of his death calmly brushed his teeth.

One day while walking from the bus stop to Betar headquarters, I heard someone call, "Get the Jewboy!" Then he shouted, "Sic 'im!" A barking dog ran toward me. I didn't turn around. *Hadar:* A Betari shows no fear.

The barking got louder. I continued walking with measured steps, trying to control my furious breathing. A whistle: The dog was retrieved. I entered the Betar basement, feeling I'd just passed my first initiation.

I became editor of the Brooklyn Betar newsletter, three mimeographed sheets on whose masthead was a sketch of a shirtless warrior with swelled chest, holding a sword and shield. I was the only volunteer for the job. I wanted to be a journalist. Jabotinsky, Herzl, Tisbi Illés had all been journalists, using the press to warn Europe's Jews of approaching destruction. A journalist's job was to be alert, restless; by becoming a journalist I might help save the Jews from the next holocaust.

I'd just gotten my first journalistic break: a piece in the *Jewish Press* about my father's wartime experiences. The paper, which often ran articles by writers for whom English wasn't quite a second language, hadn't changed a word of my twelve-year-old's prose or even bothered to correct my mistakes, like spelling "Transylvania" at least three different ways. But so what? I was a published writer.

Suddenly my father realized that he had succeeded: He'd created a Tisbi Illés. He began to manage my writing career, which meant that I'd write up his ideas and submit them to the *Jewish Press*. When he wanted to address Jewish youth about the importance of Israel, I wrote an open letter to Jewish youth about the importance of Israel. I was his translator, Aaron to his Moses, offering the prophetic stutterer fluent speech.

Giving him *nachas*, a parent's pleasure in his child's achievement, was also part of my strategy for preempting his next heart attack. The more joy I gave him, the more I would strengthen his will to live. Conversely, any aggravation could agitate his heart and kill him.

I tried to be a good son, but we quarreled anyway. And so I compensated with a profusion of articles in the *Jewish Press*. Journalism meant salvation: the way to warn Jews of coming danger, the way to give my father life.

My first editorial for the Betar newsletter was an attack on Vatican II, the papal commission that had just issued an unprecedented repudiation of theological anti-Semitism. My single source of information on the commission was the *Jewish Press*, which contemptuously dismissed it as too little, too late. As Orthodox Jews, who cherished every ritual and theological idea accumulated over the centuries, the *Jewish Press* editors might have appreciated the Catholic Church's courage in renouncing elements of its own theology. Instead, the paper insisted the change was meaningless, that Esau still hated Jacob.

Inspired by the *Jewish Press*, my editorial blithely misinterpreted Vatican II, claiming that the Catholic Church had "forgiven" the Jews for deicide when, in fact, it had dismissed that charge as baseless. I was outraged at the imagined insult: Who were those anti-Semites, those murderers, to forgive us? If anything, they should beg for *our* forgiveness!

The editorial reserved its special contempt for "liberal-minded Jews" engaged in the new Catholic-Jewish dialogue, exemplars of what we in Betar called the "ghetto mentality" — or what my father called a "stupid Jew." Stupid Jews were people who pretended they lived in a benign world and who blinded themselves to danger or insult, who assumed they were being complimented when Gentiles told them that they didn't look Jewish or that they were "good Jews," different from the others.

The old mode of Jewish survival — servile accommodation — had become unbearable, had died in the Holocaust with those who practiced it. Before any Jewish dialogue with Christians must come rage, a settling of accounts.

But where was our rage? The post-Holocaust Jew was a kibbutznik, a Nobel Prize winner, a borscht belt comic. Idealistic, funny, at peace with the world. As if nothing had changed. Only the Revisionists remained in bitter mourning; and that, even more than for their militancy, was why I belonged among them.

4.

I asked my parents to send me to Camp Betar. I dismissed their anxiety about the camp not being religious and appealed to their sense of Jewish unity. Unlike most Zionist youth movements, which were either entirely secular or Orthodox, Betar welcomed all Jews; didn't that deserve our support? The brochure Melvin Pickholtz gave me said the camp respected tradition and kept a kosher kitchen. And anyway, having just turned bar mitzvah, I was now a responsible Jew; shouldn't I be trusted to uphold my faith?

It worked. Somehow my parents were too distracted by religious issues to notice what should have been their real anxiety: Camp Betar's paramilitary training. In their concern for prayer services and Shabbos observance, they forgot to worry about guns and night maneuvers.

In early July they drove me to the Catskills, past the town of Liberty, famous for Grossinger's Hotel, to a village called Neversink. I half-hoped the camp would be surrounded by a high fence, with an armed guard at the gate checking my name from a list. While in nearby Grossinger's Jews gorged on five-course meals, I would be training for Jewish survival. Perhaps there was even a network of concrete bunkers beneath the camp, in which young people in dark blue uniforms studied maps of the world with colored pins marking areas of Jewish distress, in constant contact with Menachem Begin in Jerusalem and the editor of the *Jewish Press* in Brooklyn.

But there was no guard at the camp, not even a gate. Blue-and-white-painted bunks were clustered on grassy slopes; there was a volleyball court and a swimming pool. Camp Betar suspiciously resembled summer camp.

Danny, a junior counselor, became one of my first friends: We were among the few boys at camp who wore yarmulkes. Every week he seemed to wear a different one, knit by his latest girlfriend. The rumor was that Danny was secretly seeing a girl from Shomria, the neighboring camp of the Marxist Zionist movement, Hashomer Hatzair, Betar's arch rival. But I refused to believe that Danny — who came from a famous Revisionist family and whose father had known Jabotinsky personally — would let romance conflict with ideology.

Danny decided to teach me, ethereal yeshiva boy with heroic ambitions, how to handle a gun. He took me to the firing range at the edge of camp. "We'll begin with a nice easy gun, a twenty-two," he said. He attached a target to a distant post. Then he placed the rifle in my hands. "Not so stiff," he said. "The gun is your friend."

I missed the target. Danny said, "When you look into the sight, imagine that your eye, the bullet, and the bull's-eye are on one continuous line." I fired. Danny ran to the target. "Mazel tov," he shouted, "you hit it!" I felt the historical moment: I was the first in my family, perhaps since biblical times, to learn to use a weapon. After two thousand years of living as a pacifist among predators, Jacob was becoming Esau.

Late one night my bunk was roused. A counselor solemnly announced that, according to information just received by senior Betarim, anti-Semites from Neversink were about to attack the camp. We lay in ambush in the tall, wet grass on the border between the village and the camp. In the distance we heard laughter, shouting: "Yahoo, gonna get me a Jew!" Our counselor said, "Remember Yosef Trumpledor's last words: 'It is good to die for one's country.'"

The voices neared. They began singing — a Betar song. It was a setup, a joke — but also a lesson: Be prepared.

Yet what if the attack had been real? I'd never been in an actual fight; I didn't know how to damage another body.

I confided to Danny. "I've never even hit anyone in the face," I said glumly.

"Are you serious?" he asked. He took off his glasses. "Hit me."

"What do you mean, hit you?"

"If you don't hit me, I'm going to hit you."

I made a tentative fist.

"Hit me!"

I punched him on the nose.

"I think you've got it," he said in a muffled voice, hands cradling his face.

On Saturday nights we crowded the dining room porch and sang songs of the underground. "Today, little Sarah, I go off to war/ Don't cry, this is my fate," the marching tune stifling sentimentality. When we sang the refrain, "Mount the barricades!" we raised our fists, like exclamation marks.

Then the dancing began. A boy held a small clay drum under his arm, fingers snapping across the skin; a girl slapped her thigh with a tambourine. An obese Canadian who lived in a tree house belly danced, while the rest of us shouted, "Ya Allah!" clapping and hooting. We sang a song we considered very funny, about busting up Camp Shomria and slitting Arab throats. The crude racism didn't bother me: We were trying to harden ourselves, learn to reciprocate our enemy's hatred. Besides, I thought, we didn't really mean it: We also sang about the Land of Israel embracing "the son of Nazareth, the son of Arabia, and my son."

Indeed, Betarim seemed to be right-wing only in their insistence on Jewish power. Some Betarim even flirted with Marxism. My counselor said that, as a Zionist, he identified with all liberation movements. I was relieved that becoming a Betari didn't require me to be a right-wing conservative. Though both the civil rights and anti-Vietnam movements were happening very far from Borough Park, I supported both as a passionate spectator. I hated conservatism: What was it trying to conserve, if not the old world that created Auschwitz?

The ideological diversity within Betar wasn't really surprising. To be a Betari required the courage of nonconformism. It meant violating the Jewish consensus, the version of Zionist history in Leon Uris's *Exodus*, which idealized moderate Ari ben-Canaan and villified his Irgunist uncle, Barak. Nothing, in fact, proved Betar's marginality so much as its contempt for Leon Uris.

I was drawn to Betar precisely because of its marginality. My father had taught me that in times of crisis only individualists survived; by its very eccentricity, Betar proved it knew the secret of survival.

I had come to camp hoping to physically transform myself, to fight for Jewish survival. But except for occasional rifle practice, my training was theoretical, confined to discussions on Revisionism and sing-alongs about redeeming Judea with fire and blood.

Yet I was learning another kind of survival: how to cope with differences. Camp Betar was my entry into the world outside Borough Park. I met Reform Jews and agnostics and atheists, who challenged my instilled sense of Orthodox superiority. There were, it seemed,

many ways to be a "good Jew"; and in that prosaic realization was
my first appreciation of human diversity.

One Saturday night Israeli dancers came to camp. They wore long,
embroidered peasant shirts over baggy pants and laughed as they
flew barefoot to a staccato accordion.

Danny motioned me outside. Wordlessly he pointed to the
dancers' car: a Volkswagen. They had dared come to Camp Betar in
what we called a "Nazi wagon."

Boycotting German goods was one of Betar's most sacred commandments. The Revisionists had fought a violent but unsuccessful
campaign in the fifties against the Labor government's rapproache-
ment with Germany. Labor wanted Israel to heal the rift between
Jews and Gentiles, even Germans; while Revisionism saw Israel as
the repository of our wounds.

I considered the Jewish failure to shun Germany proof that we
were a debased people, lacking the most minimal self-respect. I hated
Germans. All Germans. Children, old people, anyone who spoke that
language and lived that culture. Nazis couldn't possibly hate Jews, I
thought, as much as I hated Germans. If I inadvertently touched
some product made in Germany, my hand recoiled, repelled by intimacy with Germanness.

My father reinforced that revulsion. The German government offered survivors monetary compensation — "reparations" — for their
suffering during the war, and every month glassine envelopes with
checks from the Bundesbank arrived in Borough Park homes. But
not in our home: Though often in debt, my father refused to accept
what he called "blood money."

A crowd gathered around the Volkswagen. Someone suggested we
smash the windows and puncture the tires. They're still Jews, someone else countered, defending the dancers. We rolled the car down
the hill and toppled it into a ditch just outside of camp.

Sometimes there were mysterious visitors from Israel, short men in
black berets, silent behind sunglasses and cigarettes. Our counselors
would discreetly identify them: That one assassinated a British intelligence officer, that one helped blow up the King David Hotel.
The anonymous men would watch us from a distance, measuring

the new generation, and then slip away. Their presence was a reminder of what opportunities for glory awaited us, if history were as generous to us as it had been to them.

A major part of our Betar education focused on why the Irgunists and Sternists weren't terrorists but freedom fighters. Their actions raised many moral questions, and Betar had an answer for every one. Why did over ninety people die in the Irgun bombing of the King David Hotel? Because the British, who were headquartered there, had ignored an Irgun warning to evacuate the building. Why did 120 Arab civilians die in an Irgun assault on the fortified village of Deir Yassin? Because an Irgun sound truck sent to warn the villagers had broken down, without the attack force knowing it.

We sang elegies about Shlomo ben-Yosef, the first "Hebrew," in Betar's nationalist language, to be hanged by the British. Ben-Yosef had thrown a grenade, which failed to explode, at a crowded Arab bus. He intended to avenge an Arab attack on a Jewish bus; and so, we were told, his act wasn't terrorism but self-defense.

We neutralized our moral dilemmas with euphemism. Murder was resistance; terrorist victims, faceless oppressors. The only blood you mourned for and exalted in song was the blood of your own martyrs.

My favorite martyrs were Eliyahu bet-Zouri and Eliyahu Hakim, the "two Eliyahus," who assassinated Lord Moyne, British colonial minister for the Middle East. Though teenagers, they faced death with the calm of old saints. When the hangman placed the nooses around their necks, he trembled; the two Eliyahus reassured him: We know you're doing your job, just as we did ours. The hangman wept.

I wanted to be like them. And though afraid I lacked the courage to kill and die, I feared an ordinary life even more.

Toward the end of summer I took the written test to become a Betari. A counselor named Winkie handed me a long list of typed questions. Then he left me alone in a room full of Revisionist books. Though I routinely cheated on school tests, I didn't cheat now. Winkie was testing my honor as a Betari.

He returned an hour later, read my answers, and solemnly shook my hand. "You are now a Betari," he said.

Every Friday, just before sundown, campers and counselors

gathered on the parade ground, to welcome the Sabbath, Betar-style. Those who had passed the Betar test wore their uniforms, standing at attention while the American, Israeli, and Betar flags were lowered from poles. The Friday after I passed the test, I too wore a uniform. Feet together, hands at my sides, I sang the Betar anthem, recalling my father in the hole: "From the pit of dust and decay will arise a generation, proud, generous, and fierce . . ."

Three

Summer of Love

I MET Glenn Richter one afternoon in 1965. He stood on a Borough Park street corner, offering leaflets to passersby. A green trench coat hung shapeless on his long, thin body, and a peddler's cap flattened and extended his head like a misplaced beak; his thick-framed glasses and thin mustache resembled a comical mask. On his lapel was a button that read "Student Struggle for Soviet Jewry."

"Take a leaflet, *read* it and give it to a friend," he repeated over and over in a staccato chant. When a woman passed him with a baby carriage, he dropped a leaflet under its canopy. "Babies can help too," he said.

He began making a speech to the impervious crowd, enunciating each syllable. "We are in a war to save a *quart*-er of the *Jew*-ish people. *You* can make a dif-fer-ence. *This* time we *won't* be silent."

I was his only audience. "I'd like to help," I said finally, enraged at my high voice.

"Yes sir!" he replied. "Glenn Richter's the name. That's G-lenn *Rich*-ter. As in the Richter scale. We're trying to create a *groundswell* of public opinion. That's a joke, man. What can I do you in for?"

"You from some organization?"

"Ah, now we come to the punch line. The Stu-dent Strug-gle for Sov-iet Jewry. Triple S-J. 'J' for Jew, man."

Then, in the pinched voice of Donald Duck, he said, "I *am* my brother's keeper! Or is it my kipper's brother?" Resuming his normal tone, he added, "But seriously folks," and then immediately quacked again, "But seriously folks!"

"I'm in sixth grade," I said. "Am I too young to join?"

His voice deep now, he said, "No one is too young, my son, to join in the great cause of helping his brothers."

He took a piece of paper from the table. "This is what we here call an official membership form. Just put your X —"

"What?"

"Your name, address, favorite TV show. Kidding. Give me your phone number, and we'll be in touch. Don't call us; we'll call you. That's because we're going to call you so often, you won't *want* to call us."

I asked for some leaflets to hand out at school.

"The man wants leaflets, we'll give him leaflets."

He piled boxes filled with sheets onto my arms: Soviet Jewry facts and figures, eyewitness reports of trips to Russia, reprints of anti-Semitic cartoons from the Soviet press. On top of those he placed boxes filled with buttons and stickers.

"Congratulations," said Glenn Richter, "you are now the Borough Park elementary school chairman of SSSJ."

Then he said, "Take some of these here leaflets, partner. It's for our next rally. The Menorah March. On Hanukkah, strangely enough. Welcome to the Student Striggle!"

I had heard of the problems Jews were having in the Soviet Union. Old people denied matzoh; young people, a religious education. But only after reading Glenn Richter's material did I realize this wasn't just one more item on a *Jewish Press* list of woes. There were three million Jews in the Soviet Union — half of six million — the last great Eastern European Jewish community.

The Soviets were destroying Judaism by outlawing memory. Even mourning the Holocaust was forbidden. Soviet Jews were in an untenable dilemma: Ordered to assimilate, they were still taunted for being Jews. Cartoons in the press showed prayer-shawled worshipers fighting over dollar bills, a grotesquely hooked-nosed Jew bowing before a Nazi boot. These cartoons weren't published by fringe hate groups but by a superpower government.

Accounts by tourists to Russia were invariably the same: Soviet Jews never spoke directly to foreigners but brushed against them, handing them notes and whispering, "They don't let us live," "We can't hold out much longer," and always, over and over, "Why don't the American Jews protest?"

And yet Soviet Jews weren't completely intimidated. Once a year, on Simchat Torah, festival of dancing, thousands of young Jews appeared spontaneously before the last remaining synagogue in Moscow, a miraculous materialization. Agents of the KGB circulated; spotlights illuminated the anonymous crowd; but still they came, to dance horas and sing Yiddish songs whose words they didn't understand, a Jewish resistance to mortality.

In his account of a trip to the Soviet Union, *The Jews of Silence*, Elie Wiesel described the young people gathered around accordions and balalaikas: A girl played an old Yiddish song on a guitar, "Buy my cigarettes, take pity on a poor orphan"; a group sang a wedding song, substituting the words for greeting the bride with, "Come let us greet the Jewish people."

In the middle of one circle, wrote Wiesel, a young woman sang a Yiddish song and then led a chant. "Who are we?" she asked.

"Jews!" shouted everyone, laughing.

"What are we?"

"Jews!"

"What will we remain?"

"Jews!"

Afterward, Wiesel asked her, What do you know about Judaism? That it is based on outdated values, she said. And about the Jewish people? That it is made up of capitalists and swindlers. And Israel? That it is racist and imperialist. Where did you learn all this? From school textbooks and the press. Why then, asked Wiesel, do you insist on remaining a Jew?

"What does it matter what *they* think of us?" she said. "It's what *we* think that counts." Then she added, "I'll tell you why I'm a Jew. Because I like to sing."

In SSSJ (which we pronounced: "triple S-J") I found my purpose. Instead of fighting ghosts like the American Nazi Party, holdovers from my father's war, I'd be playing out the next phase of Jewish history. The liberation of Soviet Jewry was my generation's chance to undo American Jews' silence during the Holocaust; in saving Soviet Jewry, we would save ourselves.

I became an activist, an obsessive. During school recess I confronted friends with facts from Glenn's leaflets, and I recruited dozens of new members for SSSJ. I'd been used to suppressing my emotions, afraid they might overwhelm me; but now I released them — in safe, measured doses — through the euphemism of slogans. I'd learned from my father that personal identity didn't matter: In an instant, history could sweep you away. And so I expressed my individuality through activism, at once losing and finding myself in an impersonal cause.

I alternated my Sundays between the Betar basement and SSSJ headquarters. The SSSJ office was two rooms — "Suite 4D," as our stationary proclaimed it — in an almost-vacant tenement awaiting demolition, near Harlem. There were only a handful of activists and no budget. The organization depended on dollar bills sent by college students, occasional checks from synagogue men's clubs, the sale of buttons at rallies. Once Glenn had to delay printing a newsletter because he couldn't afford ink for the mimeograph; SSSJ leaflets — piled on desks, in the bathtub, in the dumbwaiter — were printed on both sides of the sheet, to save paper. "We may be Jews," said Glenn, "but we're not Rothschilds."

In the early 1960s Glenn had been a civil rights worker in Mississippi. Then he dropped out of law school to become SSSJ's national coordinator, which meant being office manager, secretary, archivist, and PR director. He brilliantly concealed SSSJ's marginality, renting small halls for rallies and then issuing press releases about the overflow crowd; he set up a sound truck in Manhattan's Garment District during lunch hour, and the papers reported a rally of thousands, not realizing that most "demonstrators" were in fact passersby, stopping briefly from curiosity.

Once I asked him why he was devoting his life to SSSJ, and he said, with a rare sobriety, "In my understanding of Jewish history, someone always came along to help. So now it's my turn. No great soul-searching stuff; you just do what you gotta do, man."

Of course, there was no money to pay him. "I don't need a salary," he said, "I'm a brain surgeon on the side. No seriously, I'm independently impoverished." At rallies he avoided the stage where dignitaries gathered, taking care of details instead. He sought no recognition and got none.

The Great Menorah March, as the SSSJ leaflet proclaimed it, proceeded through Central Park and ended at the Soviet UN mission on the Upper East Side. It was a freezing December night. Glenn rushed by with a walkie-talkie and called out to me, "It's colder in Siberia!" We kept our spirits by singing the Hebrew words of Isaiah's messianic prophecy, "Nation shall not lift sword against nation and shall study war no more." We sang the sad melody in loud, earnest voices. We held flashlights covered with red foil to simulate flames, forming a ragged line of light through the deserted park.

Though barely a thousand people were marching, the procession seemed endless to me. Pressed on all sides by college students, I couldn't see its beginning or end. The very fact that we were demonstrating, breaking the timidity of American Jews, meant that we had already won. Soon we would be ten thousand, a hundred thousand; soon the streets of every city would be filled with Jewish songs.

At home later that night, I completed the activist's ritual: watching the TV news for your demonstration to appear, then scanning the screen for familiar faces in the crowd, especially your own. Suddenly I saw it: my face blank with cold, framed by a black vinyl hat with earmuffs and a visor. I had crossed the bridge from marginal Brooklyn to make my mark in Manhattan. And my generation would break with my father's in precisely that transition: We would know power.

*   *   *

By the time I'd met Glenn on a Borough Park street corner, SSSJ was a year old. Its founder and chairman was Ya'akov Birnbaum, an Englishman in his late thirties who had recently come to America to found the Soviet Jewry movement. Ya'akov was a large man with a beaked nose and a Vandyke. He imposed his presence with vast sweeps of his arms. He filled his sentences with "You see, you see," said not merely from habit but urgently, imploring you to share his vision. Like Moses, he had a speech impediment, often turning his *r*s into *w*s.

What we knew of Ya'akov's past were events that coincided with Jewish history. He had grown up in prewar Nazi Germany, then fled with his parents to England. His father, a linguist, worked as a government censor during the war and brought home news of the Holocaust. "My father was a scholar's scholar, an utterly impwactical man," he said. "His helplessness, you see, seared itself into my soul."

Ya'akov had a grand strategy: The Soviet Union, he said, would decline economically and become dependent on the West. Enter SSSJ, which would shame an apathetic American Jewry into action; and American Jewry — leading a "gweat coalition for human wights" — would in turn pressure Washington to champion our cause. Finally, Washington would present the Soviets with an ultimatum: free trade for Jewish freedom.

That, at least, was the plan. For now, though, SSSJ was an ignored fringe of the American Jewish community, which placed Soviet Jewry close to the bottom of its priorities. Though we were obsessively respectable — before a rally Glenn would mail out a list of "approved" slogans for picket signs, so that no militant note compromised our tone — the Jewish establishment considered us dangerous radicals. Some accused us of risking the lives of Soviet Jews by provoking the Kremlin with our "irresponsible" protests. Most dismissed us as fantasists.

Still, I believed in Ya'akov's prophetic powers, a result of his selflessness. Ya'akov convinced me that American Jewry would be mobilized, that the conscience of the world would be stirred, that the amnesiac and intimidated Soviet Jews would retrieve their identity and courage and return to the Jewish people. We simply had to "*shrei gevalt*," cry out in anguish, Ya'akov said in Yiddish, and the re-demptive force hidden in history would be released.

I had never met a religious person like Ya'akov. Borough Park Jews wanted nothing more than to be secluded from the world, left alone with their rituals and pain; but Ya'akov was trying to place us at the center of international events. He believed in redemption and lived his life in messianic expectation. For my father, the Messiah was invoked either as a joke or with a sigh: Anything hopeless was compared to "waiting for the Messiah." But Ya'akov was convinced that a messianic era marked by world respect for human rights was approaching, and he saw the Soviet Jewry movement as part of an awakening of oppressed peoples everywhere. His language evoked a vast messianic stirring: Demonstrations were a "great convergence"; SSSJ, a "great cry of conscience."

As with the early civil rights movement, SSSJ was moved not by rage but righteous indignation. Hope protected us from bitterness: Soon the world would respond to our pain. We would win because we had to win; there was no cause more just, no political movement more pure. We appealed to justice — to "public opinion." Ya'akov re-peated those two words so often that they evoked for me a concrete image: a disciplined and organized force waiting, in his phrase, to be "galvanized."

My father had insisted that something new must emerge from the Holocaust, an end to Jewish innocence and passivity; and Ya'akov taught me to apply that lesson. But the truly radical change wasn't just that Jews were finally protesting, but that this time we would have allies. Ya'akov implied that the Holocaust wasn't confirmation of eter-nal gentile enmity, as my father taught, but perhaps the opposite: the turning point leading to an era of peace between Jews and "the world." Ya'akov's daring premise was that decency existed; we simply had to rouse it. Gentiles of goodwill would atone for the past by helping us save our Eastern European remnant. One of SSSJ's first demonstra-tions was an interfaith fast at the Soviet mission; Martin Luther King and other civil rights leaders routinely spoke for our cause.

I watched the civil rights demonstrations on TV, the vast inte-grated crowds singing their hopeful songs; and I sensed that Ya'akov was right, that the world *had* changed since the Holocaust, that helpless people would no longer be abandoned. It was as if Auschwitz had made redemption not only necessary but possible: Having seen a working model of perfect evil, one could now dare to imagine a world of perfect good.

My father, though pleased with my activism, was skeptical. "Protest," he said to me, "by all means protest your brothers' unjust sufferings. But how much good it will do . . ."

I wanted him to understand that this was the generation of re-demption. If we could prevent another mass Jewish disappearance, then the Holocaust wouldn't be the last word on our history — and he wouldn't have been wrong, as he sometimes said he was, to bring Jewish children into the world. But he refused to be comforted. He doubted the very basis of SSSJ's strategy: that gentile goodwill could be roused for Jews. Nothing had changed in the Goy's hatred of the Jew, or ever would.

On the Sundays I spent in the Betar basement, my father's skep-ticism was reinforced by the Revisionist warning: Don't be duped, like prewar Europe's Jews were, by utopian illusions. But spending alternate Sundays at the SSSJ office was like emerging from my fa-ther's hole into a world of infinite possibility. Ya'akov and my father debated within me, and I developed two personae: the SSSJ optimist and the survivor pessimist. I believed in a messianic future of har-mony; I trusted only the hard lessons of the past. Each side was cer-tain of its truth; each awaited vindication.

                                                                        2.

Early in the morning of June 5, 1967, I found my father hovering over the kitchen radio. It wasn't unusual for him to pace the house at all hours, driven from bed by defaulting customers and Arab threats to Israel and memories of confinement in small spaces, one anxiety unleashing them all. "So what's the news?" I asked. That was our standard greeting, and it meant, What's happening with Israel and to the Jews?

"War," he said. "When I heard first the news, I saw the hairs on my arm standing."

For weeks we had been expecting war. In May Egypt had block-aded the Straits of Tiran, Israel's shipping route to the east, and

moved its army to the Sinai border. The papers filled with genocidal threats and boasts from Arab capitals. On TV we saw hysterical
Egyptian crowds leaping around banners of skulls and crossbones.
America, which had promised to protect Israel, was neutral. Everyone
was neutral, except the allies of the Arabs.

And I had to watch from a distance. The most important events
in my life were happening, and all I could do was join helpless rallies at the UN. The Holocaust was about to happen again, but this
time it would be far worse, because not only would Jews die but
Israel itself would disappear.

Israel was our last resort: Only the fulfillment of our most
grandiose fantasy, the return to Zion in the "end of days," could revive and comfort us after our history had seemed to end in 1945. If
Israel were destroyed, we would lack the strength to dream again in
history, lack the will to live.

Don't worry, my father had said just before the war, we still have
the French; they are real *ohavei Yisrael,* lovers of the Jewish people.
But then the French government joined the weapons embargo against
Israel. "French?" said my father. "The biggest anti-Semite. What do
you need more than Dreyfus?" He retaliated with his own embargo,
refusing to stock French lozenges in his warehouse.

The Six-Day War ended almost as soon as it began. The Israeli army
struck in all directions, mastering expanses and mazes, heights and
depths. We raced across the desert to the Suez Canal and took the
Old City of Jerusalem, alley by alley. We leaped up the Golan Heights
and descended to Jericho and the Dead Sea. "We": of course, we.

On Borough Park's streets, circles formed around anyone with a
transistor radio. Newspapers were public property. There were no
passersby. Even cars lost their anonymity: Drivers shouted the latest news through rolled-down windows. Though victory was certain
a few hours after the war began, the tension persisted, increased.
How far would we dare to go? Nablus, Bethlehem, Hebron: The new
map became instantly familiar, as though those places had never left
us. "When I saw the Jews on television streaming to the Wall,"
Ya'akov Birnbaum said to me, referring to the just-liberated Western
Wall, "I thought that all the millions of Jewish souls, you see, had
come together in one gweat movement."

Before I could even savor relief in Israel's survival, I was over-whelmed with euphoria at its conquests. The Arabs had coveted our few kilometers; we expanded to biblical borders. They had tried to destroy the fragile beginnings of Jewish power; we were now the Middle Eastern superpower. Just like Purim: not merely reprieve but reversal, Haman hanging from the gallows he had intended for Mordecai.

Like the Holocaust, this victory was too much, an excess of history. How could a Jew stay balanced? We seemed to be either on the edge of destruction or redemption, the world's great victims or victors. A nation of manic depressives.

My father said, "Who could believe such a thing possible?" He meant, Who could believe that the survivors and their children could win this victory? His customers congratulated him as though he had personally led the troops. But even at his moment of triumph, he couldn't resist offering a lesson in Jewish survival. "And why did we win?" he asked his customers. "Because — with God help — we were *united.*"

School collapsed. I was in eighth grade, and these were the final weeks before graduation. It was the beginning of summer, and the clear, hot days excited with newness and power. Our rabbi tried to continue teaching; Talmud study, he said, was the best protection for the Jewish people. But we were too restless to sit penned in our desks. And besides, I thought, our rabbi was wrong: The best protection for the Jewish people was Jewish guns. We left school and went to Borough Park's busiest avenue to collect money for Israel, but really just to be among Jews. I stood holding a round tin charity box. I didn't have to solicit by rattling the can; dollar bills were forced through the slit. Jews emptied their pockets into huge Israeli flags spread like nets on street corners, reckless with joy, giving not to help Israel but to touch its radiance.

One afternoon I went with friends to the Satmar yeshiva, head-quarters of the followers of my father's old nemesis, Reb Yoilish. For Satmar Hasidim, the Six-Day War was a theological disaster: If the Zionists had really violated God's plan by prematurely restoring Jewish sovereignty, why had they been rewarded with the capture of the biblical heartland? For consolation, the Satmars said that God had punished Israel by killing eight hundred of its soldiers in battle.

But that was a lame retort: Eight hundred Jews had been gassed in Auschwitz every hour; we could absorb the price of Israel's victory.

We paraded back and forth before Satmar's red brick fortress, waving Israeli flags. What better way to celebrate than by humiliating these keepers of eternal exile, mad pessimists who remained in their cells even when the prison door had opened? We sang the Israeli national anthem and shouted its final verse: "We have not lost our hope, the hope of two thousand years." We laughed at the Satmar boys wearing black clothes as though in mourning, huddled at the windows, speechless and sullen.

There were rumors around Borough Park that a Jerusalem shoemaker and kabbalist had predicted the war, to be followed by the Messiah's arrival. The Six-Day War's reversal of the natural order, the virtually instant transformation of the most meek people into one of the most powerful, was inevitably perceived in messianic terms. Any generation of believing Jews would have identified this era as messianic: moving from our worst nightmare to our most improbable dream, from the ingathering of the Jews into Auschwitz to the ingathering into Israel. We had entered the time of fantasy fulfillment.

Ya'akov Birnbaum had taught me that the messianic era meant the return of the Jews not only to Israel but to the world. And, indeed, the Six-Day War seemed to promise that, too. Even in communist Eastern Europe people cheered our victory, telling jokes about "our" Jews beating the "Soviet" Arabs — Israelis of Polish and Hungarian origin defeating the Soviet-backed Arab armies. Jewish power had transformed not only the Jews but the Gentiles. In those six days in June the world had been undone, recreated. We were admired, if not yet loved; the curse of Jewish ostracism seemed over.

Jewish power had made the world safe; now I could allow myself to feel not only like a Jew but like a human being. I'd recently discovered rock 'n' roll, which became the soundtrack of my newfound humanity. A Borough Park stationery store run by a suspicious man with numbers on his arm sold singles for a quarter apiece. Most were worthless, but occasionally a single by Bob Dylan would materialize in the pile. Dylan's voice was rasping, mocking, at once tender and taunting, a voice only a young person could love. I hung a poster of

Dylan in my room, beside a picture of the Revisionist leader, Jabotinsky. My friends and I quoted Dylan to each other; a sudden twang in our voice would announce a Dylan line: "He not busy bein' born is busy dyin'!" I bought a harmonica, just like Dylan's and magical in its lightness; I packed away my accordion for good.

The TV news veered between Israel and California, where hippies from all over America were gathering in the streets. They smoked marijuana and banana peels at be-ins and love-ins, laughing as they described how the seeming solidity of the world dissolved into colored patterns, a miracle landscape accessible to anyone who only knew how to look. Like the Jews after the Six-Day War, the hippies were celebrating simple existence. The "Summer of Love," they called it. In the San Francisco neighborhood of Haight-Ashbury, barefoot hippies with long hair and embroidered robes danced with bells and tambourines, as though the return of the biblical lands to the Jews had inspired a biblical resurrection.

I listened to FM radio, where they played songs coming out of San Francisco. The incessant music pulled me into its strangeness. Even the names of the bands were mysterious, Jefferson Airplane and Quicksilver Messenger Service and the Grateful Dead, as though language itself were being refashioned for a new kind of communication. I would turn on the radio with the thrill of anticipation, wondering what new sounds were about to emerge. And I wanted to follow those sounds to their source, go to San Francisco and dance in the festive urban streets, celebrate the transformation of the world from a place of menace to one of delight.

But I was fourteen years old, San Francisco was far away, and becoming a hippie was not an acceptable option in Borough Park. My father feared the hippies: Their flaunting nonconformism portended chaos, the return of Europe's madness. Where I saw Isaiah's messianic world, he saw Weimar Germany.

A head shop selling hippie paraphernalia opened on one of Borough Park's border streets. I looked around to make sure no Jews noticed me, then slipped into the dark purple incense room. Glass display cases offered curled pipes and cigarette paper. On the walls were posters of motorcyclists, rock bands, a black man in an Afro holding a burning guitar, hippies wearing army fatigues and satin capes and cowboy boots and top hats: Purim! For a dollar I bought a pair of granny glasses, round and blue-tinted with a thin metal frame. I wore them on Borough Park's streets only at night, when my father was certain to be home and not driving by. I was so proud: In my Borough Park exile I felt linked to messianic San Francisco, my eyes transformed into dilated blue orbs, ready for new vision.

                                                                    3.

Three weeks after the war, my father and I flew to Israel. The trip was my bar mitzvah present, in place of a fancy party. We couldn't afford a family trip, so my mother and sister stayed home.

We were met at the airport by my father's brother, Yitzchak. The two brothers hadn't seen each other in twenty years. Yitzchak collapsed onto my father and then onto me. He spoke in a high voice, almost falsetto, alternately comic and urgent.

We rode to Yitzchak's home in the Galilee town of Tiberias. Tanks on flatbed trucks slowed traffic. Even the civilian vehicles — canvas trucks and jeeps — looked military. We stopped to drink sugared grapefruit juice at a café decorated with little plastic Israeli flags strung along the walls and a handwritten sign, "*Kol hakavod l'Zahal,*" All honor to the Israeli army. The air smelled of gasoline and jasmine — a hard, sweet mingling.

Yitzchak and his wife, Henyu, and their son, Yossi, lived in a tiny stucco house, with a sloping red roof that had turned pink in the strong sun. The house was on a hill overlooking Tiberias, beside which lay the Kinneret, the Sea of Galilee. Across the still waters rose the Golan Heights. Until three weeks earlier, Tiberias had lain open before the Syrians entrenched on the Golan; sometimes they fired at Israeli fishing boats on the Kinneret. During the war, Tiberias's people came out at night to watch the white streaks over the Golan. My cousin Yossi's biggest regret, he said to me, was that he was only sixteen and hadn't been able to join the fighting.

Yossi was short but powerful. He appeared to be always smirking, his great arms folded. His nose was sharp, his lips thin, his brown hair streaked blond from the sun. He had grown up swimming and fishing under Syrian guns. Summers he swam the entire morning, net in hand, near where the fishing boats waited; and he'd return to shore with a net full of carp. Even at home he wore his bathing suit, without a shirt and barefoot, ignoring his mother's shouting pleas. "I'll tell you the truth," he said to her, "I'd walk around naked if I could." His single lapse from masculinity was his high-pitched voice, an echo of his father's; and as though shamed by his voice, he stuttered — not severely, but just enough to seem vulnerable.

Yossi spoke endlessly of the army, imagining himself in all its uniforms. Should he become a paratrooper in red beret, a scout sent before the tanks and the first likely casualty, a frogman mining an enemy port? "I'll tell you the truth," he said to me, "I'm not afraid of anything." He spoke so matter-of-factly that it didn't sound like boasting, but the objective assessment he meant it to be.

Yossi planned to travel the globe. His parents had been refugees; he would be an explorer. He tormented his parents with accounts of the countries he intended to visit. "Do you know there are still cannibals in the Congo? *That* will be interesting to see." Yitzchak and Henyu feared for this strange boy whose great ambitions were catching fish and exploring dangerous places. But Yossi was an Israeli: The world didn't threaten but entice him.

I loved Yossi's shrugs, his detached boasting, his charming and unnecessary shyness. We were brothers, both of us named for the same dead patriarch. I delighted in Yossi Klein, this Israeli — better — image of myself.

My father also loved Yossi, thrilled that our family had produced a Jew with muscles. With Yossi he arm-wrestled; with me he played chess. I had grown up physically detached, a Diaspora Jew exiled from my body.

But Yossi was slowly changing me. Every morning we awoke with the sunrise, ate a breakfast of yogurt and olives, and went down to the sea. My feet calloused on the stony shore, and even the intense summer heat was invigorating, a pressure against which the body stirred. After swimming we went to the outdoor market, lined with felafel stands offering bowls of fried eggplant, hot peppers, pickled lemons. I wore shorts and sandals, my shirt unbuttoned at the chest, Israeli-style; on a chain around my neck was a memento of the war: a bullet, sharp like an animal's tooth.

Throughout that summer Israel celebrated itself. Everyone was a hero, had performed some role in the miracle. The radio played "All

You Need Is Love," an anthem the Beatles could have written for Israel. On a kibbutz beneath the Golan whose children had been raised in air-raid shelters, my father embraced a passing teenage girl and kissed her; and no one seemed to consider his effusiveness misplaced. Israel's people were so intimate that everyone had been entrusted with at least one military secret, which they would share with you if you promised not to tell anyone. *"Habibi,"* Yossi said to me, using an Arabic endearment, "you are now in the safest country in the world."

I went with Yossi to see a documentary on the war, an instant film. The theater was packed, as if Israeli needed visual proof that the miracle had really happened. A young Hasidic recruit appeared on screen, holding up his rifle and grinning, amazed to be a soldier; and the audience clapped and laughed with him, sharing the absurd joy of Jewish victory. We sang war hymns along with the soundtrack, a staccato accordion playing rousing, sentimental songs that boasted not so much of Israel's power but of its permanence: "Tomorrow, a thousand housing projects will arise, and if not tomorrow — then the day after." Then we quieted, and sang the country's new anthem, an ode to Jerusalem, joining the harplike female voice on the soundtrack: "Jerusalem of gold, of copper, and of light."

We crossed forbidden borders. In Sinai I posed before a stalled Egyptian tank. On the Golan, whose charred ground was fenced with signs warning of mines, I climbed atop a Syrian bunker, then crawled inside and, through a slit, saw the houses and cars of Tiberias. In the deserted Golan Heights city of Kuneitra, whose people had fled the Israeli advance, I entered homes like an unannounced neighbor. In one home I found a photograph of a soldier wearing a beret and an ascot. Something was written on the back in Arabic, an inscription perhaps. I took it as a memento.

My father and I visited family, second and third cousins — approximations of relatives — who had managed to fall through the cracks and survive. Israel seemed a country of distant relatives, who clung to you like long-lost brothers. They gave us flaky Hungarian pastries and souvenir photography books of the Six-Day War, as if they were family albums.

In Haifa we went into a butcher shop. My father and the shopkeeper embraced and wept. Then we hurried out. Who was that? I asked, expecting another long explanation of complicated family status. My father said only, "That was one of the boy from the bunker" — the hole.

We traveled the narrow, hilly roads of the West Bank, seeking ancestral graves. Abraham and Sarah in Hebron, Rachel in Bethlehem, Samuel in Ramah: cool, dark, cavelike houses with humped stone tombs and blackened marble ledges on which hundreds of candles burned. At each holy site we wrapped the black leather straps of phylacteries around our arms, as though performing an ancient warrior rite; I bound the strap so tightly that it left purple lines on my skin. My father touched the stones with reverence, as though discovering the graves of his parents, the absent graves of Europe's unburied Jews. It was as if the biblical tombs of the West Bank, to which we'd been denied access by the Arabs, had gathered to themselves all that was taken from us.

Throughout the West Bank, torn white sheets hung from little stone houses. It seemed an absurd gesture of self-humiliation; who were the Arabs surrendering to and what were they afraid of? Yossi said, "They thought we would do to them what they had intended to do to us."

I didn't feel like a conqueror, but a liberator. Of course this territory belonged to us. No people had ever won back its land more fairly. The war had been forced on us by a genocidally minded enemy. At a refugee camp in Gaza I saw an exhibit of children's art, still hanging on the walls: the Israeli flag trampled by Arab boots, piles of skulls with Stars of David on their foreheads. The Arabs were cowards — not for losing wars but for provoking them and then protesting the injustice of their defeat.

In West Bank towns Arab boys gathered around us, offering hastily carved wooden camels, soda bottles filled with swirling layers of colored sand, yarmulkes, menorahs, postcards with the face of Moshe Dayan, mementos of their defeat. The boys' heads were shaved for lice and they wore shirts made of sacks stamped "UNWRA," UN refugee relief. Unshaven men leading donkeys moved slowly, as if in shock. Obviously, I couldn't regret their defeat. But neither could I despise them. I didn't want to think of them and wished they'd go away.

*   *   *

At the Wall my father wept. Perhaps he was finally allowing himself to cry for Europe, rather than rage against the murderers and bystanders and victims. The post-Holocaust struggle for permanence — his own and the Jews' — seemed finally won; now it was possible to mourn.

For the first time, I prayed. I'd always recited the prayers by rote: The Hebrew phrases would pour from me, perfectly accented but incomprehensible, as though someone were speaking through me. No one, not even my rabbis in yeshiva, had explained to me the meaning of the prayers — only to know when to cover your eyes with your palm as though concentrating, when to hit your chest with your fist as though remorseful, when to lay your head in the crook of your arm as though anguished. The key to being an Orthodox Jew was fluency: The faster you could say a prayer, perform a ritual, the more perfect your Jewish loyalty.

But now I leaned against the big stones and read the prayers slowly, savoring the words as prophesies. "Ingather our exiles from among the nations . . . Return to your city Jerusalem . . . Blessed are you, who causes the power of redemption to flourish." I wondered how Jews in the past could have summoned the strength to repeat those prayers, preserving them for their moment of vindication. And I felt grateful to be a Jew in this time, when faith and reality merged.

In those weeks my father and I discovered God. The leap from Auschwitz to Jerusalem strained one's doubt, one's faithlessness. If Jews could turn from God because of the Holocaust, then it was only reasonable to embrace him now. God had done *teshuva,* repented; and with the magnanimity of victors, we forgave him.

History, if still not explicable, had become retroactively bearable. In the end events had turned out just as the Bible had predicted, just as Jews had always believed they would. But perhaps even more strangely. We had witnessed our own resurrection, awakening from mass graves back into the Bible, to the time of our vigorous youth. What Jew, in the summer of 1967, couldn't believe in the God of Israel?

And yet, even as I was discovering God, I was breaking with Orthodoxy. The old rituals, born in Exile, seemed to me absurdly inappropriate for this time of redemption. Yossi and I mocked our fathers' piety as *shmontzes,* Yossi's all-purpose Yiddish ridicule for anything religious. On my first Friday night in Tiberias, as Yitzchak began the same hymns we sang in my home — childlike songs about the joy of Shabbos, of eating meat and sweets and all good things — Yossi and I looked at each other and burst out laughing. My father glared at me, but I couldn't stop. Just looking at Yossi could make me laugh until I held my stomach.

On *Tisha B'Av,* the fast day mourning the destruction of the Temple and the beginning of Exile, Yossi put on his bathing suit and announced he was going swimming — though according to Orthodox law, no recreation was permitted on a fast day.

"Swimming!" shouted his mother. "On *Tisha B'Av* he's going swimming!"

"That's right, swimming. How long are we supposed to sit and weep? We have the Wall back; that's not good enough for you?"

Henyu shouted in Hungarian; Yossi laughed but finally took off his bathing suit. Then he whispered to me, "Let's go."

We went down to Tiberias and saw an Indian movie, princes dueling atop elephants. "After the army I'm going to Bombay," Yossi announced. I asked how he would finance the trip. "Gambling," he said.

We bought felafels, violating the fast. It felt wonderful. We were the generation of redemption; we were permitted — obliged — to break the laws of Exile.

4.

I returned to Brooklyn in the fall, vigorous and tanned. Almost an Israeli, a renovated Jew. I'd left Israel under protest, demanding my parents allow me to stay for high school. Still, I knew my separation from Israel would be temporary, that nothing in America could hold me.

The Yeshiva University High School for Boys, otherwise known as the Brooklyn Talmudical Academy and which everyone called BTA, was located in Flatbush. It was a half-hour city bus ride from Borough Park to BTA, through non-Jewish neighborhoods. Once I would have sat close to the driver, yarmulke-covered head bent over a book, trying to become invisible. But now, a vicarious Israeli, I bopped to the back of the bus, where Italian kids in leather jackets pushed each other for fun and yelled at the passing streets. I took a window seat, propped my foot against the seat before me, and slumped, nonchalant, demonstratively oblivious to danger.

BTA was modern Orthodox. Its main premise was that an Orthodox Jew could enter "the world" by becoming a professional, yet still remain mentally ghettoized. Unlike students at ultra-Orthodox yeshivas, we were permitted to go to movies and basketball games, to watch Gentiles from a distance; but actually fraternizing with them was unthinkable. The spirit of modernity — a curiosity about foreign cultures — didn't penetrate our Judaism.

The school transmitted opposite messages. In one wing of the building was a yeshiva girls' high school — placing the sexes in such close proximity was virtually modern. But the two wings were separated by steel doors with alarms — that was Orthodox. We were encouraged to study chemistry and biology but were taught by our rabbis that the world was literally five thousand years old and that the theory of evolution was laughable. In the morning, when we studied up to four hours of the Talmud, we were supposed to be prewar European Jews; in the afternoon, when we switched to history and science, we turned into contemporary young men. The two sensibilities rarely interacted. The steel doors separating us from the girls' school symbolized BTA's compartmentalization: Set Orthodoxy and modernity side by side, but hope that neither notices the other.

Subjects like the Bible, Jewish history, and rabbinic philosophy were taught, but grudgingly: our real religious education was the Talmud. We were in our early teens, just beginning to assume the courage of skepticism. Questions pressed me: How could every religious law be considered immutable when so many of them — like those governing slavery — were outmoded? Clearly, Judaism had evolved over the centuries, yet we were expected to believe that the system had been transmitted whole from its most ancient origins. There was no one I could discuss my questions with. Instead, I was taught complex talmudic arguments about obscure points of law, who pays how much if an ox gores a cow — a religious education for a more innocent age.

There were four levels of Talmud study in BTA. The elite class was reserved for those likely to become rabbis, the boys the rest of us avoided. Then came the advanced Talmud class, whose purpose was to turn BTA's future doctors and lawyers into educated Orthodox laymen. Next came the "garbage" class — which is what everyone, including the rabbis, called it. The garbage students would never become masters of talmudic cleverness, but they might at least grow up to become good Orthodox Jews, properly performing the rituals whose meaning they wouldn't understand.

Not even that much was expected of the boys in "supergarbage," who secretly socialized with the girls next door and smoked cigarettes in the bathroom. Supergarbage was the dumping ground for BTA's spiritual charity cases: boys who weren't expelled only because their next stop would be public school, where they'd be lost among the goyim. In supergarbage the rabbis didn't try to teach, only stop students from leaping out of windows.

I found myself in the advanced nonrabbinic class. Part of the joy of Talmud study, of unraveling a difficult question, is sensing the pride of all who came before you. But I had no enthusiasm for dialogue with the rabbis. I had just returned from messianic Jerusalem, only to be squeezed back into the cramped Diaspora alleys of the Talmud. I didn't want to settle the disputes of lenders and borrowers and watchmen and thieves; I didn't want to become a lawyer, a moderator of passions. The rabbis were patching holes in the world; I wanted to tear it open and remake it whole.

The relentless rationalism of the Talmud depressed and exhausted me; when the rabbi began his swaying singsong, I lay my head on the desk and slept. I desecrated the symmetrical layout of the Talmud page — a thick block of text surrounded by thin columns of commentary — by filling the margins with drawings of Israeli planes strafing Arab tanks and with hippies playing guitars, celebrating the twin miracles of the Summer of Love.

My father warned me: "Talmud sharpens the brains. If now you don't learn, later you'll regret." He spoke in his most ominous voice, suggesting that failure to master talmudic logic would dull me, make me unfit to survive. But the Talmud hadn't saved the yeshiva boys of Nagy-Károly, so adept at subtleties that they missed the most blatant dangers.

Our rabbi was a big unhappy man we called Ollie, because he resembled Oliver Hardy. Ollie spoke in original aphorisms. If someone didn't know the answer to one of his talmudic questions, he said,

"You vos a fool in your mother's belly." When we left a bottle of mouthwash on his desk, he smashed it on the floor and shouted, "I spit in your mugs!"

I wanted to be in supergarbage. When Ollie called on me to read from the Talmud and I didn't know "the place" — as they put it in yeshiva — he shouted, "I'll throw you out to garbage!" Sadly he was only bluffing, because the two garbage classes were already overfilled.

Ollie taught us two hours a morning and then rotated with the rabbi from supergarbage, a man who threatened disrespectful students with cancer of the mouth. One day the boys of supergarbage announced to Ollie that they were planning a *siyum* — a party to celebrate the completion of a section of the Talmud. Except that their *siyum* was meant to celebrate the fact that they would never finish any section of the Talmud. Ollie shouted, "There vill be no *siyum!*" The next day the boys brought in a multitiered wedding cake from a nonkosher bakery. One of them offered a piece to Ollie, who threw the cake back at him. The boy threw another piece at Ollie, covering his face with cream.

Every BTA class aspired to that kind of legendary moment. The most flattering self-image of a BTA boy was that of a wise guy, a saboteur of order. I had gotten my introduction to the "BTA attitude" the previous spring, when I'd come to the school as a timorous eighth grader for my talmudic entry exam. A venerable rabbi with a long white beard, head of BTA's religious studies, asked me to interpret a few lines of the Talmud. Nervously, I began to read. Suddenly a blackboard eraser glided under his office door; then the door flew open, and jostling students playing the Brooklyn version of hockey kicked the eraser back out of the room and slammed the door behind them. But the truly impressive detail was the rabbi's response: He didn't glance up from his Talmud.

Twice a week we studied what was euphemistically called "Jewish philosophy" with a prematurely bald fanatic named Yok. At first Yok had seemed more reasonable than our other rabbis because, unlike them, he was American-born and spoke English without an Eastern European accent, as if he belonged to our world. He even seemed to have a sense of humor, deceiving us with puns. In fact, he was a

grim man who turned the class into one long tirade against modernity. Newspapers were "*znus*papers" — *znus* being the Yiddish word
for prostitution. Jews who ate turkey on Thanksgiving were dangerous assimilators; Jews who celebrated New Year's Eve, idolators. Yok
assured us that any step outside the rigid boundaries of the Torah,
as defined by ultra-Orthodoxy, would be severely punished. "The fires
of hell are sixty times greater than the greatest fire on earth," he
said, smiling broadly. "Since that's the hydrogen bomb, you can imagine what we're talking about."

Nothing good for a Jew could come from "the world." Yok liked
to repeat the opinion of one rabbi quoted in the Talmud: "If they
tell you there is wisdom among the nations, believe it; if they tell
you there is Torah among the nations, don't believe it." Goyim could
fix your car and send satellites into space but couldn't understand
truth, the meaning of life. Only Jews had a link with God — and
only those who studied the Torah.

Jews and goyim were locked in eternal struggle. For now the goyim
prevailed. But when the Messiah came, *we* would triumph: Twenty
goyim would cling to each thread of our prayer shawls, pleading to
serve us as protection against divine judgment. Yok's scenario was
the opposite of Ya'akov Birnbaum's generous messianism. For Yok
the world existed to serve the Jews; no event occurred that wasn't
meant for our benefit. Why was there a Vietnam war? So that Jewish
boys seeking a divinity school draft deferment would enroll in yeshiva
and study the Torah. That God would start a war in which thousands died or were maimed or orphaned just so Jews could study the
arguments of fourth-century rabbis seemed to me an inadequate explanation for the meaning of suffering. Yok offered an additional
reason for the Vietnam war: God was trying to cleanse the world of
illegitimate children by killing them off.

Yok's contempt for non-Jews was ultra-Orthodox, not modern
Orthodox; and no other BTA rabbi spoke quite so crudely. Some
even noted that the Jewish idea of chosenness was to serve the world,
not rule it. Still, Yok's Judeocentrism was only a nastier, more extreme version of BTA's sensibility. Jews were the center of the world;
and while perhaps not every minor event in every forlorn corner was
intended for our glory, anything extraneous to Jews was of no real
interest to us or, by implication, to God himself.

Despite my recent conversion to the human race, Yok's insistence that every aspect of a Jew's life be "Jewish" seemed to me compelling. I admired his absolutism. I wanted to be a good — a perfect — Jew, worthy of all who sacrificed before me. Inspired by Yok, I told my parents that I refused to attend my aunt's Thanksgiving dinner, an annual family tradition, because Thanksgiving was "goyish."

I assumed that God cared for all peoples, not just the Jews. And yet my view of history wasn't really so different from Yok's: that the billions of people who lived and suffered and died were no more than extras in a Jewish drama, that the human experience was really the Jewish experience. Didn't Christianity and Islam — religions I knew nothing about but dismissed as watered-down derivatives of Judaism — prove that we were the moving force in history? I believed the anti-Semites were right, except in reverse: Jews *did* secretly control the world, but benevolently. How else to explain the Holocaust and the pathological persistence of anti-Semitism, if not as evil trying to destroy the source of good? I was ready to concede that there were decent people who weren't Jews. But decent *peoples?* Only the Jews.

5.

The letters from Soviet Jews began arriving in the West after the Six-Day War. The first was written by Yasha Kazakov, a Moscow university student, and addressed to Soviet leaders: "I consider myself a citizen of the State of Israel. I demand to be freed from the humiliation of Soviet citizenship."

A voice, a name! Suddenly "Soviet Jewry" wasn't a silenced abstraction anymore. Kazakov's letter, exhilarating in its daring, was smuggled abroad and published in the press. A few days later he was given a visa and materialized in Israel. With a single incident, SSSJ's entire premise had been validated: that despite decades of forced assimilation, young Soviet Jews still wanted to be Jewish; that eventually they would fight back; and that, with enough Western attention to their cause, the Kremlin would relent. Silence had doomed European Jewry in the 1940s; protest would save its remnant. That was the equation, the law of redemption.

Next came an open letter to Soviet authorities written by Boris

Kochubiyevsky, a Kiev engineer: "As long as I am capable of feeling, I will do all I can to leave for Israel. And if you find it possible to sentence me for that, then all the same. If I live until my release, I will be prepared to go to the homeland of my ancestors even if it means going on foot."

Kochubiyevsky was sentenced to three years in prison. After his trial a copy of the letter was smuggled out to the Western press. In SSSJ we were convinced that had Kochubiyevsky's case been noticed by the West before his arrest, he too would have gone to Israel instead of to prison, just like Kazakov. The difference in the fate of the two Zionist dissidents confirmed SSSJ in its optimism: "Public opinion" — the goodwill of humanity — would save Soviet Jews.

With Kochubiyevsky's arrest, SSSJ now had its own political prisoner — a "prisoner of Zion" we called him. Instead of protesting abstract human rights abuses like the ban on matzoh or the closing of synagogues, we finally had a living symbol of Soviet oppression.

Glenn called a "Free Kochubiyevsky" rally at the Soviet UN mission, during school hours. I asked BTA's principal, Rabbi Abraham Zuroff, whether students could attend. Zuroff routinely spoke with a terrible slowness, as if about to impart tragic news. "Mr. Klein," he said to me, pausing. "If I give you permission to go to this rally, where will it end? Next week, someone will want to go to a basketball game. We can't very well have anarchy, can we, Mr. Klein?"

"But Rabbi Zuroff, how can you compare Soviet Jewry to basketball! I mean, Boris Kochubiyevsky is in jail right now waiting for us to save him — "

And then I did it: I began to cry. Oh God, I thought, I can't believe I'm doing this. Zuroff feigned impassiveness. But he couldn't hide the unease in his shifting eyes.

"You can have five students," he said.

"Ten," I countered.

"Seven. And I want a note from every boy's parents. We won't make a habit of this, will we, Mr. Klein?"

New letters appeared. I learned the key phrases of every appeal, the particular quality of its desperation. Most were signed, taunting the KGB with their writers' fearlessness. They were addressed to "World

Jewry," to "Women of the World" — nonexistent entities. The situation had reversed: Now Soviet Jews had public, individual identities, and we in the West were an anonymous mass.

The miracle had happened; the lost Jews were stirring. But for American Jewry it was business as usual. Establishment groups didn't mobilize their enormous resources and memberships to make the names of the letter writers known, to protect them from the KGB with what SSSJ liked to call "the glare of publicity." They didn't publish the letters in newspaper ads or organize giant rallies or hunger strikes. The Soviet Jewry issue stayed close to the bottom of the American Jewish agenda, useful for inclusion in rabbis' New Year sermons and in press releases from establishment organizations. American Jews lacked the imagination to understand the courage of Soviet Jews, as if writing a protest letter to the Kremlin was no different than writing one's congressman. Americans were trapped by their easy lives, afflicted with an impaired sense of empathy.

Emboldened by the Six-Day War, Soviet Jews were daring the Kremlin with an insane recklessness, gambling their lives on the near-impossible prospect of an exit visa from the most sealed country in history. Young Jews walked the streets wearing Israeli flagpins — even as the Soviet government press denounced Israel as the world's most evil state. In the Moscow Metro someone posted handwritten advertisements for classes in Hebrew, an illegal language, complete with address and phone number.

Formally, I remained a Betari, occasionally still going to meetings in our basement headquarters and wearing the Betar uniform to the annual Salute to Israel parade on Fifth Avenue. But my ideological passion had shifted to SSSJ. Betar, with its unforgiving memories, represented the past; SSSJ was the messianic future.

Soviet Jewry became my centerpoint, virtually my identity. I set up a recruitment booth for SSSJ in the BTA basement, which functioned as a combined lunchroom/gym/auditorium/locker room. I was a freshman, an easy target for ridicule. How much are you selling that Soviet jewelry for, seniors asked. Where can I get my free Kochubiyevsky?

I phoned the rabbis of Borough Park synagogues, asking to address their congregations. Then I wrote a speech and rehearsed it before my father. "Slowly, slowly," he said. "Look up from the

paper. And look me in the eyes." When I admitted I was afraid to
face an audience, he said, "There's nothing to be afraid! What are
those people better than you? Are you asking for yourself? No! Only
for your unjust suffering people."

My standard speech spoke of walls of apathy, crimes of silence,
perpetrations and perpetuations of oppression. I cherished rhetoric,
impersonal passion, the safest way to share emotion with my father.

6.

On Sundays I helped my father deliver orders to customers. Our
route passed through the East Village, whose streets were transformed into a foreign land: There were macrobiotic restaurants and
Indian boutiques, posters announcing rock concerts in balloonlike
letters, men in orange robes beating eggplant-shaped drums strapped
around their necks.

I wanted to leap from the car into the strangeness, into the "east"
of the East Village. I had recently decided that I despised the West,
that Western civilization had died in Auschwitz. My mother tried to
interest me in her collection of classical records, but I refused to listen: The Nazis had played Beethoven in the camps. I was drawn only
to the new and unfamiliar — to rock 'n' roll, whose relentless drive
exorcised a poisoned culture.

I wanted my father to understand that the hippies were harbin-
gers of a new world, that only ecstasy, an extravagance of life, could
defeat the old Holocaust world. But he reacted like any adult.

"Look at that hair," he said, pointing to a hippie. "Is it girl or
boy?"

I rolled my eyes.

"What do they know, these spoiled children," he continued. "They
have it too good, that's the whole problem in this country."

As the sixties turned anarchic, he increasingly feared for the sanity of his beloved adopted country; and he regarded hippies as the
ultimate "stupid Americans." A stupid American was someone who
took comfort as his or her birthright, who confused America for human reality. Like the American Jew who once said to my father: "I
know all about the Holocaust, Mr. Klein. I was a kid in Brooklyn

during the war. We didn't have no meat in the house; my mother had to ration butter. We suffered plenty, too, don't kid yourself."

My father shook his head in disbelief at the products he sold to stupid Americans. There were multicolored twirl pops the size of a person's head, giant chocolate pacifiers wrapped in gold foil. Americans were children, constantly in need of stimulation. "Something new, Mr. Klein," his customers pressed him. "What do you got that's *new?*" Referring to his fellow survivors, he said to me, "The dumbest refugee is smarter than the biggest American professor."

When we were Jews together, we saw the world identically. He and my mother had even begun joining me at SSSJ rallies, bringing folding chairs to rest on between rounds of picketing. I'd finally convinced him that saving Soviet Jewry wasn't a lost cause, that his pessimism was inadequate for a messianic era of Jewish power and renewal; implicitly, he conceded that his survivor wisdom wasn't infallible.

But when we stopped being Jews together and switched to being Americans, we fought as bitterly as any father and son in the 1960s, saying things we quickly regretted. He would lose himself in shouting, his rage at history focused on my teenage irritations.

Though we argued over "American" issues, the subtext was always the Holocaust. He wanted me to have "nice short hair" and not look like a "sheggie," a shaggy hippie — because the hippies were anarchists who undermined civilization and risked provoking a fascist reaction. I wanted flowing hair: It was no coincidence, I thought, that the first brutality imposed on camp inmates was to shave their heads, strip them of beauty, power, self.

I bought bell-bottom jeans. Being hip meant separating myself from the nebbish yeshiva boys I'd grown up with, victims in training for the next holocaust. But my father wouldn't let me wear hippie bell-bottoms; he told my mother to taper the flair. "You're killing me!" I screamed.

We fought about the Vietnam War.

"All these demonstration against Vietnam are controlled from beginning to the end by KGB," he said.

"That's the most ridiculous thing I ever heard," I replied.

"What do you know," he countered. "You": an American.

"You think you know everything," I said. "You": a victim of the past.

I bought a bag of marijuana from someone in supergarbage and split it with a friend named Joe. We cut school and went to his house. We listened to the pagan exhortations of The Doors and rolled a joint.

The world receded. I mentally repeated my name but didn't recognize the sound. I stared at my face in a mirror: It looked familiar, but not intimate. I panicked: I was surrendering to something I couldn't control, entering the totalitarian experience. If my father saw me now he would think: My son has become a stupid American, preferring illusion to reality. And yet it felt like a holy moment, in the way that profanity can be mistaken for holiness because both transcend limits.

Joe was the ideal drug companion, unobtrusive yet sympathetic. He liked people but didn't need them; his self-containment was mistaken by our classmates for aloofness. During school recess he read philosophers and poets the rest of us hadn't heard of, and he considered himself a poet. Tall and slightly stooped, with long, thin blond hair, he had the bearing and generosity of a poet. But he lacked the poet's language, filling his verses with unusual words he found in the thesaurus.

Joe, who'd grown up in Poland, reinvented himself, banishing the burdens of his past. He never mentioned his Polish childhood. I was certain it must have been traumatic, filled with anti-Semitic taunts and beatings, but he seemed to have no bitterness toward Poles or other non-Jews. He didn't even call them "goyim." People were people, he said. The absence of rage in a Jew from post-Holocaust Poland didn't seem to me nobility but a character flaw, as if his benign nature lacked the courage to confront evil.

I resolved to become his teacher in Jewish emotion, a healer in reverse who would tear open wounds. I would teach him to keep a part of himself inconsolable, just as religious Jews leave a corner of their homes unpainted to mourn the destroyed Temple.

But Joe seemed immune to rage. He even called himself a universalist. In Borough Park's language, "universalist" was a synonym for traitor. Thousands of young Jews in prewar Europe had abandoned their people at its most desperate time and joined universalist communism, and we sneered at their concern for social justice as mere pretext for escaping their Jewishness. They seemed to us cowards and hypocrites: They spoke of the suffering of humanity but did nothing for their own suffering people. When Jews proclaimed themselves lovers of humanity, we suspected they meant: everyone but Jews.

Joe said it was possible to be both a Jew and a universalist. Maybe so, I said. But what was your *main* identity, Jew or human being? Other people might take their humanity for granted; but Jews, at least in Borough Park, felt certain only of their Jewishness.

Joe said, "I'm a human being who happens to be a Jew. It's quite simple, actually. I also happen to be male and have blond hair."

How could Joe elevate the amorphous identity of "human being" above the concrete identity of "Jew"? Human beings died accidentally; Jews were murdered. And that demanded a special Jewish solidarity.

"The Jews are my family," said Joe. "But can I love every Jew just because they're Jewish? That's absurd. Actually, I feel closer to Herman Hesse than to many Jews I know."

Joe's argument tempted me. A Jewish human being, "Jew" as adjective, not noun. Why not admit it: Ethnicity was a mere variation of our common humanity. And what a relief it would be to stop filtering every experience through suspicious Jewish eyes, to relax one's vigilance against the next attack.

Still, Joe's universalism frightened me. If the Jews were really no different than other peoples, then what was the meaning of our suffering? The mere preservation of one more ethnic group wasn't good enough; there had to be some higher purpose worthy of our effort to survive. The notion of Jewish chosenness, however vague to me — chosen for what? — at least challenged the unbearable possibility that our martyrdom had been senseless.

Granted, I said to Joe, Jews are human beings like everyone else. But look at our place in history: Our ideas affect the whole world. Doesn't that mean we're different — better?

"You say we affect the *whole* world?" said Joe.

"The Christians, the Muslims, everybody steals their ideas from us."

"You seem to have forgotten the Hindus and Buddhists. Two billion people in the East have never heard of Jews."

For days afterward I brooded about those two billion people denied even a diluted experience of Judaism. What was to be done with them? Finally, I found the answer: communism! Social justice, messianic utopia — Jewish ideas, albeit in distorted form, that were conquering the East.

With triumph and relief, I offered Joe my solution. No matter how you looked at it, I insisted, the Jews were central. I waited for Joe to concede. But he just smiled.

One day, driving with my father in Manhattan, we passed a booth with a banner that read, "Keep Biafra Alive." Biafra was fighting a losing secessionist war against Nigeria, which was trying to starve it into submission. The pictures of swollen-bellied Biafran children formed a backdrop of the late sixties, to be avoided as reminders of our inadequacy.

I asked my father to stop, and I jumped out of the car. A black boy, perhaps the same age I'd been when I first joined SSSJ, stood alone behind the booth. I gave him what money I had.

When I returned to the car, my father's voice was a barely controlled hysteria.

"And what is that your business?" he demanded.

"Millions of people are starving," I said.

"You don't have enough to worry about your own people? You have to go chase? How many Jewish boy run to demonstrate for the civil rights? But *shvartze* you won't see demonstrating for the Russian Jew!"

A Holocaust survivor was berating me for caring about starving people. But what if he was right? Was it a *moral* flaw for Jews to get involved in other peoples' problems? Non-Jewish causes would always find their champions; but if Jews didn't defend other Jews, who would? Even more galling, chances were that the very people you helped now would later turn on you — precisely what had happened to American Jews who'd fought for civil rights and were then "paid back," as my father put it, by black anti-Semitism. The worst sin post-Holocaust Jews could commit was to allow themselves to be taken for fools.

But weren't Jews equally forbidden to be bystanders to genocide? The Holocaust had been so vast that it could hold the suffering of humanity; to keep its lessons for ourselves seemed not merely selfish but a terrible waste. When did the "lessons of the Holocaust" demand that I be only a Jew, and when a human being? And when was it possible to be both?

At the Biafran booth I'd picked up a pamphlet that seemed to intuit my dilemma and offered a blatantly selfish rationale for Jews to help Biafra: The Arabs and the Soviets were aiding the Muslim Nigerians, while the Christian Biafrans were pro-Israel. I seized the pretext and wrote articles for the *Jewish Press* advocating an alliance between Biafra and the Jews. My father suspected a trick, but couldn't rebuke an appeal to Jewish self-interest.

Biafra starved, surrendered, died. It found no champions. "The world" didn't care — not for Europe's Jews, the Biafrans, or anyone else. That realization was subversive; for it meant that "the world" hadn't necessarily *wanted* the Jews to die in the Holocaust, as I always assumed, but simply didn't intervene because it never does. Still, I couldn't concede the point and clung to the self-importance of belonging to a uniquely abandoned people.

7.

In 1968 the Jewish Defense League (JDL) was founded, and Brooklyn Jewry's fears found a home.

The JDL began as a street patrol to protect poor and elderly Jews stranded in urban areas that were turning black — euphemistically called "changing neighborhoods." Its obsession was fighting black anti-Semites, with occasional diversions like beating up Nazis and pro-PLO demonstrators. Its instinctive solution to every problem was violence; at times it resembled a street gang more than an organization. One JDL newspaper ad featured a photograph of self-consciously menacing young men in sunglasses, tightlipped and posing with chains and baseball bats, with the question, "Is this any way for nice Jewish boys to behave?" and the answer, "Maybe, just maybe, nice Jewish boys help pave their own road to Auschwitz."

The JDL gathered those peripheral Jews who believed that American Jewry's success had been earned on their backs: the urban poor abandoned by neighbors fleeing to suburbia, Orthodox Jews ignored by the liberal Jewish establishment, Holocaust survivors and their children bitter over the abandonment of European Jewry in the 1940s.

In one form or another, those grudges overlapped in me. I was a Borough Park Jew, not an American Jew. I despised Grossinger's Hotel and chicken soup jokes and bar mitzvah pageants and sonorous rabbis — a culture of self-abasement and vulgar excess. In this of all centuries, American Jews had turned Judaism into something laughable, pathetic.

I should have been an obvious candidate for the JDL. But I didn't immediately join, partly because I already had my cause. The defining struggle of our generation was saving the last Eastern European Jews. I resented the JDL for squandering the emotions of the Holocaust — and its powerful slogan, "Never Again" — on historically meaningless street skirmishes. And the JDL campaign for American Jewish safety seemed to me self-indulgent. American Jewry was safe enough. Too safe: A little anti-Semitism might shake up its smug certainty of being the great exception to the law of Diaspora impermanence, might even encourage Jews to move to Israel.

The leader of the JDL was a thirty-eight-year-old rabbi named Meir Kahane. An editor of the *Jewish Press,* he wrote sharp, sarcastic columns mocking assimilationists and Reform Jews, whose massive temples he compared to mausoleums and whose rabbis he labeled bar mitzvah caterers.

Kahane was familiar to me: We came from similar backgrounds. In the 1940s he'd been a BTA boy and a Betari, helped smuggle guns to the Irgun underground, and had been beaten by police for throwing tomatoes at the visiting British prime minister. He infused the JDL with Betar's anti-utopianism, its disdain for liberal and left-wing Jews active in "alien" — non-Jewish — causes, like the civil rights and antiwar movements. Jews have no responsibility to the world, he insisted, only to their fellow Jews.

The JDL and the *Jewish Press* shared the same hysteria. All Jewish problems were equally urgent, all enemies equally dangerous. The BTA boys who joined the JDL liked to practice karate kicks on each other and swing their nunchakus — two clubs joined by rope — in the locker room, creating a cordon of untouchability around themselves. Their favorite word seemed to be "nigger": Most of them lived in terrorized neighborhoods that were turning black, and by daring to say "nigger" they empowered themselves. Kahane exploited their fear: The JDL, he wrote, was fighting "Nazis in black shirts and Nazis in black skins."

I wasn't totally immune to the JDL's appeal. Any outbreak of passion was a welcome relief from the American Jewish nothing; the JDL brought drama to a community dying of boredom. If mediocrity was American Jewry's great sin, the JDL at least offered street theater. And though B'nai B'rith and the *New York Times* denounced it as a Jewish Ku Klux Klan, the JDL also brought a certain status to Jews. In the late sixties no ethnic grievance was respected unless accompanied by TV images of twisted faces and waving fists; and the JDL gave tame American Jews — "Nice Irvings," as Kahane contemptuously called them — the glamour of an aggrieved minority. Along with the Black Panthers and the Weathermen, we too now had our outlaws. The JDLers dressed the part: light blue berets and olive army jackets with rows of Jewish political buttons pinned onto their breast pockets. Brooklyn had finally produced angry Jews.

One Halloween night — traditional time of teenage egg attacks on Jews — I joined a JDL patrol. We drove around Borough Park looking for gangs, baseball bats in the backseat. More than the fear of getting hurt in a fight, I was afraid my hands would freeze and be unable to bring the weight of a bat onto a human cranium. Afterward I joined a JDL karate class, to train my body in instinctive aggression. No matter how I ridiculed the JDL, I couldn't entirely escape it. Despite myself, I kept an interested eye on Kahane and his boys.

8.

The hundreds of protest letters from Soviet Jews became thousands. One of them was a group appeal by eighteen families from Georgia, which read like a *piyut*, a prayer poem:

We are not afraid of anything; dead or alive, we are the children of Israel.

We will wait months and years, we will wait all our lives if
    necessary, but we will not renounce our faith or our hopes.
We believe: Our prayers have reached God.
We know: Our appeals will reach humanity.
For we are asking little: Let us go to the land of our fathers.

In SSSJ we planned our biggest demonstration ever, the Exodus
March, Passover 1970. We pasted "Exodus" stickers on buses and
subways, creating the illusion of a mass movement. We even made
"Exodus" buttons, like the antiwar movement did for its rallies. For
SSSJ to invest in a button that would be obsolete in a few months
was an unknown extravagance, proof that this demonstration would
be special.

The Exodus March was cosponsored by the American Jewish
Conference on Soviet Jewry, an umbrella group for establishment
organizations like B'nai B'rith and Hadassah. The conference existed
mostly on paper. It was run by a single part-time staffer and had no
fixed budget, subsisting on small handouts grudgingly given by its
constituent organizations. Its expenses were small because it sponsored only a few minor rallies a year — just enough activity to give
the establishment an alibi of involvement. Its real intentions were
embodied in its name: a "conference," not a struggle. Impoverished
SSSJ organized far more rallies and published far better educational
literature than all the powerful establishment groups combined.

Ya'akov Birnbaum took me to a conference meeting. Representatives of organizations with multimillion-dollar budgets pledged
five hundred dollars to the Exodus March; some delegates said they
had no authorization to offer any sum at all. "This is outwageous!"
shouted Ya'akov. "You're trying to save Soviet Jewry on the cheap!"

The Exodus March was held on a warm spring day. The area
around the Soviet UN mission was filled with Jews. Instead of posters
with slogans, we held large white cards, each naming another Soviet
Jewish letter writer, covering Manhattan's streets with names.

The march ended at the UN. On a podium in the middle of First
Avenue stood Rabbi Shlomo Carlebach, troubadour of the Soviet
Jewry movement. Shlomo — that's what everyone called him —
wrote songs of longing for redemption. A Shlomo melody could be
so compelling, so obvious, that after a single hearing one seemed to

have always known it. His songs seeped into the Jewish people almost anonymously, becoming instant classics, as though transmitted from a distant, vital past.

Shlomo was the poet of the lost Jews. He traveled the world, inspiring miracles of Jewish renewal. In communist Prague he danced all night with young Jews surrounded by secret police and then in exhausted ecstasy wrote the SSSJ theme song, "*Am Yisrael Chai,*" the people of Israel live. He danced in the streets of Haight-Ashbury with the hippies, whom he called by his own Yiddish endearment, "holy *hippalach*."

Shlomo taught that Jewish redemption would come not from the self-satisfied Orthodox with their three-piece Shabbos suits and kosher Chinese restaurants but from the periphery — the hippies looking for God in material America, the Soviet Jews and the SSSJ kids throwing themselves against either side of the Iron Curtain, all those trying to tear down walls and staking their lives on a miracle. At concerts he told a story of a young woman in Moscow who summoned him into an alley and then whispered the first five letters of the Hebrew alphabet, the only Jewish sounds she knew. "Her holy letters will *mamish* — really — help bring the Messiah," he said.

Shlomo had a big gray beard and long, curly gray hair in which were tangled his Hasidic sidecurls; a large belly; a fleshy, sensuous face; and intense, charismatic eyes. A giant Star of David hung on a chain across his shirt, as if he could be mistaken for anything but a Jew. He seemed to remember everyone he ever met, as though he'd decided to embrace the whole Jewish people by befriending each of its individual members.

I had met him at a Soviet Jewry rally when I was a boy and requested his autograph; he pulled me toward him, kissed my forehead as though blessing me, and laughingly called me "holy brother Joe," insisting on the English name for "Yossi" as a private joke between us. Afterward he would greet me at rallies with a hug and a mischievous smile and, rolling his eyes in feigned ecstasy, shout, "Hey, holy brotha' Joe, *mamish* the highest Jew in Borough Park!" sounding at once like a hipster, a Hasid, a Baptist preacher, and a parody of Shlomo Carlebach.

Though I knew Shlomo only from those fleeting embraces, I cherished him like an old friend. Shlomo created his own messianic reality through exuberant goodwill, turning passing acquaintances into instant intimates. Other Orthodox Jews measured their spirituality by the thickness of their walls, while Shlomo sang his Hasidic songs in prisons and Indian ashrams and black ghetto schools. In Shlomo's world there were no strangers, no borders between people or nations, certainly no enemies, only souls waiting to be revealed. In Chicago he gave a mugger his wallet and then hugged him; the mugger broke down weeping and returned the wallet. In Moscow he waved to KGB agents who were tailing him, and they waved back. It didn't matter whether every detail happened exactly as Shlomo said it did; for Shlomo was saying that this *could* be the time of redemption, of the triumph of good, if Jews used the miracle of their survival to help heal the world.

Shlomo stood before the "Exodus" marchers gathered at the UN and said, "Friends, I want you should know that the two holiest Jews in the world are Yankeleh Birnbaum and Glenn Richter. I know a lot of rabbis who won't be sitting on the dais when the Messiah comes. But Yankeleh and Glenn will be up there with the highest."

With a sudden vigorous strumming, his voice deep and sure and sweet, Shlomo sang, *"Am Yisrael Chai."* He began slowly, prolonging each word. Then he paused. Before the song could really begin, the words must be properly introduced, their power acknowledged. *"Am — Yisrael — Chai."* Again; he held each word until it swelled, then released it, not breathless but reluctant.

"Holiest friends," said Shlomo, interrupting himself, "I want you to really sing, our souls should go straight up and tear apart Heaven until God opens the gates of Russia for our brothers and sisters."

Then the song broke through. *"Am Yisrael Am Yisrael Am Yisrael CHAI!"* Shlomo jumped up and down and shouted, "Come on, let's go!" The random crowds organized into circles. We braced each other's shoulders and spun. I was instantly breathless, unable to sing. Someone stood in the center of our circle and waved a giant blue-and-white Israeli flag on a pole, and it looked as if the blue glass obelisk of the UN and the white river behind it were absorbed by our flag. We spun until the ground fell away, nothing left but ecstasy, miracle, the certainty of flight, spiraling to a place without borders. . . .

Four

The Ecstasy of Rage

THE ARRESTS in Russia began in June 1970. A brief report on the radio said that twelve Jews had been seized at the Leningrad airport while attempting to hijack a plane to Israel. Glenn Richter called: "Comrade Kleinski? Bad news for the Jews."

Glenn said the hijacking was probably a frame-up. But what if it wasn't? What if some Jews had become so desperate that they were ready to force their way out of Russia? If the hijacking were real, then Soviet Jews had moved from letter-writing to violence. And our peaceful, "responsible" demonstrations would no longer be enough.

A SSSJ all-night vigil at the "Isaiah Wall" — a small plaza opposite the UN, on whose wall was engraved Isaiah's messianic prophesy of a world without war — drew less than fifty people. No reporters came. I called a radio news station for the third time and said, "If you want us to smash windows, we'll smash windows." Twenty minutes later, a reporter appeared. "Who's the window-smasher?" he asked.

We sat on the winding steps leading down into the Isaiah Wall plaza and spent the night debating our next move. We were convinced that the hijacking arrests were just the beginning of a KGB campaign to destroy the Zionist underground and that anything was possible now — pogroms, even mass deportations.

We needed a hundred thousand people in the streets immediately. But only the Jewish establishment had the power to summon a real protest movement; and its single response to the Leningrad arrests was a press release, deploring and denouncing. Instead of rallying outside the UN, I said, we should be taking over the offices of B'nai B'rith and Hadassah.

The next morning we left the Isaiah Wall and walked to the nearby headquarters of B'nai B'rith's Anti-Defamation League (ADL). We laid our torches, stinking of gasoline, around the lobby. "We demand a meeting with ADL leaders," I said to the receptionist.

Policemen entered the building. Glenn began photographing. The cops left.

We were invited to a conference room. We sat opposite a half-dozen ADL officials at a long table. Disheveled and sleepless, our very appearance proclaimed a state of emergency.

"We do more for Soviet Jewry than anyone," began a man who called himself ADL's foreign affairs expert. "We gave two thousand dollars last year to the American Jewish Conference on Soviet Jewry."

"Out of your budget of how many millions?" asked a SSSJ activist named Noam.

"Of course we can never do enough for our brethren in Russia."

Noam rolled his eyes.

"You kids don't know what you want," the foreign affairs expert said.

"We want you to buy a full-page ad in the *Times* about the Leningrad arrests," I replied.

"The Soviet Union could financially ruin us by arresting twelve Jews a week," said the expert, laughing.

"Ha, ha," said Noam.

"I don't understand this concern for twelve Jews when there are three million in the Soviet Union."

"What about when the number was six million?" I asked.

"Yes, we lost the battle for the Six Million."

"You didn't lose the battle," I said. "You never fought it."

"What are you doing for Boris Kochubiyevsky?" demanded Noam.

"We have information," said the foreign policy expert, "that Kochubiyevsky is doomed."

"He's doomed," said Noam, "because of people like you."

The only real response to the Leningrad arrests came from the JDL. Meir Kahane led twenty followers into the Soviet trade office in Manhattan, waving lead pipes and physically expelling its staff. Unlike our peaceful SSSJ vigil, the takeover made headlines.

The JDL had entered the Soviet Jewry struggle. Its members chained themselves to the wheels of an Aeroflot plane on a Kennedy Airport runway and toppled police barricades at the Soviet UN mission. They disrupted appearances by visiting Soviet artists, releasing mice during a violin concert, rolling marbles onto an ice-skating performance, dancing a hora onstage during a ballet recital. Kahane had expropriated the tactics of the radical Yippies, the violent pranksters of the New Left, orchestrating acts of rage for the TV cameras.

In one sense Kahane's strategy resembled Ya'akov Birnbaum's: The JDL was trying to free Soviet Jewry by threatening Soviet-American relations, making it more worthwhile for the Kremlin to release its Jews than hold them. But Ya'akov believed in an incremental campaign of education and peaceful protest, mobilizing American Jewry and sympathetic non-Jews; whereas Kahane launched a campaign of terror against Soviet-American relations — guerilla war, or at least violent guerilla theater.

Kahane despised SSSJ's faith in gentile decency. Instead of cultivating public opinion, the JDL deliberately flouted it, playing Black Panthers to SSSJ's Freedom Riders. Kahane didn't care if the *New York Times* condemned JDL violence or if ballet aficionados booed JDL disrupters. What mattered was getting noticed. Kahane understood the demonic side of media: The uglier you behave, the more coverage you receive.

Politicians invited to SSSJ rallies were almost always liberals, speaking the rhetoric of civil rights; we shunned cold warriors, whose anticommunism would allow the Kremlin to dismiss us as politically motivated. But Kahane brought far-right congressmen to JDL rallies and joined with Eastern European anticommunist exiles whom he despised as closet Nazis. Where Ya'akov envisioned a messianic coalition of goodwill, Kahane preached a coalition of cynicism. The Jews, wrote Kahane, have no friends, at best temporary allies of convenience.

Ya'akov bitterly resented him. "I know Meir, heh, heh," Ya'akov said to me, with an insinuating, nasty laugh. "He came to a few of our rallies in the beginning, made a speech or two, very passionate and all the rest of it. But no substance, you see. He's ruining *years* of our work with wild acts of self-aggwandizement. Meir is a violent soul; he dweams of chasms of blood."

How would we free Soviet Jewry: by alliances of expedience, or by those of goodwill? By violent acts that won publicity for our neglected cause, or by patient coalition-building that cultivated rather than alienated potential supporters?

I trusted Ya'akov. And I mistrusted Kahane as an opportunist, using Soviet Jewry to get headlines for himself and his group. And the JDL could be so embarrassing: One TV news report about a JDL riot at the Soviet mission focused on a hysterical woman with glasses shaped like slanted eyes repeatedly shrieking, "Jewish blood! Jewish blood in the streets of New York!"

And yet I envied the JDL's audacity, its ability to manipulate the media. The JDL was bringing a new level of desperation into the Soviet Jewry movement, transforming it into a "real" cause for which protesters went to jail. I'd always prided myself on being at the center of the movement; but now I felt that center shifting, from SSSJ to the JDL. Suddenly there were people whose names I didn't even know who were sacrificing more for Soviet Jewry than I was. How could I miss the intensity?

2.

I finally made it into supergarbage. I was now a high-school senior. By my junior year I'd no longer even bothered cheating on Talmud tests; I spent my mornings in the bathroom with friends who'd been thrown out of other classes. My rabbis assumed I lacked some essential Jewish quality, making me unsuited for talmudic logic. They pitied my parents and left me alone.

Supergarbage was a celebration of anarchy. Someone would shout, "Choo choo train!" and we'd instantly form our desks into a single line and shuffle out the door. We threw fake birthday parties for each other, tooting blowers and snake-dancing around the room. We proclaimed one morning Camera Day and took pictures of our rabbi, Elmer Weisfish, pulling would-be photographers by the hair.

Despite his — entirely understandable — violent outbursts, Rabbi Weisfish was BTA's kindest teacher; and we delighted in tormenting him. We hid his lunch and fedora. We left ransom notes on his desk, purporting to come from the kidnappers of his son. In honor of his Canadian origins, we burned the Maple Leaf in class.

Weisfish raced about the room, one hand holding up his pants, the other grabbing and smacking us. In desperation, he'd read aloud from the morning's *New York Times* to calm us; and we would quiet for a few minutes, a temporary lapse into sanity. Weisfish pleaded with us in the name of God, the Jewish people, the Six Million. "You behave like *shvartzes* in Harlem!" he shouted.

One day he began to weep. "I don't know what's wrong here," he said, "maybe it's me."

"Maybe it is," called out a student. Weisfish shoved him out the door.

We formed a supergarbage branch of the Jewish Labor Bund, Eastern Europe's antireligious workers' movement destroyed in the Holocaust. We interrupted Weisfish's teaching to sing "L'Internationale" in Yiddish; on the blackboard we wrote our adopted slogan, *"Arbeit Macht Frei,"* Work Liberates, the words the Nazis had placed on the gates to Auschwitz.

No matter how often Weisfish threw you out of class, he always let you back again — because after supergarbage there was no place left to go. He never held a grudge. He seemed to understand that there was nothing personal in our disruptions, that we were in fact immensely fond of him. We just couldn't help ourselves. Maybe he forgave us because we were children of Holocaust survivors, equating any kind of obedience, even to teachers, with a fatal passivity; maybe he realized that he was merely a victim of the blind thrust of our life force.

*   *   *

The arrests continued. Leningrad Jews smuggled out a letter to the West, warning that "a trial is being prepared" — a show trial to destroy the Zionist movement.

I expected an outcry of pain from the Jewish community; instead, it offered only token gestures of protest. At a meeting of the American Jewish Conference on Soviet Jewry, Ya'akov pounded the table and shouted, "Jews! A twial is being pwepared!" But no campaign emerged to stop the trial. The establishment, I told Ya'akov, was driving me to Kahane.

A letter arrived from a Riga Jew named Ruth Alexandrovich: "One by one my friends are arrested, and evidently, soon it will be my turn. I don't know how many years of life, how much health and strength, the prison will take from me. But I promise that I will never betray my friends or my people." A week before her wedding, Ruth Alexandrovich was arrested.

But not even Ruth — in SSSJ we called Soviet Jews by their first names, as if our concern granted us a claim on their intimacy — seemed to move American Jewry. Together with a few friends I invaded closed meetings and receptions held by Jewish organizations, distributing accusatory, ink-stained leaflets filled with typos. We walked into a ballroom in the Waldorf-Astoria, where a rabbinic group was honoring itself with a banquet, and handed the tuxedoed spiritual leaders our leaflets: THIS IS NO TIME FOR CELEBRATIONS. We disrupted a meeting of the American Jewish Conference on Soviet Jewry, shouting, "Murderer!" at the chairman when he tried to speak.

A dozen of us entered Hadassah headquarters in Manhattan and decorated the lobby with blow-up photographs of Ruth, a kerchiefed young woman with a sad smile and distant gaze, resembling a heroine in the Yiddish theater. Reporters came, intrigued by young Jews demonstrating against their grandmothers.

The president of Hadassah, an imposing woman with gray coiffed hair, entered the lobby, screaming, "What the hell is going on here?"

"What are you doing for Ruth Alexandrovich!" I shouted back.

"Who are *you* to tell us what to do?" she demanded.

"We won't let you do to Soviet Jewry what you did to the Six Million!"

"We don't take direction from you. Youth have no right to come here."

I folded my arms, tilted my head back to keep the hair out of my eyes, and smirked.

                                                                    3.

Moish Mandel, short and muscular, wasn't conventionally cool. He didn't dress fashionably or know the latest music. His coolness was more subtle and powerful: He never showed surprise. Whether taking a final exam or standing alone late at night on a deserted subway station, he remained nonchalant. I imagined him a commando, executing some meticulous task with total self-control.

Everyone wanted to be Moish's friend. He wasn't so much funny as sharp, especially toward authority figures. He bantered with his teachers and mocked them to their faces; he sat in their chairs and put his feet up on their desks, just to feel their power. And they took it, drawn like everyone else to his charismatic chutzpah.

If there was a fight with anti-Semites, he was among the first to join in. His courage came, in part, from exaggerated self-esteem. He was fascinated with himself, and he expected everyone to share his fascination. He spoke with deliberate slowness, allowing his listeners to savor every word. He considered himself a leader by right; he was certain that he was smarter, braver, more competent, and more charming than anyone else. But he was an egoist who was willing to take personal risks, endanger his precious self; and that paradox was the source of his charisma.

Moish projected patience. "What's the problem?" he'd say with a slow half-smile, then pinch your cheek or pat you on the head, as though he were a wise elder. But beneath his seeming equilibrium lay rage, some hidden wound to his sense of preeminence — a wound that he might one day blindly avenge. He was, I felt, capable of awesome ruthlessness. And that suppressed frenzy added to his power.

I knew Moish, who lived in a "changing neighborhood" in the Bronx, through SSSJ. One afternoon I left school early to meet Moish at a Manhattan hotel for a SSSJ action. It was November 7, the anniversary of the Russian Revolution, and we were planning to disrupt a celebration of the Soviet-American Friendship League.

We joined the ticket line. At first I thought we'd come to the wrong place: Almost everyone was speaking Yiddish. In fact, they were old Jewish Stalinists, the faithful remnant, coming to honor the oppressors of Jews.

Members of SSSJ — yarmulkes removed, incognito — scattered throughout the hall. A professor spoke of the Soviet Union as a model of ethnic fraternity, and the old Jews clapped. Then the Soviet ambassador appeared and received a standing ovation.

"Stupid fucking Jews," Moish whispered to me. Here in this room one could begin to understand why the Holocaust had caught its victims so unprepared. Europe's Jews were masters of self-deception; they forgot how to distinguish enemies from friends, forgot how to survive. I felt obliged to despise universalism and espouse a hard ethnocentrism, to repudiate these communists' fatal innocence.

A member of SSSJ stood and hesitantly interrupted the Soviet ambassador, "Uh, excuse me, but what about the Soviet Jews?" Even SSSJ disruptions were polite.

The audience roared. We put on yarmulkes and chanted slogans. A big-bellied security guard stood over Moish and me, shouting, "Here they are! They're right among you!" The guard put his hand on Moish's shoulder. He opened his jacket and showed Moish his gun. "Be a good boy," he said.

The guard turned to me. "You got one of those for me?" he asked, pointing to my yarmulke.

"Are you Jewish?" I asked stupidly.

"What do you think 'Richie Lettleman' is?" he replied.

A piano was wheeled onto the stage, but the old Jews refused to be calmed. They ran about the hall looking for yarmulkes, nursing-home patients on a pogrom. Shaking fingers clawed at me. Someone spat in my face. "Fesheest!" shouted an old man in Yiddish English. "Fesheest peeg!"

Moish pulled me away. "If we don't get out of here," he said, "I'm going to hit an old Jew and never forgive myself."

We made it outside. Moish said, "In a few days they may start killing Jews in Russia. And here we are, fighting our grandmothers." Pinching my cheek and using a Yiddish endearment for my name, he added, "Yossel, don't waste my time anymore with bullshit. When you're ready to do something serious, give me a call."

*   *   *

A pipe bomb exploded outside the Manhattan office of Aeroflot, the Soviet airline. Someone phoned the media and said, "So long as Jews are on trial in Russia, Russia will be on trial before the world. Never again." Suddenly the Soviet Jewry movement — that most gentle of protest movements — had its own terrorists.

A few hours later Meir Kahane appeared at a crowded press conference, which he'd just happened to schedule a week earlier for this very time. Reporters asked whether the coincidence didn't prove he'd known of the bombing in advance. Kahane smiled. "We take no responsibility," he said. "But we applaud the act."

I was thrilled. No one could dismiss us now. We were just like the anti-Vietnam movement: *serious*. Thanks to the bombing, the Leningrad trial had finally become front-page news. I refused to speculate about what might have happened had passersby been in the area during the explosion. Instead, I fantasized about placing a bomb outside a Soviet office, then slipping home and turning on the radio, waiting for the news.

I called Moish to share my excitement. I told him that I blamed the establishment Jewish leaders for the bombing. If they'd done their job and organized big peaceful rallies, no one would feel desperate enough to blow up Soviet offices.

Moish was bemused. "Still busy with the establishment, Yossel? Forget the establishment, Yossel. A dozen 'Exodus' marches won't do as much as one *meshuggener* with a bomb."

The hijacking trial began on December 15. Glenn Richter organized an emergency rally at the Soviet mission, during school hours. I went to the three senior Talmud classes, asked their rabbis for permission to make an announcement, and said, There will be a mass walkout at recess.

The principal of BTA, Rabbi Zuroff, positioned himself by the front door and glared, trying to intimidate us with his presence. One by one, we passed him and walked out. Then Melvin Pickholtz — my old Betar comrade, still the most timid boy in class and nominated every term for student president as a joke — tried to leave. This was too much for Rabbi Zuroff. "Mr. Pickholtz," he said, "I'm warning *you* especially: Don't go." Pickholtz stayed.

We picketed on the usual corner, in the usual orderly circle. Despite the crisis, SSSJ didn't escalate its tactics. No sit-downs blocking traffic, no chain-ins at the Soviet mission gate. I met Moish, leaning against a barricade, blatantly bored. "Ain't no one gonna give a shit about our nice little rallies," he said.

Meir Kahane appeared, surrounded by followers. Despite the bitter cold, his white trench coat was unbuttoned, a man apparently too absorbed with important issues to tend to his own comfort. His smooth young face was handsome but unexceptional. He wore a large black yarmulke over short black hair. When someone greeted him, he smiled and then quickly looked to the ground, his thin shoulders stooped, as if embarrassed by the attention.

I couldn't take my eyes from him. I was drawn, of course, by the charisma of his notoriety, but equally drawn by the paradox of a seemingly shy man who sought media attention. I assumed he was selfless, sacrificing even his humility for the cause.

The TV cameras gathered around him. Brooklyn Jewry — BTA! — had produced a world-class outlaw, a man whose very appearance made news. Europe's Jews had died unnoticed, and Kahane was the antidote to our marginality. Thanks to him, Jewish suffering was now headlines. He was the terrorist hero, who finds for his dispossessed people an ephemeral home in the media.

Glenn was addressing the crowd when the chanting began, "Kahane! Kahane!" Moish and I joined in, heckling Glenn with the JDLers. We had crossed the line.

Glenn yielded the mike. Kahane spoke with a stutter. "If Jews d-die in Leningrad," he said, wincing with the repetition, "New York is gonna burn!"

"Never again!" we shouted, raising our fists, empowering our stuttering savior.

"It is time to take the Soviet Jewry issue off the obituary page and put it where it belongs — on page one! I want to see a thousand young J-Jews ready to go over the barricades. But," he turned to Glenn and smiled, "not today."

Moish approached Kahane, and they went off to the side, whispering. Then they left together, Kahane's arm around Moish's shoulders. A few days later a dozen Kahane followers, Moish included, took over a synagogue facing the Soviet mission. They barricaded themselves on the balcony, shouted through bullhorns at the Soviet diplomats, and announced they were remaining until the end of the trial.

Underground accounts of the trial revealed that the defendants had indeed intended to hijack a plane. They'd booked every seat of a small aircraft used in internal flights, so as not to endanger innocent passengers. One of the Jews, Mark Dymshitz, was a licensed pilot; he was to take control of the plane and fly it to Sweden. The night before the anticipated hijacking, the plotters realized they were being tailed. Though the scheme was now doomed, they persisted, hoping their desperation would draw world attention to Soviet Jewry. They were arrested before they even boarded the plane.

The prosecutor demanded the death penalty for two defendants, Dymshitz and Eduard Kuznetzov, who'd already spent years in prison for organizing illegal poetry readings. The verdict came on Christmas Eve: death for Dymshitz and Kuznetzov. Death for a hijacking that never happened.

A few nights later the JDL rallied in a college auditorium near the Soviet mission. Several thousand people filled the hall. JDLers in tight jeans and berets and green army coats wore buttons with the borrowed slogans of black militants, "Jewish Is Beautiful" and "Jewish Power," and the words "Never Again" printed over the tiny repetitive names of Nazi death camps. I wore my favorite button, "Up Against the Wall Mother Russia," a takeoff on the Yippie slogan that ended with the word "motherfucker."

A man with a long mustache extending to either side of his jaw wore a leather jacket with an Israeli flag sewn on the back, like a motorcycle gang emblem. A young black Jew in a yarmulke paced the aisles, waving a giant Israeli flag on a pole. A fat man in a football helmet — ready for action — grinned at anyone who looked at him, raised his fist and said, "Never again!" Across the stage a banner displayed the JDL symbol, a fist cut through a Star of David.

There were rumors of what was about to happen: We would march from the auditorium and divert the attention of the cops, while the group still barricaded inside the synagogue rushed out and forced its way into the mission.

I greeted friends with the black-power handshake, angled as if for a handwrestling match, grasping hands turned into a single fist. A Borough Park acquaintance, Yankel Shlagbaum, held two small American flags. *"Nu,* Yankel," I said to him, "what's the joke?"

"You think the cops are gonna beat someone holding *two* American flags?" he said, laughing.

Meir Kahane appeared onstage. He looked around at the largest crowd any JDL rally had ever drawn, smiled slightly, and pronounced in Hebrew: "Blessed are you, Lord our God, who has kept us and sustained us and brought us to this day."

"Never again, never again, never again," we chanted. Amen, amen, amen.

"American Jews have a hang-up," said Kahane, moving his yarmulke over his head, back and forth, as if stoking a fire. "It's called respectability. *Re-spect-abil-i-ty.* The year is 1943. Stephen Wise and the other American Jewish leaders have just approached Roosevelt to bomb the train tracks leading to Auschwitz. Roosevelt refuses. The Jewish leaders have a problem. What is to be done, now that each day, each day as American Jews celebrate their weddings and revel in their expensive bar mitzvahs, thousands of Jews are being gassed?"

Remarkably, his stutter was gone. He spit his words, not holding them long enough to falter over them. And by repeating words and even entire phrases, he transformed his stutter into rhetoric.

"What would have happened — what would have happened! — if Stephen Wise and all his wise men had called for a hundred thousand Jews to fill the streets of Washington and sit down in cold anger and *not move* until Roosevelt agreed to bomb the train tracks? What if rabbis had chained themselves to the White House gates singing that well-known Jewish song, 'We Shall Overcome'?

"Two things would have happened. Two things. They would have all been arrested. And the train tracks would have been bombed.

"But they didn't get arrested. Jews don't do such things. It's not *respectable.* And so six million Jews died, and American Jews kept their respectability. I say it's time to bury respectability before respectability buries us!"

This was my father speaking. His lonely indictment of American Jewry was finally being heard. I felt the thrill of his vindication.

Kahane continued: "I know Jews who can't sleep at night because of their concern for humanity." He smacked his lips, savoring the sarcasm. "I know Jews who go to jail for blacks and Puerto Ricans and Chicanos and Pygmies. I know rabbis who went to Selma to get arrested. But I don't know of a *single* rabbi who broke the law when the crematoria were being fed with *twelve thousand* Jews every day. Not *one* Jewish leader even thought of doing what every self-respecting black leader did for his people when the issue wasn't life or death but permission to sit in the front of a bus.

"Never again will Jews watch silently while other Jews die. Never again!"

"Never a-gain! Never a-gain! Never a-*gain!*"

"Tonight we have a different Jew, a fighting Jew! But this fighting Jew drives the respectables, the Nice Irvings, up their wood-paneled offices. 'Violence is unJewish! The Bible says so!' In the Bible we find the story of a man named Moses, who saw an Egyptian beating a Jew. And what did Moses do? Set up a committee to investigate the root causes of Egyptian anti-Semitism? The Bible says, 'And he smote the Egyptian.' "

Kahane raised a fist and slowly twisted it. "Listen, Brezhnev, and listen well: If Dymshitz and Kuznetzov die, Russian diplomats will die in New York. Two Russians for every Jew!"

"Two Russians for every Jew! Two Russians for every *Jew!*"

We filled the exits and pushed outside. The night blinked with rotating police lights. In the bitter air our slogans turned to smoke: "We are *Jews,* we couldn't be *prouder,* and if you can't hear us we'll shout a little *louder!*" Helmeted cops formed a barricade along the curb, clubs horizontal across their bellies. We were dangerous with rage, no longer pathetic little Jews, no more Nice Irvings.

We practically ran the single block to the Soviet mission. I tried to get close to the head of the line, but not too close: to see what was happening; to be touched by danger, the possibility of pain; but still be far back enough to run when the cops began swinging.

We packed onto the pavement, prevented by the cops from spreading into the gutter. There was no room, but still the crowds kept coming, pressing from behind.

A young man in a white karate jacket tied with a black belt shouted, "Let the Reb through, let the Reb through!" They called Kahane "the Reb" — the teacher. The dense crowd somehow parted, and the man in the karate jacket escorted Kahane to the front of the line. Camera crews ran alongside.

Kahane leapt over the farthest barricade and disappeared into a line of cops. I thought: That guy has balls.

The cops charged the crowd, swinging. We linked arms. "They're calling us kikes!" someone shouted. "Nazis! Nazis!" we chanted.

Glass shattered. A young woman fell through a Christmas display window; she lay in the glass, screaming. The cops clubbed randomly. I led someone with a bloodied head into an apartment building, down to the basement. The janitor tied a wet towel around his head. We returned to the street.

There was no one to tell us what to do next: The JDL leadership was either in jail with Kahane or barricaded inside the synagogue. We wandered aimlessly, chanting. Irate neighbors shouted at us from above; bags of garbage fell on our heads. Demonstrators pushed into the apartment building, pounding on doors and screaming obsceni-ties, forgetting the cops, the mission, Kuznetzov and Dymshitz. I headed for the subway.

I was home for the eleven o'clock news. We were, of course, head-lines. I moved close to the screen to spot myself in the crowd. Instead, I saw Yankel Shlagbaum, blood on his face, glasses skewed, in ei-ther hand an American flag.

4.

The death sentences were the Kremlin's great miscalculation. Twenty-four governments, and even Western communist parties, protested. The Soviet Jewry movement had entered the big time. For days the words "Soviet Jews" appeared in newspaper headlines. In school there were conversations about Soviet Jewry I didn't even ini-tiate. On New Year's Eve the Leningrad court commuted the death sentences to fifteen years in Siberia.

I emerged from the Leningrad trial a follower of Meir Kahane — "the Reb," I called him now. Kahane promised to resolve the con-tradiction between my internal life as a surrogate Holocaust survivor and my objective life as an American. Kahane was telling us, young American Jews, that our comfortable lives were an aberration, a meaningless interlude between times of persecution, and that by confronting New York cops and risking beatings and arrest we could reenter Jewish history and experience its menacing intensity. The key transition from privileged American to vulnerable Jew was to see the government not as your protector but your enemy. Even more than for trying to free Jews from the Soviet Union, I loved Kahane for trying to free us from America.

And yet nothing proved our Americanness more than our craving for experience — within relatively safe limits, of course. Like the New Left protestors resisting an imaginary Nazi "Amerika," we flattered ourselves with absurd comparisons. If New York cops were storm troopers and FBI men KGB agents, then we were resistance fighters and dissidents. There *were* moments of genuine danger at a JDL rally: One could get clubbed or arrested, spend a few hours or days in jail. But even the JDL elite, the underground boys who bombed Soviet buildings, knew that, if arrested, they wouldn't face a Soviet court but an American one.

I wanted to be a Jewish outlaw, at war with history. But I was also an American, raised on *Easy Rider* and *Bonnie and Clyde*. Americans of my generation longed to be outlaws, and America let you pretend to be whatever you wanted. I had already taken the first step toward counterculture recklessness: smoking marijuana and wearing a denim jacket with angry political buttons pinned to its pockets. The next inevitable step was arrest for some minor offense like a street sit-down, a misdemeanor without consequence but that bestowed a whiff of prison, menace. Young Americans established a reverse respectability: the less legal, the more admired. Only a generation pampered by history could aspire to outlawhood.

The JDL offered me entry into both the danger zone of Jewish history and the fun house of America, allowed me to become at once my father's contemporary and a Yippie. Indeed, the JDL was the most fully American of any Jewish organization, for it tested, without anxiety, the limits of American tolerance toward Jews. We relied on the basic restraint of the police even as we provoked them, trusted in the protection of the American government even as we threatened its interests.

Kahane announced a new anti-Soviet tactic: harassment. Teams of JDLers would follow Soviet diplomats and their wives, "questioning" them about the treatment of Soviet Jews. If Jews weren't free in

Leningrad, insisted Kahane, then Soviet diplomats won't be free on the streets of New York. The harassment campaign was intended to sabotage President Nixon's policy of Soviet-American détente. Kahane summed up his contempt for détente with a slogan, "Don't build bridges over Jewish bodies."

I cut school to hang out on the corner of East Sixty-seventh Street and Third Avenue, waiting for diplomats to emerge from the nearby Soviet mission — "the mission," we called it. The scene went like this: A black limousine with "DPL" — diplomat — on its license plates pauses at the corner of East Sixty-seventh Street. We surround the car, point our middle fingers, spit at the hastily rolled-up windows. Then someone spots a Russian-looking man in a fur hat walking quickly across the avenue. "Hey Igor! Got one of those hats for me?" Igor confesses he's Russian by bowing his head. We're just behind him now, lewdly smacking our lips and shouting Russian curses that inflame his ears: *"Roosky khoy!"* Russian prick. Two cops stroll behind us. "Okay, boys," one of them says, not unfriendly. "That's enough fun for today."

We charged long-distance calls to the Soviet mission and in the bathrooms of bars pasted stickers that had drawings of naked women and read, "Sonya is man-hungry and waiting for *you*," followed by the number of the mission.

I phoned the mission at all hours: A wary voice answered, "Yes?"

"I'd like to speak with Boris and Natasha," I replied.

"Plis?"

"Roosky khoy!"

The Soviet Cultural Center in Washington was bombed, and then the Soviet embassy in Amsterdam. On the corner of East Sixty-seventh Street, we sang, to the tune of "Volga Boatman," "Soviet mission — boom! Soviet mission — boom!"

The press denounced us as hoodlums, even as it encouraged us by paying far more attention to violence than to peaceful protest. When Kahane was arrested at the mission for disorderly conduct, the *New York Times* — which usually consigned coverage of SSSJ rallies to well within the inside pages — reported the incident on page one. It was an unspoken pact: Kahane provided the spectacle, and the media rewarded him with publicity.

The Soviets retaliated — not against Soviet Jews, which might have forced us to pause, but against American diplomats in Moscow. Groups of "irate Soviet citizens" organized by the KGB surrounded Americans on Moscow streets, cursed and shoved them, and smashed the windows of their cars. Détente was in danger; cultural exchange ruined. Just as Kahane had predicted: The only way to make the Soviet Jewry problem a world problem was to violently threaten Soviet-American relations. The JDL harassment and Soviet counterharassment were headlines for weeks. One newspaper wrote that the JDL was the main topic of conversation at cocktail parties in Washington and Moscow. A few yeshiva kids shouting obscenities on a street corner had caused the worst superpower crisis in years.

Kahane appreciated the joke more than anyone. As the crisis intensified, he became more jovial, his speeches full of irony: "FBI agents ask me what I know about the bombing of some Soviet office or another. I say that I don't know anything, offer them tea with lemon, and we talk about politics."

At the height of the harassment campaign, the *New York Times* published a front-page exposé of Kahane's past. The article portrayed a tormented man who had lived a double life: He'd worked for years under a pseudonym, Michael King, trying at one point to create a pro–Vietnam War campus movement; his former colleagues hadn't even known that he was an Orthodox rabbi. The article strongly hinted at an adulterous affair with a non-Jewish model, who then committed suicide, presumably because of Kahane. One especially pathetic anecdote described Kahane's short-lived attempt to settle in Israel before founding the JDL: He assured friends that he, an unknown rabbi from Queens, would soon be made an Israeli cabinet member. The Kahane who emerged from the *Times* portrait was a self-obsessed man desperate for recognition as the embodiment of Jewish destiny, but who lacked control over his own life and seemed unsure of his most basic identity.

Kahane didn't sue the *Times* or even bother refuting the charges. And yet I accepted the JDL line, because I wanted to: The exposé was a smear. When, after all, had the sober *Times* ever run a front-page story about the personal life of a public figure? The *Times*'s

assimilated Jewish editors, I thought, felt threatened by our as-
sertiveness; the Nice Irvings were panicking.

The JDL office was located in a warehouse at the edge of Borough
Park, a few blocks from where I lived. The area was an Italian en-
clave, and until the JDL appeared, I'd been afraid to walk there wearing my yarmulke. The office was called the Jewish Identity Center,
known simply as the ID. Across the street from the ID, men in short
hair and mirrored sunglasses stood for hours before shiny cars. After
leaving the ID, I looked around to see if I was being followed.

You entered the ID via a steel door into a small foyer. A secretary eyed you through bulletproof glass before buzzing you in. You
came to a large room, with a punching bag and karate mats and bullet holes in the wall. The JDL boys were deliberately reckless with
guns, as if compensating for generations of Jewish timidity.

On the wall of Kahane's basement office was spray-painted in un-
even black letters, "Office of the 'Reb' "; in the middle of the room
was a boiler. An obese young man named Sheldon sat next door editing the JDL newsletter, a collection of accounts of JDL riots and bad
but earnest poems about the Holocaust. In Sheldon's office lay a coffin
left over from some JDL march, and in which he sometimes slept.

My neighbor Sol Gottleib belonged to JDL's elite *chayas,* or animal, squad, which fought anti-Semitic street gangs and broke up
Nazi rallies. Sol would stand on his rooftop with a hunting bow and
imagine felling pogromists as they invaded Borough Park. He patrolled Jewish cemeteries against vandals and was the first to give
chase when hoodlums threw rocks at the stained-glass windows of
our synagogue during Shabbos morning services. When not defending Jews, Sol hung out in a limousine with a fat Hasid who held or-
gies at the Waldorf.

Sol wanted each of America's six million Jews to tattoo a number
on his or her arm, as a living memorial for Europe's Six Million.
"Yos," he said to me, "pick a number."

"I'm not sure I want numbers on my *arm,*" I said.

"All right," said Sol, reasonable, "so we'll print the numbers on
cards."

Everyone seemed to have a scheme, some grand idea to save the
Jews. Al Erenreich, a big red-faced man, was one of those middle-

age, American-born JDLers who so strongly identified with the Holocaust that only his Brooklyn accent revealed that he wasn't a survivor. One day he phoned me at home and summoned me into his car for a secret meeting. We drove awhile without speaking; he turned the radio up, a precaution JDLers took in case their cars were bugged.

"Stalin," he said finally.

I nodded.

"Svetlana Stalin," he said. "Stalin's daughter."

"Right," I said.

"That bitch. Living in the freedom of these United States while her father's victims lie ten feet under in frozen graves. Have you ever heard her make *one* statement for Soviet Jewry? Just one? Eh? Don't you think she owes us?"

He paused and smiled — that JDL mannerism heralding a confidential revelation about "doing something crazy for Jews," as we put it.

"So here's what we do," he said. "Drive out in a caravan of cars to her home in Arizona, with *big* signs on the hoods: "Shameless Svetlana! Redeem Your Family's Lost Honor and Speak Out Against Red Fascist Oppression of Jews!"

He waited for my reaction.

"Mr. Erenreich," I said, "why couldn't we talk about this on the phone?"

"You never know who's listening," he said.

Moish had emerged from the synagogue siege at the Soviet mission a JDL leader. He became secretive, hinting at underground activities. Sunday afternoons he went shooting, and he was absent from home for days at a time. "We're doing good things for Jews, Yossel, good things," he said and then smiled.

He spoke like Kahane, a slow, sarcastic speech that mimicked gangster talk. He referred to FBI agents as "feds" and called agents assigned to the JDL by their first names. Anyone he considered an enemy of the Jews or of the JDL was "a bad guy, a *bad* guy"; while a friend was "a thousand percent, a *million* percent." Understated menace and exaggerated praise: a reckless speech that despised exactness, truth.

"So *nu*, Yossel," Moish said to me, pinching my cheek, "don't you think it's time to get serious? JDL is hungry for smart guys; anyone who can spell his name without too many mistakes can walk in and take over. Your heart's in the right place, Yossel, you're a thousand percent. But when are you going to start *doing* for Jews?"

In fact, I wanted desperately to become a JDL leader. I wanted to know the movement's secrets and be admired for my daring, to stand at rallies with a megaphone and incite the crowds against the cops. I wanted to be a confidant of Kahane and call him "Meir," just like Moish did. And yet I couldn't commit myself to the JDL's inner world of guns and feds. Despite Moish's insistence, I hadn't even met Kahane. I knew that if I did, I'd have no choice but to immerse myself totally in the JDL. And the reason I couldn't do so — though I was ashamed to admit it to Moish — was that my father didn't want me to.

My mother warned me, "Daddy is worried sick about you getting into trouble and ruining your life." "Worried sick" was meant literally: He could get another heart attack. In trying to save Jews, I might kill my father.

The job of a child of survivors was to keep his or her parents alive by providing *nachas*, parental pride. To transform their survival from mere fate into miracle. Our lives were borrowed: Our parents weren't supposed to have survived, and we weren't supposed to have been born. I had no choice; I deferred to my father's health and happiness.

Of course, I resented him. He'd raised me to sacrifice for the Jews; what better *nachas* could I give him than to become a JDL leader? But prison wasn't any survivor's idea of *nachas*, not even my father's. "Let the other boy do the wild thing," he said to me. "You can do more for the Jewish people with your brain." As an inspiring example, he invoked his own childhood hero, the Zionist journalist Tisbi Illés, who had roused Nagy-Károly's Jews with speeches and articles. My generation's moment in Jewish history had come; the Soviet Jewry movement had turned dangerous, hip — and he wanted me to be Tisbi Illés.

"Take it easy," he said to me, stroking my cheek. "Go slow. Don't get so exciting. No extreme are good; always go to the middle path."

His advice angered and confused me. *He* of all people was preaching moderation? And yet, though I didn't realize it, he had changed.

He was still capable of great bursts of anger — at the anti-Israel UN, at Satmar Hasidim, at his rebellious son. Yet he was no longer committed to rage as an ideal, but rather bound to it by habit. He had softened enough to recognize anger as an imperfection. And he was trying to spare me the same self-inflicted wound.

I equated extremism with passion, life. Anger would keep me from becoming a stupid adult, dulled by small needs and ambitions. My father was trying to smother me with moderation, but I would resist him. If I couldn't become a JDL leader, I could at least be part of the scene, inhaling the ecstasy of rage.

One afternoon, while I was hanging out at the ID, a call came that Puerto Ricans were about to massacre Satmar Hasidim in Williamsburg, the Brooklyn neighborhood where most Satmars lived. As much as the JDL despised their anti-Zionism, Satmars were still Jews; and we valued ethnic solidarity as the ultimate ideal.

We got into cars and headed to Williamsburg. We gathered on a block of burned-out tenements, stood in military formation with hands clasped behind our backs and waited for pogromists who never came. Moish sat at a ground-floor window in an abandoned building behind us, shotgun on his lap. A police detective assigned to the JDL approached the window. "What you got there, Moish?" he asked.

"You come any closer," said Moish, "I'll blow your fucking brains out." The detective backed away.

In Moscow, on Purim, a hundred Jews entered the Soviet Parliament and announced a hunger strike. It was too much. Nothing like this had ever happened in the Soviet Union. I fantasized about leading a sit-in of American Jews inside the Kremlin, proving our commitment and our fearlessness.

One Sunday in March, together with my sister Chani, I rode a chartered bus from Borough Park to a JDL Soviet Jewry rally in Washington. It was my first visit ever to the capital — civics education, Borough Park–style.

Though rumors had predicted six hundred busloads of demonstrators, no more than twenty buses were parked on the Ellipse across from the White House. We filled a corner of the huge park, listening to a speech by a young Russian Jew who had recently managed to emigrate to Israel. His name was Volodya Shlechtman, and for

the last week he'd been sitting in a cage on a Washington street, os-
tensibly on a hunger strike. I met my friend Sol, who'd spent the
week with Shlechtman and who said that Shlechtman secretly ate
when no one was around. "This guy ate more in the past week than
you or I eat in a month. I'm telling you, Yos, when he finishes with
his hunger strike, he's gonna need a diet."

We forgot about the low turnout and strolled to the Soviet embassy, happy in the sun and wind. The cops rerouted traffic and let
us march in the street. We shouted "Never again!" and chanted the
dates of Israel's military victories, " '48 — '56 — '67 — anytime!" daring the Arabs, the Kremlin, the UN, anyone foolish enough to take
on the Jews. Then someone combined the two chants, " '48 — '56 —
'67 — never again!" and we responded enthusiastically, until we realized our mistake and fell into awkward silence.

We stopped at an intersection near the embassy, and Kahane
spoke through a megaphone: "I'm asking you to do today what Jews
didn't do while the gas chambers were burning: Sit down in the
streets of Washington."

The crowd lowered to the ground. Some people squatted, ready
to leap when the cops came.

"The police are going to tap you on the shoulder," Kahane continued. "I ask that you go with them willingly. No violence."

"No violence! No violence!" chanted the JDL marshals.

It turned into a party. A friend of mine played Grateful Dead
songs on the guitar, and we sang along. We were elated to be sitting in the streets of Washington, retroactively undoing the shame
of American Jewry. Even the police were infected by our joy. One
cop approached a teenage girl and asked, "May I have this arrest?"
A cop tapped me, and I rose with my fist in the air, just in case a
photographer was around.

Those of us already arrested waited by police buses with barred
windows, joking with the cops who took our mug shots. One JDLer
put his arm around his arresting officer, posing for the picture. I
asked my cop if I could have a copy of my mug shot as a souvenir.
"Your first arrest?" he asked. I nodded. "Maybe the judge'll go easy
on you, say, ten years and a fine."

I boarded a bus and sat by the window. The JDLers stood on the
seats and pounded the roof rhythmically to chants: "One, two, three,

four, open up the iron door! Five, six, seven, eight, let my people emigrate!"

We were packed into small cells, and the overcrowding excited us with the power of our numbers. We cheered with raised fists each new group brought past our bars. Someone in the cell had a transistor radio, and we listened to the news about us: over a thousand arrested — "busted," we called it, to sound like blacks and left-wing radicals — the largest mass arrest in Washington's history. We each paid a ten-dollar fine and were back on buses that same night. When Chani and I came home, there was a sign on the door: "Welcome Heroes."

Two months later Kahane appeared at a press conference with Joe Colombo, alleged head of a New York Mafia family, and announced an Italian-Jewish alliance of the fringe. From now on, the JDL and Colombo's front group, the Italian-American Civil Rights League, would support each other's causes. Colombo's ostensible cause was ethnic dignity: fighting the stereotype of Italian-Americans as mafioso. But Colombo's real goal was personal rehabilitation: By campaigning for the good name of Italian-Americans, he hoped to obscure the fact that he was among those who'd blackened it. Colombo was so unsavory that even an alliance with the JDL offered a measure of respectability. Outlawhood was apparently relative.

Colombo's cynicism was matched by Kahane's. Though Kahane insisted the bizarre alliance was good for the Jews — Italian-Americans would protest for Soviet Jewry, Jewish kids in Brooklyn wouldn't be beaten by Italian teenagers — his real reason for joining with Colombo was that it was good for Meir Kahane. He'd just been indicted for constructing a bomb at the JDL summer camp in the Catskills — for educational purposes, he said — and faced a possible five-year jail term; Colombo had paid his bail.

The pact was the logical conclusion of Kahane's Jewish isolationism. An alliance of despair: Who else but fellow outcasts would want anything to do with Jews? Kahane's implicit message was that all goyim were gangsters anyway, and better to deal with blatant hoodlums than with those who claimed to be civilized but would in the end betray you.

I hated the alliance, which was a parody of Ya'akov Birnbaum's

messianic vision of the Soviet Jewry movement uniting Jews and
Gentiles in reconciliation. The Colombo link also threatened the le-
gitimacy of the Soviet Jewry movement, lent communist attacks on
JDLers as "Zionist gangsters" a literal credibility. I recalled Ya'akov's
warning to me about Kahane's dreams of "chasms of blood." What
kind of man had I allowed to become my leader?

I confided my reservations to Moish. He patted me on the head.
"Yossel, Yossel," he said, "what are you worried? Isn't it better to
have the Mafia with you than against you, Yossel? The Mafia has
money, connections, guns. Everything a good Jewish boy needs. Trust
me, Yossel: We're doing good for the Jews."

I wasn't convinced. But I swallowed it. The alliance was a quirk,
a footnote to the JDL's historic struggle for Soviet Jewry. And who
knew? The Reb had been right about tactics until now; maybe he
really did know what he was doing.

Kahane's charisma came from a willingness to violate every limit;
and in that sense, the Mafia alliance actually enhanced his appeal.
Nothing, insisted Kahane, must stand in the way of our cause. Jews
had been abandoned by humanity during the Holocaust and would
inevitably be abandoned again, so conventional morality didn't bind
us. The only moral measure that mattered was whether a given act
was good for the Jews. Or for the JDL. Or for Meir Kahane.

The Mafia connection became a kind of joke at the ID. Some
JDLers wore Civil Rights League caps. One day my friend Sol accompanied Kahane and Colombo to a golf game. "They're good guys,
those Guineas," said Sol. "A thousand percent."

Barely a month after the deal was made, Colombo was shot and
badly injured at a Civil Rights League rally. Kahane was one of the
few non–family members admitted into the wounded man's room. The
Civil Rights League, and its JDL alliance, faded shortly thereafter.

5.

In the fall I entered Yeshiva University, YU, which I called, "Why
me?" Orthodox and all-male, YU was my last choice of college. But
activism had ruined my high-school grades. Even the city-sponsored
Brooklyn College, with its generous admissions policy, rejected me;

while YU admitted almost any graduate of BTA, which was under its auspices.

YU was located in "uptown Manhattan," as the school brochures put it, meaning past Harlem, in Washington Heights. The "campus" consisted of a few buildings along Amsterdam Avenue, interspersed with kosher restaurants — a tiny Jewish strip that felt itself besieged by the Hispanics around it. Most YU students dormed, huddled in our four-block refuge. Weekends I returned to Borough Park, riding the subway through hostile territory on my shuttle between Jewish enclaves.

When I left the YU safety zone for the subway, I would take off my yarmulke. Until then I'd never walked the streets bareheaded. I felt thrilled with lightness, with invisibility. I hated being the Jew on display, constantly monitoring the effect of my presence on passersby and trying to distinguish stares of curiosity from those of distaste; always half-expecting some anti-Semitic outburst that forces your identity into exaggerated, defensive pride. It felt exhilarating to be without a yarmulke, just another potential New York victim of random, impersonal crime.

Though wearing a yarmulke was a custom, not a religious law, it had become a defining act of an Orthodox Jewish male. Its original purpose was to remind its wearer of God's hovering presence but had since become a sign of ethnic loyalty, reminding the Jew of his otherness.

I didn't want to be marked apart. I took any opportunity to escape my YU ghetto. Saturday nights I drove around Greenwich Village with friends from BTA who were now in Brooklyn College. We took off our yarmulkes, getting high in the car and then tentatively venturing into the bars and clubs and nonkosher restaurants. Among these friends I could be a teenager, being more passionate about a Dylan album or some drug than about saving the Jewish people. They were fellow children of survivors, acutely conscious of impermanence and therefore without ambition — "bums," as parents said in Borough Park, one of the few English words to enter the survivors' vocabulary of dread.

An activist, I couldn't be as cynical as my friends were. But I shared their need to break out of Orthodoxy, inhale experience.

Activism and drugs were the most accessible opportunities, and I used those as stimulants for testing myself against the world.

By the fall of 1971 thousands of Soviet Jews were emigrating to Israel. Though many more were still being denied visas, we were clearly winning. We had done the impossible: broken the Soviet Union. The combined pressure from without and from within, of Western Jews protesting and Soviet Jews defying prison, had proved irresistible.

The Soviet Jewry movement taught me that evil has no substance, cannot endure against a vigorous good. And my faith was confirmed in the God of Israel. Judaism was born in a public and collective revelation at Sinai and was experienced in holidays rooted in historical events; and so I looked for signs of God not in nature but in history. I prayed in the streets with slogans, and God's answer came through the newspapers.

One morning the *Times* reported that Boris Kochubiyevsky, the "prisoner of Zion" who once wrote he was ready to walk to his homeland, had been freed from jail and flown to Israel. Then came Ruth Alexandrovich, the imprisoned activist on whose behalf I'd sat in at Hadassah. Jews from Soviet Georgia, descendants of lost Israelite tribes, landed in Lod Airport, near Tel Aviv; kissed the runway; and then sat down on strike, demanding choice apartments in Jerusalem. The miracle was becoming concrete.

I went to hear Elie Wiesel speak. He recalled his encounter with a young Jewish woman in Moscow, which I'd first read as a boy in SSSJ: "I asked her why she was a Jew, and she said to me, 'Because I like to sing.'" Then, a few months ago, Wiesel had gone to Lod Airport to see the arrival of Russian immigrants. One woman looked familiar; Wiesel approached her and asked, "Do you still like to sing?"

Meir Kahane emigrated to Israel. He'd just been convicted of conspiracy to construct a bomb and been given a five-year suspended sentence. Kahane's career in America was over: One more arrest and he'd get sent away.

I joined the hero's send-off at Kennedy Airport. We sang and danced around our leader, restraining him from boarding his plane until the last moment. Afterward some JDL boys ran along a bal-

THE ECSTASY OF RAGE

cony where flags of all nations hung and, to our cheers, removed each one bearing a hammer and sickle or an Islamic crescent. They could just as well have uprooted most of the other flags, too, for almost the whole world had aggrieved us. At one time or another I had demonstrated against not only the Soviet Union, Poland, Iraq, Lebanon, and Syria, but France, Germany, the United States, and, of course, the UN, which alone could contain such generous rage.

Kahane's absence left an aimlessness at JDL rallies, a charismatic void. His departure seemed to come at the worst possible time for us. Though the exodus of Soviet Jewry had begun, the gates could be shut at any time. Thousands were being allowed out, but tens of thousands were not. And Zionist activists were still being sent to Siberia. More pressure was needed precisely now when the Kremlin seemed vulnerable, to force the gates fully open.

One Sunday I was arrested at a JDL sit-down at the Soviet mission. The next day a New York tabloid published a picture of me, waving my hands and shouting from the back of a paddy wagon. I bought half a dozen copies of the newspaper. But the picture I was most proud of was inaccessible: As I'd stood there shouting, Joe Beatty, a New York detective assigned to the JDL, aimed his camera at me; I raised my middle finger in response. With that gesture I proclaimed myself a young man worth watching.

6.

Moish called.

He said he had an article for an activist newspaper I was planning to publish with some friends. I asked him what the article was about and he said, "It's not for the phone."

"You can publish it in a newspaper but you can't talk about it over the phone?"

"Patience, Yossel, patience. Soon you'll understand everything."

We met, at his suggestion, in front of the Jewish Agency, Manhattan's central office for pro-Israel activity. Instead of greeting me, he asked, "What did you think of Hunter College?" He meant the recent sniper attack into the Soviet mission from the roof of neighboring Hunter College; a caller had said the shots were fired in response to a report that Sylva Zalmanson, a former defendant in the Leningrad trial, was dying in prison.

"I don't see anyone doing anything better for Sylva," I replied.

"That's good enough," Moish said. He pulled out some sheets from his denim jacket pocket and said, "Read."

The carefully handwritten article was entitled "Hunting Russian Bears at Hunter." I stood in the street and read:

> The four shots fired by the brave Jewish militant were meant only as a warning. More acts such as this will follow, with much more violent intention.
>
> The silence on the part of the American government, the world, and most of the world's Jews as Sylva Zalmanson dies proves only one thing: The battle to free Soviet Jewry lies in the hands of those few who are willing to sacrifice their own lives for their people's freedom.

"You're a good shot," I said, not knowing what else to say.

Moish laughed, modest and knowing. "I'll pass on the compliment."

"Was it Jakobovitz?" I asked. Jakobovitz, a dopey Borough Park teenager who performed magic tricks at birthday parties, had just been arrested for the Hunter shooting, although he would later be released. A front-page picture showed him being led into court, holding up his manacled hands and grinning.

"Give us some credit, Yossel. I'm talking about a serious underground. One thing you learn very quickly in this business: The feds ain't no smarter than you. They've really made assholes out of themselves with Jakobovitz."

I'd always flattered myself that I belonged at the center of my generation of Jews; now Moish was admitting me, at least partly, into its inmost circle of commitment. I looked at the passersby on the street; I knew something none of them even suspected. I felt exalted above the transparent lives around me.

We crave knowledge of hidden things. A human being is ignorant of the most basic facts of his existence; and entry into a secret society offers empowerment over mystery, the illusion of mastery.

And yet, proud as I was, I felt deeply anxious. Why was Moish confiding in me? Just knowing about his group was a kind of initiation. What was the price of admission into his knowledge?

"What can I do for you," I said rather than asked, deliberately nonchalant.

"I want you to do what you're supposed to do: Publish a newspaper. And I want that newspaper to be a vehicle for our group to communicate with young Jews. It's important for us to have a paper we can trust. It also won't be bad for your circulation, Yossel. Consider this article our first communiqué. From time to time I'll pass on other articles to you. If the feds come around asking questions, you don't know nothin'. These articles appear anonymously in the mail. And when they ask you for the originals, Yossel, you've thrown them out. Capish?"

I thought constantly of Moish. Sitting in class was painful while he and his friends were risking their lives for Soviet Jewry. They had taken empathy to its ultimate, turned themselves from American citizens into hunted Jews. Of course, I wanted to join them; but that was impossible. Becoming a terrorist meant being followed by FBI agents and leading an obviously secretive life. My father's heart would never survive it.

But was I using my father as a pretext? Could I really place a bomb and then return to routine without constantly fearing I was about to be arrested? And, if arrested, could I endure a trial without cracking, resist making a deal with the DA to save myself and betray my friends?

I feared I lacked the courage of hardness. In my fantasies I placed myself inside the Warsaw Ghetto or a cattlecar and dared myself to survive. Nothing I achieved was ever good enough, because my imaginary obstacles were always insurmountable. I needed to test myself against evil: match my power of endurance against its capacity to wound, my commitment to save against its commitment to destroy. What I feared most was precisely what I felt most drawn to.

I called Moish and asked to get together. We met in a Manhattan public library, where we could whisper without seeming suspicious. Moish wore a peddler's cap low over swollen eyes; he hadn't shaved in days. He'd just spent a week in prison for alleged illegal gun possession, only to be released for lack of evidence. "It was nothing," he said. "A vacation. My cellmate was this roly-poly *shvartze* who happened to like cocaine. When he heard what I was in for he said, 'Man, by the time you get outa here, pussy's gonna be outa style.' A good *vort*, no? The feds are trying to hang me, but I don't look dead yet, do I, Yossel?"

I told Moish why I'd asked to meet: I wanted to interview him — anonymously, of course — for a book I'd begun writing about Jewish activism. The book would be a polemic justifying our grievance against the Kremlin, the Arabs, the Vatican, the Jewish establishment — the world.

If I couldn't join the terrorists, I could at least be their voice. I aspired to being my generation's chronicler. After every Soviet Jewry demonstration I would send in a report to the *Jewish Press,* which rarely paid me but usually published the repetitive stories. I was a compulsive note-taker, recording incidents on the picket line and even in jail, writing on my palm when I had no paper.

"Ask," said Moish. "What I can answer, I'll answer. What I can't answer, I won't answer."

And so it went. We met in the library or in a park for our interviews. I asked questions I thought were daring but were really meant to give Moish a platform, and he responded with answers he thought were insightful but that any terrorist for any cause could have offered.

YOSSI: How can you justify endangering innocent people?

MOISH: When you call the press and tell them there's a bomb set to go off, you're doing your best to prevent injury. So far, someone up there is on our side, because no one has ever gotten hurt from our actions.

YOSSI: After the Amtorg bombing [a 1971 attack against the Soviet trade office, Amtorg, in Manhattan], the papers said that the cop who defused the bomb was almost blown to pieces.

MOISH: So what you're really asking is why the life of Sylva Zalmanson is worth more than the life of Patrolman Joe Shmuck. Obviously, it isn't. But you can't look at it just as a life for a life. It sounds ruthless, but the whole situation involves much, much more.

We believe that Soviet Jewry is in great physical danger. People forget that Stalin almost shipped a million Jews to concentration camps in Siberia, and the only thing that stopped him was his death. How can we be so sure that another Stalin won't seize power next Monday?

The whole world is made up of innocents. I'm not saying you have to become an unfeeling, unthinking animal. But you have to condition yourself to deal in concepts.

YOSSI: How far are you willing to go?

MOISH: You should know we're totally crazy. We've got plans to kill the Syrian ambassador to the UN if the Syrians don't free their Jews. We also want to kill Nazi war criminals — by gassing them. We've been experimenting on dogs. Great stuff.

The *anti-semitin* ain't got no limits for what they're ready to do against Jews, so we ain't got no limits neither, Yossel. [Half-smiling.] The boys in the group have a saying: "If you can't fuck it, blow it up."

There was nothing holier than a terrorist underground, I thought, standing at the center of world attention but anonymously, fame without ego.

And yet had I been less gullible, I might have asked myself some obvious questions. Why, for example, had Moish suggested the Jewish Agency for our first meeting, where we could have easily been spotted by someone we knew, rather than a more obscure rendezvous? It was almost as if he were trying to expose himself.

And why had he agreed to be interviewed for my book? Why, for that matter, had he contacted me in the first place? A basic rule of an underground is not to reveal itself to outsiders. I'd accepted without question Moish's rationale for confiding in me: I was to provide his group with a safe media link. But how necessary was that? Why not phone in anonymous messages to the wire services? What possible propaganda benefit could outweigh the danger of involving me? Obviously, I wouldn't turn Moish in; still, I was hardly risk-free. What if I got high with a friend and fell into one of those foolish revelatory drug talks? What if I wanted to impress a date with how much danger my life held?

The truth was that Moish needed to talk. Terrorists measure their effect by the media attention they summon. Yet only the projection of their rage is noticed; while they themselves remain hidden, famous in absentia. That paradox between living for publicity and being forced into absolute secrecy had to be especially painful for a teenager. Moish was doing big things, yet he couldn't brag about them. By exposing himself even to a single outsider, he personalized his group's glory. I was his safe exit from anonymity.

Perhaps Moish even had moments of ideological weakness. He was, in his way, a sensitive person, willing not only to kill but to die for human rights. Obviously, his line of work could tolerate no ambivalence. Still, he must have needed to talk to someone outside his group, to test his moral premises.

He chose the right person. I accepted his line uncritically. I shared his contempt for authority. Official justice could easily turn demonic: The Holocaust had been planned by men in business suits, endorsed by the courts, executed by the army and police. I empathized with the Black Panthers and the Weathermen, outsiders imposing the justice of the fringe. Like Moish, I was caught by the romance of the outlaw. And like Moish, I believed you could borrow the tactics of evil to empower the good and still remain immune from becoming evil yourself.

7.

On January 26, 1972, someone threw a firebomb into the lobby of the Manhattan office of Sol Hurok, impresario of the Soviet-American culture exchange. A secretary named Iris Kones, a Jew, died of smoke inhalation.

My first thought was for Moish's safety; his group must have been behind the attack. I didn't think about Iris Kones. It's not that I tried to put her out of my mind because I felt remorse; I simply didn't think about her. I didn't believe she was Jewish; I didn't believe she was dead; I didn't believe she ever existed. If I felt anything at all toward Iris Kones, it was anger for giving the Soviet Union and the Jewish establishment the chance to villify the JDL.

The night of the bombing, I was visiting my parents' home. My father came into my room and said, "The FBI are here to see you."

"Right," I said.

"I mean it, in the living room are waiting now two men for you."
He was pale, but his voice was steady.

Two shorthaired men in trench coats were sitting on our plastic-
covered velvet couch; as if for honored guests, the chandelier had
been turned on, allowing them to admire our Austro-Hungarian
decor.

The men rose when I entered. One of them introduced himself
as Bob Nixon. "No relation," he said.

The bantering quickly ended. "You've heard the news, Josef," said
Nixon.

"Josef" was the name on my birth certificate, the name I used for
formal occasions like registration for the draft and police bookings.
No one called me Josef.

"What do you think about it?" asked Nixon, pressing.

"What should I think? It's a terrible tragedy."

"The girl was Jewish, Josef."

"What does that matter?" I replied. "She was a human being."

I thought that was a very funny remark.

"Do you support this kind of act, Josef?"

"I'm against violence. We should write letters to our congressmen
instead."

They're playing with me. When are they going to ask about Moish?
Why else have they come to me so soon, on the night of the bombing? Maybe Moish is already in jail. Had they bugged our meetings
in the library?

"Where were you this morning at nine-thirty, Josef?"

"Here, at home."

"Do you have witnesses?"

"My mother, my sister."

"That's good."

"You haven't wasted any time coming to see me," I said.

"We're talking to anyone who's been arrested at a JDL rally. Do
you understand our position, Josef?"

"We're all doing our job."

"This isn't a question of Jewish ideology. We're after murderers
here. Do you know anyone who might do something like that?"

"I can't imagine anyone I know doing anything like that."

"If you happen to come across information that might be help-ful, would you pass it on to us, Joe?"

"No."

If you led them on, they might somehow entrap you.

My father, who'd stayed with me for moral support, suddenly spoke. This was his chance to address the American government on behalf of his people. He said, "You have to understand why these boys do such thing. They are desperate to end their brothers' suf-ferings. If the American government would help the Soviet Jews, no-body would have to do anymore such terrible thing."

Nixon wrote quickly in his pad. I wondered if my father had be-come a suspect.

Not a word about Moish. Maybe they really didn't know; maybe they'd come to me because I'd drawn attention to myself by giving Joe Beatty the finger from the back of the paddy wagon. Whatever the reason, the visit raised my stature as an activist and confirmed my childhood fantasies: Now I really was at war with my govern-ment.

Yet is that all I felt: self-important and protective of my friend? No remorse for a dead young woman, no queasiness about terror-ism? Apparently not. I blamed JDL violence on the Soviet oppres-sor, the apathetic Jewish establishment, the sensationalist media that ignored peaceful protests — on everyone but those who had caused Iris Kones's death.

Moish called.

We met at the library. He was more tense than I'd ever seen him. "The heat is unbelievable," he said. "You can't imagine what this Hurok thing did to us. Everything's on hold."

"What went wrong with the bombing?" I asked.

"What bombing? You think there was a bomb? Don't believe every-thing you read in the papers, Yossel. A few kids putting a smoke bomb together in the basement of the JDL office — capish? That's how serious it was: in the basement of the ID, with J. Edgar listen-ing in. It wasn't supposed to do anything more than cause a lot of smoke. A smoke bomb, not a bomb that goes boom. So what hap-pens? They throw it into the lobby, it lands on a couch, the couch catches fire — and a poor Jewish girl dies of smoke inhalation."

"You mean it wasn't you?"

"God forbid! What do you think, we're amateurs?"

"So what's gonna be, Moish?"

"What's gonna be is that we have to get these stupid kids out of the country fast. That's why I called you. We need a mailing address for these kids' false passports. I wanted to know if we could use your dorm room."

I was delighted: I could share in the glory of the underground without actually having to bomb anything.

No passports came, and Moish didn't call again. I had no luck raising money for the newspaper that was to print Moish's communiqués, and I felt embarrassed to call him. On visits home I listened for clicks on the phone, watched the street for men sitting in cars.

8.

That summer the Ukrainian Dance Company came to the Metropolitan Opera House. I waited for the JDL to disrupt the performances, which were sponsored by the Soviet government, but it seemed paralyzed. Moish and his friends were deep underground; Kahane was in Israel. And most active JDLers were either training at the group's summer camp in the Catskills or hanging out in Jerusalem.

Ever since Moish had confided to me about his group, I'd felt the need to prove myself worthy of his trust. And now, if only by default, it seemed my time had come.

I went to the Borough Park pizza shop to see who of "the boys," as JDLers called themselves, was still around. The pizza shop was where Borough Park's religious culture, its veneer of intactness, collapsed. On any given evening, the sidewalk before the pizza shop would be crowded with JDL boys waiting to be summoned to a fight; drug pushers with tiny knitted yarmulkes worn close to their foreheads like visors, slurring their words from the sides of their mouths; chain-smoking yeshiva wise guys with fedoras pushed to the back of their heads and suit jackets draped over their shoulders like capes, slapping each other's palms and asking, "You got for me maybe a *jointeleh?*"

The only JDLer I found was Yankel Shlagbaum, who'd been

clubbed at the Soviet mission during the Leningrad trial while holding two American flags. Yankel wasn't willing to risk arrest, but he
agreed to help me from a distance.

We went to the Metropolitan Opera House the next night. I carried an attaché case with an alarm clock inside, a fake bomb. My
choice of tactic was revealing: I wanted to share in Moish's drama.

I bought a ticket, while Yankel waited across the street at a phone
booth. I sat through the first few minutes of the performance, placed
the briefcase under my seat and walked out. When Yankel saw me,
he phoned the Met, said there was a bomb in the hall, and gave my
seat number. He ended with an inevitable slogan: "When Sylva
Zalmanson is dying in prison, there will be no Soviet culture in New
York. Never again!"

We waited for the large glass doors of the Met to fill with fleeing
people. Nothing. Yankel called again: "You've been warned a second
time. We're not going to be responsible for what happens if you don't
evacuate the hall." He spoke with such menacing authority that I almost believed the building might explode. Still nothing. Was the
management heartless? How could they risk innocent lives?

A few nights later I returned to the Met, with three new accom-
plices. We entered the building, wearing suits. In our pockets were
plastic bags filled with chicken blood, obtained from a Brooklyn
slaughterhouse.

Throwing blood at Soviet representatives was a JDL tradition. One
JDLer had poured blood on the head of a Soviet diplomat at a
Washington cocktail party and received enormous press coverage.
The media loved blood, and we tried to give the media what it wanted.

I had no moral qualms about throwing blood at dancers. The
Kremlin was exporting culture to humanize its image and divert
Western attention from its oppressive regime, so I considered its cul-
tural representatives fair targets. I lived in a world of symbols:
Dancers were jailers; chicken blood, Jewish suffering.

We split into pairs. Eli and Sholom sat together toward the front,
Avi and I in the middle. Avi always grinned. Even when he got upset he kept grinning, unable to stop, torn between wanting to be nice
and not wanting to be ineffectual.

Avi and I walked up the center aisle, toward the stage. The
Ukrainian dancers were in a spinning frenzy. Eli and Sholom stood

up, shouted "Never again!" and threw their bags. All heads seemed to turn toward Avi and me, exposed in the middle of the aisle.

Eli and Sholom disappeared through a side exit, unnoticed. Avi and I threw our bags at the stage. We turned around and ran toward the main exit. A foot extended into the aisle and I fell on my face. A man held my arms while others kicked me. *"A shande fur der goyim!"* someone shouted in Yiddish, A disgrace before the Gentiles. I tried to scream back, *"You're* the disgrace!" but my mouth was pressed to the floor. Finally, I was rescued by detective Joe Beatty, who'd been sitting in the audience, waiting for something to happen.

Beatty handcuffed me and led me to a paddy wagon. "You bastards are keeping me from sleeping with my wife," he said.

"Who's your wife, Joe," I asked, "Hermine Ryan?"

Hermine Ryan was a Queens housewife recently exposed as a former death camp guard.

"No," said Joe, "Eva Braun"—Hitler's mistress.

I found Avi inside the paddy wagon. When he saw Beatty, he began screaming, "You stole my yarmulke! Give me back my yarmulke!" I tried to calm him, but he worked himself into a fit; he even stopped grinning.

A detective sitting beside us told Beatty, "Too bad you got to him first. I would have thrown the fucking bastard down fifty flights of stairs."

I took a yarmulke from my pocket and bobby-pinned it to my hair. Even JDLers who ordinarily didn't wear a yarmulke made sure to put one on in jail, to prove that it was no longer an invitation to an easy hit but a symbol of the tough and fearless Jew, the Jew who knew prison. I wasn't tough, but I was trying to be fearless.

At the precinct we phoned a volunteer JDL lawyer named Harvey. Though it was late, Harvey rushed over. He told us that the cops were not only charging us with disorderly conduct but resisting arrest — a felony. "What, are you kidding me?" I said. "I practically *ran* into Joe Beatty's arms!"

"The cops are pissed at Avi for carrying on about his yarmulke," said Harvey.

Thanks to Avi, we would be held overnight and brought to court the next morning, rather than be released on bail immediately.

Harvey said he couldn't join us in court, and we had no backup. He suggested we take a legal aid lawyer.

I called my parents and explained why I wouldn't be coming home that night. They took the news calmly: Though they'd tried to keep me away from the JDL, they had no hesitation about supporting me now that I was in trouble. My mother assured me she'd be in court the next day.

A cop led Avi and me to separate cells. The cop opened the iron door and said to me, "Don't worry, it's not a gas chamber."

The next morning Avi and I were handcuffed again and taken to the Tombs, holding cells located below the central courtroom complex in downtown Manhattan. We were stripped of our belts and shoelaces, to keep us from hanging ourselves in remorse, and led into a large cell filled with black teenagers. I felt like an albino, my skin fluorescent, my blond hair flaming. A cop passed, looked at me in my yarmulke and said, "For what? For *what?*"

"JDL," I said.

"No shit!"

Avi and I stood in a corner. The only other white in the cell was a man with a shaved head, and he was the only one still handcuffed. He stared at Avi, slowly walked over to him and kicked him in the groin. Then he walked back just as slowly to his place. No one seemed to notice what had happened, so I pretended not to notice either. I wasn't entirely displeased to see Avi bent over in pain; his big mouth had brought us here.

I don't know how long we waited in the cell, because the cops had also taken our watches. I thought of the biblical Joseph in the pit, alone among snakes and scorpions. You could be attacked here, mutilated, and the distant guards would remain oblivious. If you were guilty enough to be brought to the Tombs, you would know how to take care of yourself; certainly, you didn't expect the guards to *protect* you.

We were led before a judge and charged with disorderly conduct, violation of the city health code ("throwing a noxious substance"), and resisting arrest. My mother smiled at me nervously and waved.

The judge interrupted the prosecutor's account of our crime and said, "I heard about it on television last night. I'm Jewish and I think these kids are contemptible." There was good news and bad news:

We'd made TV, but the judge was Jewish and thought we were contemptible.

Avi's grandmother, who was sitting beside my mother, suddenly spoke, in a heavy Yiddish accent, "Your honors, I'm the grandmother and I hope you teach mine Avi a lesson he should never soon forget. The Soviet Union is for the Jewish and for everybody good." *Mazel tov:* a communist.

My mother pinched her arm and whispered, "If you don't shut up I'll break your bones." The old lady shut up.

A legal aid lawyer asked permission to represent us. "These kids have bank accounts," said the judge, "let them hire counsel."

The lawyer persisted: "I regularly represent women who earn fifty dollars an hour." The judge said no.

The prosecutor requested a hundred-dollar bail for each of us. The judge said, "I'd send them to Riker's Island pending trial." Riker's was where they penned junkies and South Bronx gang members. Even JDLers from the animal squad spoke of Riker's with respect.

The prosecutor — not a Jew, fortunately, but an Italian — told the judge he didn't think Riker's was necessary, since neither Avi nor I had a serious record. "If that's your decision," said the judge. We were each released on a hundred-dollar bail and later ordered to pay that same sum in a brief trial before another judge.

Five

Crossing the Border

THE EXODUS ended. In August 1972 the Kremlin imposed a "ransom tax": Would-be émigrés had to reimburse the government for their state-sponsored education. Few Soviet citizens could afford the extortionist rates the Kremlin was demanding. Moscow Jews appeared at a press conference with price tags around their necks.

We needed to do something spectacular, unprecedented. But almost every conceivable tactic had already been tried. And the JDL was paralyzed. Moish had dropped out of "the business," as he called it, and his group ceased functioning. The FBI pressure was relentless. Four JDLers were arrested for the Hurok attack and charged with murder; another seven were arrested for bombing a Soviet office in Manhattan two years earlier. The JDL became preoccupied with defending its own prisoners.

Then one day I read this polemic in a Jewish magazine:

JDL members strike like petty thieves in the night where there is no risk to their safety. Throwing rotten eggs and stink bombs in concert halls is cowardly mischief. I shall withdraw and apologize for referring to the Jewish Defense League as the League for Jewish Cowards if they were to transfer at least some of their activities to Russia.

Of course: A demonstration *inside* the Soviet Union. Force them to arrest *American* Jews. That would prove we were unstoppable, more committed to saving Soviet Jews than the Kremlin was to oppressing them.

And I would prove to myself my dedication and courage: If I couldn't be a terrorist, I could at least take conventional protest to its farthest extreme.

By demonstrating in Moscow, I would join the frontline of the war for Jewish survival. In our family album was a photograph of my cousin Yossi as an Israeli soldier. I considered us soldiers in the same army, fighting the same enemy on different fronts. The Soviet Union armed Arab terrorists and crushed Judaism within its borders, trying to reverse Zionism and turn us back into victims. But the Holocaust, that excess of exile, had made Jewish vulnerability unbearable. Yossi and I, each in our own way, were fighting the post-Holocaust war against powerlessness.

On Yom Kippur I sat in synagogue beside my father. He wore a *kittel*, the shroudlike white robe that is the Yom Kippur symbol of mortality, of emptying yourself of small needs and fears and accounting your life before God.

I confided the plan to him. "Russia is not like America," he said quietly. I replied that in this era of superpower détente, our American passports would protect us; even Soviet Jews had demonstrated at the Kremlin and not been sent to Siberia. My heroic ambitions were tempered by a canny calculation of the risks.

"You never know with the Russian," he said. "You could go to jail for many years. Are you prepared?"

"Yes."

"Then I'm behind you."

He seemed so pale, so vulnerable. How could I do this to him? But he knew that I had no choice. I'd grown up in a secure Diaspora, with a Jewish state as backup should America become cursed. The vast disparity between my father's reality and mine made me feel inauthentic. *I had never suffered.* But by demonstrating in Moscow, I would become, however briefly, an Eastern European Jew.

2.

On the ceiling of Alan Krup's room was painted what he called his motto in dripping red letters, "Life is wandering from shithole to shithole until you get bumped for the ultimate fuck." Krup headed a JDL chapter in a "changing" Brooklyn neighborhood of monolithic high-rises, separated by elevated train tracks from the black ghetto of Coney Island; and Krup's surroundings reinforced for him the truth of his motto. The windows of his room shook from speeding trains, whose Day-Glo graffiti proclaimed the urban apocalypse. Every day Krup rode those trains to Columbia University (where he studied history), passing a gauntlet of gangsters and junkies who taunted, shoved, and occasionally mugged him at knifepoint. He kept a shotgun in his bedroom and felt absurdly vulnerable on the train carrying merely a canister of mace.

The motto on Krup's ceiling was partly inspired by his father, a struggling toy manufacturer. Mr. Krup had taught his son from an early age to expect betrayal from his fellow human beings and that all pleasure ends in pain, all life in death. Krup savored repeating his father's advice to him when he was a little boy: "Alan? It's a dog-eat-dog world." The only proper response, concluded Mr. Krup, was to look out for number one.

Yet despite his father's best efforts, Krup had become an idealist. He was determined to "do what's right," as he put it. A revolutionary, he believed that a moral elite, defined by self-sacrifice, had always changed history. His first political action occurred in fifth grade, when he led a student strike demanding the installation of a candy machine. In high school he'd been a Trotskyite; then he switched to the JDL because it was an organization of Jewish revolutionaries, the Jewish SDS. For a while after joining the JDL he continued to demonstratively wear red — red socks, red handkerchief hanging from the back of his jeans, and even, on the rare occasions when he wore one, a red knitted yarmulke.

In the JDL Krup found a compromise between his father's cynicism and his own idealism: "Looking out for number one" meant caring only for your own people, and to hell with the rest of the world. By turning the Jews into an extension of himself — "*my people*" — Krup could sacrifice for others while maintaining his father's wariness of ideals.

Krup's father had taught him almost nothing about Judaism; Krup grew up ignorant of the most basic religious rituals. But Mr. Krup did insist on one Jewish lesson: If a goy hits you, hit him back. And so Mr. Krup grimly approved his son's involvement in JDL street fights with anti-Semites and, before Krup had gotten his license, would even drive him to fights. Still, Mr. Krup thought that getting clubbed at the Soviet mission for persecuted Jews in faraway places was ridiculous. "The Jews will screw you worse than anyone," he warned Krup. Worry about yourself, he advised; go to school and make money. But Krup had only one ambition: to save Jews.

His parents were American-born, not survivors; but the Holocaust was the event through which Krup viewed the world. With its absolute division between evil and good, the Holocaust satisfied his judgmental nature. He seemed to have a definitive opinion on every person, national group, and subject. Blacks were "niggers"; Italians, "Guineas"; Poles, "Jew-hating Polacks." Pet owners who coddled their animals while Third World children starved were criminals — "You could call them a pet peeve of mine."

But Krup reserved his special contempt for the real or imagined venalities of his fellow Jews. Bob Dylan was a "middle-class kike masquerading as Woody Guthrie"; Elie Wiesel, a "shyster making a fast buck off dead Jews." Those who died in the Holocaust without fighting back were cowards, "plain and simple," as Krup liked to say. Worst of all were Jewish liberals, like the editors of the *New York Times* who'd written pious editorials in the 1940s about the fate of the Jews rather than rage in the streets.

Krup wasn't handsome, but his face was charismatic with an intense intelligence. Beneath his strong chin, almost hidden from view, grew a line of hair meant to be a beard. His eyes, magnified through thick lenses, were alternately tender and unforgiving, full of empathy for human suffering and ridicule for human stupidity. It was startling to discover such power in the face of an eighteen-year-old, and his expression seemed to dare you to shock him with some horror he hadn't encountered or at least imagined.

And yet Krup was very funny. He cherished puns and irony; the irony of sharing his name with the German armament-industry "Krupp," which helped run the Nazi death camps, especially pleased him. He would search his substantial collection of Holocaust books for references to Krupp's war crimes, then read the details to his friends, cackling, as though uncovering some family scandal.

Despite his absolutist stance toward almost any issue, Krup was able to laugh at himself. He could see all sides of a debate and knew that his own certainties were, perhaps, no more valid than the contradictory truths of others. Still, he believed that those who affected history were successful precisely because they suppressed self-doubt, their empathy for opposing views. Relativism created middle-age liberals, people who never risked their lives to change the world. And so he deliberately crippled himself, denying his fine mind the pleasure of complexity.

That is why Krup was almost brutally unforgiving of the Jews who'd died in the Holocaust without physically resisting. As a self-taught Holocaust expert, he knew how difficult resistance had been: that the Jews had first been isolated and starved in ghettos, then deceived about the destination of the cattlecars and depleted by the nightmare journey to the camps. He knew, too, that many *had* resisted — not violently, since weapons were almost impossibly scarce, but in more subtle ways, like smuggling food into the ghetto and people out. And yet those facts seemed to him mere excuse. The context didn't matter, only the result, which was that millions had died without fighting back. Krup forced himself to be severe toward the victims, to ensure that he would act differently were he ever in their place.

Jewish passivity didn't merely shame but enraged him. "How could a father watch his family walk into a gas chamber and not jump the first SS guard he saw?" It was as if Jews lacked some basic quality of self-preservation, and Krup's own experience reinforced that suspicion. The previous year on Halloween he'd organized a JDL patrol to protect his neighborhood's synagogues from "trick or treat" egg attacks; the officers of one synagogue complained to police that the JDLers were trespassing. Krup, outraged, announced he was through protecting Jews. "Fucking kikes," he'd said to me afterward. "My father was right, oooh, was he right. When the Nazis round them up again, I'll be cheering."

But I knew Krup's pique was only temporary, that he couldn't help sacrificing for Jews. All he needed was a project to inspire him, something worth risking his life for.

I ran into him one Shabbos afternoon, strolling with JDL friends in Borough Park. "Krup," I said, "we gotta talk. Private." My first security lapse: Now everyone would know I was planning something.

"What do you think about doing a sit-in in Moscow?" I asked when we were alone.

"You mean like inside the Kremlin?"

"Yeah, like inside the Kremlin."

"You got a group behind you?"

"Nothing."

"Money?"

"Not a dime."

Krup was silent.

"So what do you think?" I asked.

"Klein? You're out of your fucking mind. It's the greatest thing I ever heard in my life."

Krup and I became obsessed with going to Moscow. We spent hours discussing different scenarios. Could we really get into the Kremlin? It wasn't like the White House, after all, with organized tours of Premier Brezhnev's dining room.

Alternatively, we considered buying a ship, sailing to Odessa, and inviting Soviet Jews to board for Israel. But that, too, we decided, was impractical: It cost a lot of money to buy a ship.

I suggested we take over Moscow's last remaining synagogue and declare it liberated Jewish territory. "No way," said Krup. "The kikes who run the joint all work for the KGB. They'd denounce us as Zionist fascists and beg the commies to arrest us. It would be Halloween all over again." Synagogue officials collaborating with police were a sore point with Krup; we dropped the plan.

We decided to take over the Moscow emigration office, OVIR. We had no idea where OVIR was or how to get into it; we'd simply heard that's where Soviet Jews went to apply for visas.

Krup and I had been friends for a while; but now that we were joined by a project, an act of Jewish service, we became inseparable. The only thing Krup valued as much as Jewish loyalty was friendship, and both were based on the same premise: you and me against the world. Friends had to compensate for humanity's meanness with an abundance of love. He constantly measured his friends' devotion — to the Jewish people and to himself, an indivisible loyalty. Would his friends give their lives for the Jews as he was ready to do? Would they kill for Krup as he would for them? "A friend," Krup liked to say, "is someone you can call at two in the morning, tell him you need him for a fight, and he's *there*." If you failed his loyalty test, you were banished to the vast category of worthless human beings. And if you dared betray him, he would be as relentless an enemy as he was a friend.

Krup found his model for friendship in a JDL cult book called *The Deed*, an account of two teenage assassins — the "two Eliyahus," my childhood heroes as a Betari — who formed the ultimate heroic friendship, ascending the British gallows with an exalted graciousness, smiling and singing. When they were hanged, they were about the same age as Krup and I were then; going to Moscow was our way of approximating their self-sacrifice.

The premise of our friendship was the assumption that we formed an idealistic elite. Together with a few friends, only we were smart enough to understand the nature of the times and were tough enough to appropriately respond. The rest of the Jewish people — to say nothing of humanity — was either corrupt or stupid; and we emphasized that venality to underscore our exalted chosenness. We reveled in exposing hypocrisy and pettiness, in ridiculing entire ethnic groups — especially Jews — with their most negative stereotypes. We would scan the newspapers for outstanding examples of human vileness, then read them to each other over the phone, laughing wildly.

Our cynicism was meant to counter a fatal Jewish naïveté. If the Jews had been so totally unprepared for the Holocaust, it was because they'd trusted — civilization, progress, the enlightened twentieth century. German Jews trusted *Deutsche Kultur*; Soviet Jews trusted Stalin; American Jews trusted Franklin Delano Roosevelt. Everyone and everything had lied.

And so Krup and I fought a private war against Jewish gullibility with a relentless, cynical knowingness. We tried to exorcise whatever faith in human good remained in us. Had we chosen a motto, it would have been this line from Krup's favorite rock band, The Who: "We won't get fooled again."

We phoned each other at all hours, just to read aloud passages from Holocaust books.

"Klein, are you ready? This is the absolute ultimate greatest." He began reading from a memoir written by a death camp prisoner who worked in the body-burning brigade: " 'The *Untersturmführer* orders the three leather craftsmen in the brigade to make two hats with horns, like those of a devil. From then on, we march to work with the fire chief —' "

Krup paused here and cackled appreciatively at the Nazis' humor: They called the head of the body-burning squad the "fire chief." He continued: " 'We march to work with the fire chief and his assistant leading us, wearing their horns and carrying the hooks they used to stir the fire. The two men were always singed from the fire, and this gave them a charred, blackened look. They were tall and slim, and normally dressed in black fatigues and black shoes; and now, with their horned hats, they truly looked like devils. Our *Untersturmführer* was determined to lighten our mood.' "

There was a long silence on the line. Finally, Krup said, almost shouting, "Klein, do you understand? *Do you understand?*"

"Unfuckingbelievable," I said.

We had discovered the key event that explained Jewish — no, human — history. No one, we assured each other, not even the Jews, really understood the Holocaust. We alone appreciated its enormity, its uniqueness: not merely the vast numbers of victims but the systemization of death, the co-option of the most basic elements of civilized society, like order and bureaucracy, for the creation of necropolis. Krup and I believed we inhabited a world of total barbarism, without relief: Civilization itself was poisoned.

In Krup I found a friend who, like me, was trying to order his life by the knowledge that Auschwitz had happened. I had no choice: The Holocaust had been imposed on me. But Krup allowed himself to be possessed: Someone in our generation had to be not merely affected but transformed by the war, discard personal ambition, and devote himself to the Jews. We'd inherited a revelation of the power of evil, of the true nature of the world and the Jews' place in it; and those insights couldn't be confined to a corner of our being.

We tried to live with the constant awareness of the Holocaust, the way a mystic invokes the presence of God. And we did so for the same basic purpose: to transcend ordinary consciousness. We believed we could attain selflessness, a kind of sainthood, by entering the Holocaust and offering ourselves to it. In place of God we centralized the demonic; our vision wasn't divine light but the night fires of Auschwitz, not heaven but hell.

We believed that we'd penetrated the Holocaust so intimately, took on its pain so brilliantly, that we even had the right to joke about it. We would phone each other collect, identifying ourselves to the impassive operator as "Mr. Eichmann" or "Mr. Hitler," and, without bothering to say hello, launch into one of our Holocaust routines. How do you get six million Jews into a Volkswagen? Men to the right, women and children to the left. How do you get them out? Empty the ashtray.

Part of the pleasure of the "joke" was its privacy: People would recoil from our crassness, but most wouldn't even understand the joke's reference — the process of separating young men from women, children and old people on the "selection" line to the gas chambers. Through those jokes we laughed at the world, its false pieties and ignorance. And we proved our toughness: We could enter the Holocaust without squeamishness. We lived in a shattered world, and we despised ordinary decency — politeness, rather than prophetic rage — as a lie that denied the void.

3.

One by one we initiated recruits into our group, until we numbered some two dozen. Thanks to the Moscow trip, I was now a JDL insider, hanging out with Krup and his friends, some of whom joined the group. I no longer identified with the moderate SSSJ; tellingly, I didn't confide the Moscow plan to Ya'akov or Glenn.

We gathered for our first meeting one weekend in Borough Park, standing in a conspicuous huddle among crowds of Shabbos strollers. Some JDLers who weren't part of our group approached us with knowing smiles: "You guys plannin' a fight or somethin'?"

We retreated to a park on the edge of Borough Park — known locally as an "Italian park," unsafe for Jews. We stood around, waiting for someone to say the word "kike." Our very presence was a dare. In our yarmulkes and Shabbos suits we looked like regular Jews, easy targets. But just let them say "it," and they'd be confronting brass knuckles and nunchakus.

Nothing happened. One of our boys began a Yiddish chant: *"Alleh goyim in d'erd,"* All goyim into the earth. *"Afilu der guter?"* we responded in unison, Even the good ones? *"Nisht du kan guter!"* he shouted, There are no good ones!

No good ones? I was alive because a "good one" had saved my father. And yet I fully entered the chant; more than anything, I wanted to be one of the JDL boys.

Among Krup and his friends I spoke with a kind of swagger, mimicking their intonations and key phrases, bidding for acceptance. They spoke either in superlatives ("outrageous," "unbelievable") or in exaggerated understatement ("The Holocaust was a bad thing, a *bad* thing."). I emphasized my Brooklyn accent, speaking in constricted, nasal sounds that I assumed made me sound tough like them. Even my laughter was borrowed from Krup, a near-hysteria that tried to convey recklessness. When I caught the sound of my voice, it startled me — as if somebody else were speaking.

I feared I'd become an imposter: I pretended to be a nonconformist but in fact craved approval. And I sensed that my "political" self was inhibiting some unknown, more authentic self from emerging. In any situation where I couldn't hide behind politics, I felt clumsy and exposed. It was so easy for me to shout from the back of a paddy wagon; but when asked a simple question in class, I'd turn red. At times I felt so tense, so self-conscious, I had to remind myself to breathe.

Self-doubt threatened to undermine my activist persona, the only identity I knew; so I laid those anxieties aside. But I couldn't

entirely suppress them and feared that a time would come when I'd
have no choice but to confront myself.

The OVIR boys, as we called ourselves, began hanging out together,
moving in a large cluster, feeling our power. Our favorite spot was
Bernstein's, a kosher Chinese restaurant on the Lower East Side.
We would sit in Bernstein's until the cash register closed, smoking
cigars and telling pornographic jokes to the Chinese waiters and
singing our favorite Yiddish song about how good it is to be a Jew
and beat a goy. (In fact the song was more pathetic than aggressive:
A Jew slaps a goy, and the goy cries, "Oy!" — a wishful reversal of
ghetto Jewish reality. That is what remained for us of Yiddish culture: its fantasies of revenge.)

The presence in Bernstein's of respectable Orthodox Jews — YU
students, families from Long Island — only incited us to act up more,
to prove how different we were from them. We mistook their deco-
rum for passivity, our vulgarity for daring. We were tormented by restraint, obedience, images of orderly lines — lines at the cattlecars
and the gas chambers. Through our excesses, we retroactively tried
to stir a Jewish insurrection.

Krup and I led the group. He was in charge of fund-raising; I,
logistics — finding out where OVIR was and how we might take it
over.

Krup had one promising lead, Herbie Schwartz, a businessman
who contributed to the JDL and whom we code-named "Fat Boy,"
not only for his obesity but his extravagence: His home was said to
include a room-sized pantry stocked with sweets. Fat Boy was also
known to have an appetite for publicity; Krup said we might have to
wear signs at OVIR proclaiming, "This arrest sponsored by Herbie
Schwartz."

Krup and I sat for hours making lists — which media to contact
after the takeover, what slogans to paint on banners, what to bring
and not bring to Russia (bring blank sheets and markers for banners; don't bring books or religious objects identifying us to the border guards as Jews), lists of lists we needed to make.

School became incidental to my life. I was now in my sophomore
year; thanks to decent grades, I'd transferred out of YU to Brooklyn
College. I took easy courses, mostly in Judaic studies — history of

the Holocaust, literature of the Holocaust, courses whose books I'd already read for pleasure. I didn't care about an education. There was nothing I wanted to study or become. I wanted to be what I already was: a server, someone worthy of Jewish history. Still, a Jewish boy was supposed to get an education, and college was a congenial atmosphere for an activist; so I went.

My classes were filled almost entirely with Jews. During breaks I sat in Kosher King, the campus's Jewish hangout, McDonald's without cheeseburgers. Like me, my friends were all lapsed Orthodox Jews. None of us wore yarmulkes anymore or practiced religious rituals. Almost our last trace of Orthodoxy was ethnic insularity. "Nonpracticing Orthodox Jews," we ironically called ourselves. At age nineteen I'd still never made a non-Jewish friend. I could probably count the number of times I'd had a friendly conversation with a Gentile.

Brooklyn College was comfortable; its only problem was the draft. At YU I'd been given a divinity student deferment — a standard YU courtesy to its students, whether or not they intended to become rabbis. But now my deferment was gone. It was 1972, and the Vietnam War was on. The draft was determined by lottery, and I had a winning number.

I asked around Kosher King for a "draft dodger yeshiva," as the institution was commonly called, that didn't require its students to attend, only to pay tuition. An entire network of such yeshivas had arisen in Brooklyn, as though America were czarist Russia and Jewish boys had to be rescued from the enemy regime's draft. One story circulating told of a student who'd been late with a payment to his draft dodger yeshiva. The rabbi said to him, "I had a dream about you: I dreamed I saw you marching in the Veterans Day parade."

I found a rabbi whose yeshiva had a name but no location. The rabbi, a little man with a pinched black fedora, came to my parents' home to discuss tuition. He offered us a bargain: four years for the price of three, if we paid up front.

"Very smart," I said, "the newspapers are already saying the draft won't last another year."

"So it's a gamble," he said.

My father interrupted. "If we're already paying, maybe my son can learn by you even once in a week?"

"I'll tell you the truth," the rabbi replied, "if he's looking to learn, our yeshiva is not for him."

We paid a year's tuition and thereby ended my talmudic education.

Fat Boy stopped returning Krup's calls, and eventually we found out why: He'd been indicted for tax fraud.

I was at a dead end with logistics. I told Krup I had to fly to Israel, to find Soviet émigrés who could tell me about OVIR. He said, "We can't afford to send you to the Bronx."

One night Krup and I and a third member of the group named Lev drove out of town. Krup wouldn't say where we were going or who we were meeting: "We're getting serious here about security."

We stopped at a traffic light, and a car filled with teenagers pulled beside us. They pointed to Lev's yarmulke and then patted their own heads, laughing. We got out of the car. Krup opened his trunk and retrieved three crowbars. The other car took off. "Goy bastards!" we shouted.

We pulled into the lot of a kosher restaurant. Waiting inside was Bert Zweibon, cofounder with Kahane of the JDL. Zweibon, a lawyer, a heavy man with sleepy eyes, served as the JDL spokesman when the organization wanted to appear reasonable. With Kahane now living in Israel, Zweibon in effect headed the JDL.

"There aren't enough jails in America?" he said to me as we shook hands. "To Russia you have to go?"

Wordlessly, I looked to Krup for an explanation of what was happening. One of our first decisions had been to keep the OVIR plan out of official JDL hands: It was almost impossible to maintain a secret in the JDL, which was thoroughly infiltrated by the FBI; and since we intended our sit-in to sabotage President Nixon's détente policy, we feared the feds would warn the KGB.

Krup explained that he'd turned to Zweibon because we had nothing left to lose. Only Zweibon's connections, he said, could get the project moving.

"From now on your only worry is the KGB," said Zweibon, with a half-smile resembling a grimace. "Money, legal advice — whatever you need, you'll get."

"Sounds good," I said, wary.

"You're going to Israel next week," Zweibon continued. "The person you're to meet there is named Shabbtai. A lawyer. Very close to Menachem Begin. An Irgun veteran. He'll give you all the information you need. He's a *thousand* percent. He's so smart, he probably has the floor plans of the Kremlin in his desk."

Krup said, "Klein, I want you should understand something here: We're playing the big leagues now. Listen, learn, and don't ask too many questions."

"Should I look up the Reb in Israel?" I asked, meaning Kahane.

"What are you crazy?" said Krup. "The Reb is a wonderful man. A million percent. But he can't keep a secret. You know the first thing he'd do? Call a press conference: 'Don't ask me for details, but we're about to do something unbelievable. Okay, a demonstration in Russia. Where? At the Moscow emigration office. But you didn't hear it from me!' "

"Will Shabbtai be expecting me?" I asked.

"You'll get the royal treatment," said Zweibon.

A week later I was in Israel. I phoned Shabbtai; he'd never heard of me. I mentioned Zweibon's name. "All right," he said, without enthusiasm.

Despite the tepid welcome, I went to his law office as though on a pilgrimage. Shabbtai had been an Irgunist; and I venerated the anti-British underground, a legacy of my Betar education. Menachem Begin's picture still hung in my room, a blow-up of a British wanted poster, his unshaven face desperate and hard.

My meeting with Shabbtai was the ultimate activist moment: I was about to plan an illegal act with an Irgunist. I confided to him about our project, expecting the shared pleasure of conspirators. But instead he seemed annoyed. "If you hadn't mentioned Zweibon's name, I wouldn't give you a minute," he said. "After the business with Paglin, anyone who comes to me from Kahane gets thrown out the door."

"The business with Paglin" referred to the recent arrest of a group of Israelis, including Kahane and an Irgun veteran named Amichai Paglin, who'd planned attacks on Arab targets in retaliation for PLO terror. Shabbtai blamed Kahane's security lapses for the group's exposure. "In my life I never met such a big mouth," he said.

I told Shabbtai that Kahane knew nothing of the project. "What do you want from me?" he asked. Information, I said: the address of OVIR, a diagram of its layout, the number of its guards and office workers, an assessment of our likely punishment.

"This isn't an action for Americans," said Shabbtai.

"What do you mean?"

"You Americans have no sense of security. You don't know how to operate in a closed society."

"I was sent by a very serious group of people," I said. "If you won't help me, I'll go somewhere else."

Shabbtai knew, or could well imagine, that we weren't really *that* serious. Still, it seemed the appropriate thing to say.

"Call me next week and I'll have answers for you," he said.

When we met again, he was almost friendly. "It seems you chose the right building," he said.

He handed me a diagram of OVIR. A small staircase led to the first floor, where Jews went to apply for exit visas. Then he revealed this remarkable detail: In an upstairs office, foreigners went to renew their tourist visas. That meant we could enter the building without causing suspicion; our presence in OVIR would be entirely natural.

Shabbtai said the most probable scenario was that the Soviets would expel us. "But you never know with them. You have to be prepared for anything." Getting shot by a nervous guard? "Unlikely," he said.

I returned to New York with a notebook full of diagrams and information: a map of the area where OVIR was located, the name of the closest subway station, the Moscow phone numbers of foreign journalists and of the American embassy.

Krup, too, had been productive: He and Zweibon were actually raising money. And yet, by confiding our plan to prospective donors, we were taking an enormous security risk. The results were inevitable: Everyone in the JDL seemed to know about Moscow. A JDLer who was on trial for an anti-Soviet bombing and therefore hadn't been invited to join our group, approached me one Shabbos afternoon on Fourteenth Avenue, handed me a subway token and said, laughing, "For your trip."

We booked two dozen places on a tour leaving for the Soviet Union on April 15, the day before Passover. The exodus theme would provide obvious symbolism for our sit-in. Four days in Leningrad, then four days in Moscow. We would arrive in the Soviet capital on Thursday morning, April 19; we would spend that day familiarizing ourselves with the city and send a scout to check out OVIR. Friday, April 20, was OVIR day.

And yet it was possible we might never leave New York: The Soviets could simply deny us visas. Most of us had police records for anti-Soviet activity, and we assumed that the Soviet embassy screened tourist applications with the KGB. The only question was how much the KGB knew about us. We applied for visas and waited.

4.

Joey Levy was on trial for falsifying applications for gun permits. The maximum penalty was thirty years. Joey, blond and stocky, had been one of Kahane's first recruits. He'd heard the Reb speak about the need for Jews to defend each other because no one else would, and it made sense to him; so he dropped out of high school and devoted himself to the JDL. The word was that Joey had been involved in "everything," which in the JDL meant bombings. Joey seemed to laugh with a delightful fullness, which drew you in and disarmed you, while his eyes remained sober, watching. He never laughed so carelessly that he couldn't instantly retrieve himself.

The trial didn't look good for Joey. Laid evenly on a table like a firing squad were at least a dozen shotguns, which Joey had allegedly bought under a false name. A JDL friend who had taught him to shoot turned out to be an undercover cop. Joey, out on bail, swore to his friends that the cop was lying, that he hadn't forged those forms. Krup said to Joey, "It's the only thing you're *not* guilty of and that's what they're going to hang you on."

"Unbelievable," said Joey, laughing, as if discussing someone else's problems.

Joey's lawyer, a JDL volunteer, had almost nothing to say in court. "Is he mute or what?" demanded Krup. "Forget about it, Joey, they're gonna cut your balls off."

"He's a summation lawyer," said Joey, reassuring Krup. "Wait till the end of the trial. Just when you think he's a complete asshole, he blows everybody away."

Mornings Krup and I went to the federal courtroom in downtown Manhattan, to give Joey moral support. Joey sat through the proceedings rigidly impassive. My brief experience in the Tombs made me feel reverence for him: He managed to remain outwardly calm even as he faced years in prison among the *chayas*, the animals, the Yiddish word we used for the underclass.

Krup decided we should confide to Joey about OVIR, and I agreed; Joey was, after all, an expert in underground affairs. And yet involving Joey, even as a consultant, could have been a security disaster: Joey was constantly tailed by feds, and anyone in his company became suspect. One night we held a birthday party for him at a friend's house. The bell rang: A man said his car had broken down and asked to call a tow truck. He looked slowly at each of us and only then went to phone.

We asked Joey whether we should passively sit in or "liberate" OVIR and expel its officials. Not surprisingly, Joey opted for the hard line. "If you're already doing it, then *do* it," he said. Though Joey was obviously not going to Moscow — he was on his way to an American, not a Soviet, jail — he was, I thought, one of the few people who had the right to urge risks on us. I told him that if we acted violently inside OVIR, the guards might panic and shoot; Russian police weren't used to demonstrations. Joey laughed and said, "Think of all the publicity you'll get if they kill you."

One day after court we went with Joey to Bernstein's. Krup wrote some numbers on a paper napkin and handed it to Joey. "My license plate number," said Krup. "You might as well make some for your friends." Then, to the tune of "We Shall Overcome," we sang, "We Shall Be Paroled."

The table filled with numerous main courses, and Krup and Joey began a food-eating contest. Gorging food and planting bombs were expressions of the same impulse: a defiance of limits.

Unlike Krup, who despised rich people, Joey admired them and wanted to be rich himself. But Joey, an unemployed high-school dropout, had to suffice with symbolic gestures of wealth, like ordering grandly at restaurants and traveling by taxi. "Imagine how much you'll save on cabs when you're sitting," Krup said to him. Krup for-

gave Joey his love of wealth; in fact, it only heightened Joey's nobility: "Joey dreams of living in a penthouse on Fifth Avenue, but he's
willing to sit with the *chayas* for Jews. *That's* sacrifice."

The visas came; no one was rejected. Krup raised more money,
though still not enough; my parents paid for my ticket.

At the beginning of April, a member of the group consulted a
lawyer and discovered that we could face severe penalties on our return from Moscow, for conspiring to use an American passport to
commit a crime abroad. At the very least, our passports would probably be confiscated.

The prospect of time in an American jail frightened me far more
than prison in Russia. Siberia seemed like a joke, too remote to be
real; but American jails were tangible. Now when I went to Joey's
trial, I imagined myself in his place.

The threat of criminal charges in America almost destroyed the
group. More than half our members dropped out; we were left with
nine demoralized people.

On the last day of Joey's trial, his lawyer appeared drunk. He made
a speech about the Six Million and broke down weeping. The jury
found Joey guilty.

At our final meeting, I distributed Russian lyrics of Zionist songs sung
by Soviet Jews. I thought it would be poetic to sing them inside OVIR.

After the meeting, Krup called me aside. "I'm not going," he said.

"Are you kidding me or what?"

"My girlfriend's driving me crazy. If we're sent away for a few
years, she'll fall apart."

He was lying. The real reason was that he'd decided to join a new
underground that was forming to succeed Moish's group; by demonstrating in Moscow, he would draw FBI attention to himself. But I
learned about that only later.

"I can't lead the group myself," I said.

"There's nothing to talk about. I'll be your back-up man here.
Whatever has to be done, I'll do. Finished. End of discussion."

The next day I met with Joey. "The whole thing's a joke," I said.
"Instead of twenty-four guys we're going with eight. We *still* haven't
paid for all the tickets, and I don't know where the money's

supposed to come from. Zweibon promised us press contacts, top legal advice, everything. But we're going with nothing behind us. And the whole JDL knows about it. We'll show up at Kennedy and be greeted by your FBI buddies. I can't do it, Joey."

Joey said, "Yos, you *gotta* do it."

He meant, If I'm going to jail for Jews, so can you.

"If I gotta do it," I said, "I gotta do it."

A few days later the Soviets abolished the "ransom tax." They were responding to pressure from the American Congress, which was about to pass the Jackson Amendment, denying the Kremlin trade credits so long as Jews couldn't emigrate. Soviet Jewry was now at the center of Soviet-American relations, just as Ya'akov Birnbaum had predicted years ago.

With the suspension of the ransom tax, some congressmen — and even, incredibly, some establishment Jewish leaders — now agreed with President Nixon that the Jackson Amendment was unnecessary. Yet the Soviets had merely rescinded the tax, not opened the gates or freed the political prisoners. Suddenly the timing of our trip seemed perfect: Just as the Soviets would appear to have outmaneuvered us, along come eight American activists who prove that the emigration problem remained acute.

The night before our departure we held a farewell party in Bernstein's. Krup brought party hats and blowers, Joey brought champagne, and we sang Zionist songs in Russian.

One of our boys displayed a pair of gnawed gloves and said, "I'll be lucky if I have gloves like these in Siberia."

"You'll be lucky if you have *hands* like those in Siberia," I said.

"Don't forget to bring long underwear," said Joey. "It gets cold on those Arctic nights."

"I'll send you a postcard from the Gulag," I said.

"If they hold you," Krup whispered to me, "the Soviet mission goes bye-bye."

5.

On Sunday morning, April 15, I said goodbye to my parents. They restrained their emotions: Our parting demanded courage. I realized with relief that my father wouldn't physically collapse as a rebuke to my adventurism. He had raised me for this moment; each of us would fulfill his role.

Our group — "the Moscow Eight" — gathered at the airport. Krup came to see us off. Joey had wanted to come, too, but decided it was better not to bring along his FBI tails.

Krup met our travel agent at the airport to make the final payment, which we'd somehow just raised. That's how we operated: through last-minute reprieves.

Krup took our pictures — posters for a future "Free the Moscow Eight" campaign. We pinned American flags to our coat lapels, blatant tourists, incognito Jews. Those of us with Hebrew first names now assumed English ones. I became "Joe."

Security men with walkie-talkies rushed about. "You see what I see?" I whispered to Krup.

"Tonight we're in the Tombs," he said.

The announcement came to board; no one tried to stop us. Krup said, "They can still pull an Eisenberg on you." Eisenberg was a JDL member arrested for allegedly buying the gun used in the Hunter College shooting. The feds had waited until he boarded a flight to Israel before they arrested him. Late at night they drove him to the East River and swore that if he didn't reveal who pulled the trigger at Hunter College, they'd dump his body in the water. Krup loved repeating Eisenberg's response, which he called an eloquent example of Jewish heroism: "Fuck you."

We entered the tunnel leading to our plane. An alarm sounded. We looked at each other and kept walking.

We boarded. In the seat beside me sat a tall man with short hair; he looked like a fed. "So you finally made it," he said to me. I froze: They're pulling an Eisenberg.

I forced myself to say, "What do you mean?"

He said, "You seemed to have had trouble finding your seat."

First stop: Frankfurt. Reluctantly, we disembarked onto German soil. Germany was ground zero of my hatred. One of my favorite books was *Forged in Fury*, a true account of survivors who'd tried to poison German reservoirs in 1945; I deeply regretted their failure. I wanted Germany to die, its soil plowed with salt like ancient Carthage, and its people, if not murdered, at the very least dispersed.

"The wandering Germans," symbols of evil, everywhere hated and pursued. The name "Germany," a curse and a warning: Let all who contemplate mass murder consider Germany's fate. If the world remained unchanged by the Holocaust, it was partly because Germany hadn't sufficiently suffered. Only by uprooting Germany from the nations would humanity be cured of its genocidal temptation.

It was painful to walk through the antiseptic airport, to breathe the poisoned air. I wanted to scream at passersby: Stop speaking *that* language!

One of our boys, Harvey Friedman, whispered to me, "We gotta do *something*." He meant some symbolic act of revulsion against this place.

Harvey lived in an Italian enclave in the Bronx, surrounded by Puerto Ricans and blacks; his friends were Italians, an alliance of embattled whites. "We get along fine," Harvey would explain. "They call me Jew-boy, I call them Guineas."

Krup had said when he first brought Harvey into the group, "Harv's the kind of guy you want to have at a fight."

Harvey agreed. "I'm the strong silent type. Dumb, but a good guy." He was powerfully built and wore T-shirts cut at the sleeve. But there was nothing brutal or intimidating about him: He was shy and spoke with surprising softness.

Harvey and I went to the bathroom. We stood by the urinals and aimed at the white-tiled wall just above them.

We flew to Leningrad. As we landed, soldiers with submachine guns, fur hats, and frozen faces surrounded the plane. They've come for us, I thought. We disembarked into the cold gray morning. The soldiers made no move to separate us from the other passengers. Their presence was apparently standard greeting for tourists entering the Soviet Union.

We approached customs. The only Jewish objects we'd brought were yarmulkes, sewn into the lining of our clothes. We intended to wear them inside OVIR; we couldn't imagine getting arrested without yarmulkes. Though our trip would coincide with Passover, I'd instructed the group not to bring matzoh, which would draw customs' suspicion.

"Book?" a guard asked me. Did he mean Bibles, prayer books? I showed him a paperback copy of the novel, M*A*S*H, with a woman's legs forming a V sign. "Americanski book!" he said, laughing. We passed through.

On the bus to the hotel, Rivkie Fogel, at sixteen the youngest of our group, said to me, "You know what I have in my suitcase, Mr. Big-Shot Leader? Matzoh."

"I can't believe you did that!" I whispered angrily to her.

"Just because you don't give a shit about the Torah doesn't mean I can't," she said.

Though Rivkie was what they called in Borough Park a rebel — she'd pin up her long religious-length denim skirt as soon as she stepped out of yeshiva — she remained a loyal Orthodox girl. She seemed fearless, which is why I'd invited her to join us. Once, Rivkie and I had been part of a group arrested at a sit-down near the Soviet mission; and she'd announced in the paddy wagon: "Any time you guys are planning something crazy, lemme know, yeah?" Later, when I proposed the OVIR sit-in to her, she immediately agreed.

"Rivkie," I'd said, "are you sure you're ready for this? I mean it's not like a sit-down at the mission."

"Sure I'm sure," she said. "Oh God, are my parents gonna kill me."

We drove past massive concrete apartment blocks surrounded by marshlands. The gray was relieved only by red banners with Russian slogans. Perhaps against Zionism, against *us*. Only now did the implications of our trip hit me: We had entered a country run by an anti-Semitic regime, and we were placing ourselves in its hands.

We came to Leningrad. Long rows of yellow buildings faded along the Neva River. Somewhere in this city lived thousands of Jews. We would have to ignore and even avoid them, spending the next four days in museums and concerts, dutiful tourists evoking no suspicion. How would we bear it?

We were part of an organized tour group. Most of its members were Jews; but there wasn't a hint from those Goldbergs and Shapiros that they recognized in us fellow Jews in a hostile place, that on the eve of Passover we were vacationing in the land of the Pharaohs.

The afternoon of our arrival, we walked the streets on our own, to escape the cheerful Jews on the tour. A tall man in a Vandyke stopped us. "Shalom!" he said. None of us looked at each other. We all knew what we had to do; we'd discussed it in New York: If approached by a Soviet Jew, we smile politely and say we're not interested in politics.

"My name Maxim!" he said. "I am Jew!" We nodded. "Come to my apartment and we smoke hashish." A provocateur. We walked away.

From then on we suspected the KGB was tailing us. We tried not to look over our shoulders, conspicuously agitated. We laughed a lot, simulating a grand time.

Passover began that night. Everyone gathered in my room, and we took turns in the bathroom with Rivkie's matzoh, reciting a Hebrew blessing that we hoped was out of reach of hidden mikes. Shabbtai had warned me that all hotel rooms were bugged. When we wanted to speak about OVIR, we wrote notes and then burned them in an ashtray. This wasn't paranoia: On every floor of our hotel sat a grim woman who took the keys as you left, so that "they" always knew your movements.

I bent over the matzoh and felt its condensed power. Then I said, "Blessed are you, Lord our God, who has kept us and preserved us and brought us to this day."

Around the world Jews would be reading the Haggadah, which commanded us to relive the Exodus "as if you yourself left Egypt." But only now, I felt, was that really possible. In our generation, metaphor had become reality.

The blessing over matzoh was our single acknowledgment of Passover. The next morning we were on tour, admiring the Hermitage and the Winter Palace. We stopped at monuments to the Red Army's victory over the Nazis; our guide, an unpleasant young woman who didn't bother smiling, spoke about the suffering of the Soviet people in World War II. Propaganda, I sneered to myself. Twenty million Soviets had died, many of starvation, in their war against the Nazis. But I couldn't allow myself to feel Russia's pain, partly because its regime was denying my pain — banning any mention of the Holocaust, even from memorials at sites of Jewish genocide, which recalled only "Soviet martyrs." In some sense I shared with the Soviets the same sensibility: We wanted our people's suffering to be unique.

*   *   *

On Thursday we flew to Moscow. We'd chosen the next day, April 20, as OVIR day by default: Our tour was leaving on Sunday, which meant we had one day to find our way around Moscow, check out OVIR, and tend to last-minute details like turning bedsheets into banners.

After we settled into the hotel, I sent Lev out with a city map, to find OVIR. Lev — we shortened and Russified his name from Levenberg — was an ideal secret agent. He looked deceptively straight: boyish smile, short hair, polyester pants. Yet he simultaneously maintained opposite lives, moving between different groups of friends — Talmud study partners, drug addicts, JDL activists — and keeping them apart and even unaware of each other's existence.

He could bluff his way out of any situation. The classic story of Lev's coolness was this: He'd once been sent to spy out a Soviet diplomatic office that the JDL planned to shoot at. Wearing a blond wig and dyed blond eyebrows, he entered a hot, crowded elevator. On the way up, his eyebrows began to run. Instead of panicking, he smiled pleasantly at the people staring at him, pressed the ground-floor button as though suddenly recalling another engagement, and slowly walked out the building.

While Lev was searching for OVIR, I bought a guitar in the hotel gift shop. I intended to bring it to the sit-in, to prove to police that we weren't dangerous and that there was no need to shoot us. Rivkie laughed at me: "God, are you paranoid."

Lev returned a few hours later. We left the hotel to avoid hidden mikes. "Check," he said. "It's exactly the info you got from Shabbtai. There's one guard at the door. On either side of a corridor there are two offices. At the end of the corridor there's a waiting room where the Jews go. Over and out."

We finalized the plan. We would enter the building, flash our banners toward the Jews in the waiting room, and then disappear into one of the offices off the corridor. Shabbtai had warned me not to initiate any contact with Jews inside OVIR; we had no right to compromise them.

At two-thirty the next day, banners wrapped around our bodies, we left the hotel. Lev led us to Kolpachnyy Peregluk, a quiet side street of old houses just off Dzerzhinsky Square — KGB headquarters.

We stopped before a two-story building. "OVIR," said Lev.

Waiting across the street was one of our boys, Phil Kornbluth. He had left the hotel earlier, to avoid being seen with us. He was our outside man: He would phone the foreign press, contact Krup in New York, and then alert the American embassy. I laughed when I saw him: He was wearing a Russian fur hat and "reading" the Communist Party daily, *Pravda*.

We entered the building. We walked up three small stairs and through swinging doors that reached only up to our waists. At the end of the hall, in a waiting room directly before us, were Jews — actual Soviet Jews, my life's passion.

"*Gut yontiff, Yidden!*" Lev shouted in Yiddish, Happy Passover, Jews. We put on yarmulkes and unfolded our banners: "Let My People Go" in Russian, Hebrew, and English. Before I could discern the faces before us, we turned into the small office on our left.

A secretary was sitting at a desk. "Get out!" I shouted, pointing to the door. She didn't move. "OUT!" I screamed in her face. She reached for the phone. Rivkie grabbed it from her hand and scratched her with long, black-painted fingernails. She left.

Lev and Harvey tried pushing a filing cabinet against the door, but the cabinet barely moved. "This fucking thing must have a file on every Jew in Russia," said Harvey. We all pushed and finally slid it against the door. Then we sat on the floor. My guitar resisted tuning; I compensated with vigor, playing for the Jews outside. "*Pharaonu gavaryu*," we sang in Russian, To the Pharaoh I say, Let my people go!

We waited. Any moment the *New York Times* reporter, alerted by Kornbluth, would appear as a witness, no doubt with a photographer for a front-page picture.

Suddenly the door opened. Surprise: In Russia office doors opened *outward*. The room filled with men. Giants. We linked arms, but they easily pulled us apart. I held on to a leg of the desk; my fingers were pried loose. Someone ripped the lapel of my coat. We were kicked and dragged out of the building; one of our girls was thrown through the low swinging doors. "Go," a giant said in English. "Go to home."

Who were these giants? What do you *mean*, go to home! Back to the hotel, to the Jews on our tour? "Where were you boys this afternoon? We missed you at Lenin's Tomb." This was the worst, the most unimaginable, of all scenarios: We had just pulled it off, actually *done* it, traveled to the heart of the enemy and entered triumphant with banners and songs, only to be thrown out through swinging doors like saloon drunks!

They couldn't get away with this; we *had* to get arrested. When we wanted to get arrested in New York, we'd sit in the street and block traffic. So that is what we did: sat in the middle of Kolpachnyy Peregluk. We didn't shut down Moscow: The few cars that passed simply swerved around our small circle.

A crowd gathered. Some laughed; a man spit at us. I thought I heard the word *zhid*, kike; but really, I couldn't hear clearly. My senses were functioning as though underwater; my hand was moving on the guitar, but someone else was playing.

Two black cars pulled up. Thin men with sharp faces, leather jackets, and greased hair dragged us in. Too soon: The foreign press hadn't yet arrived. As we were driven away, we sang Jewish songs. A KGB man put his fist close to Harvey's face. "Come on and hit me," said Harvey, pointing to his chin.

We were taken to a police station and separated. A cop led me into a large office. A man in civilian clothes sat at a desk, binding a book with glue. He didn't look up when I entered. The cop moved a chair into the middle of the room and motioned me to sit. I sat down and crossed my legs. He pushed the top leg off my knee. Then he straightened his back to show me how I should sit. I laid my hands on my lap: I wanted him to see they weren't shaking.

I looked around the room; the cop grabbed my head and motioned me to stare toward the man binding his book. Finally, he put the book down and sighed. He walked over to me slowly. He looked tired, a resigned expression I mistook for kindness. He held his hand out to me. "Port," he said. I knew he meant "passport" but pretended not to understand. He showed me his own passport, helpful. I relented. He walked back to his desk, heavily, and spent a long time studying my facts.

The cop motioned me to stand. I was led out of the building, to a parked bus. Inside, alone except for a guard, sat Lev. He showed neither pleasure nor surprise at my appearance. "I saved you a seat," he said.

We were driven to another police station and taken to a room. The door closed behind us. We sat alone for several hours. "Maybe they've forgotten us," said Lev. We considered walking out and leaving the station, just to see what would happen.

A man entered. Narrow eyes, gray suit with thin lapels: KGB. "I hope you are enjoying hospitality of Soviet people," he said.

"Great hospitality," said Lev. "Your goons beat us up and ripped our clothes."

"You have beat up yourself and tore your clothes," he said, smiling.

A cop appeared with a plate of cookies. "Now you can tell everyone in West about Soviet prison," said the KGB man. I assumed the improved treatment was related to Kornbluth's appearance at the American embassy. "We're on a hunger strike," I said. Lev looked at me, wordlessly asking, "We are?" I shrugged.

The KGB man said to Lev, "Come plis with me." I stayed behind. It was Friday night: Shabbos. I stood in a corner, hoping I was facing Jerusalem, and sang the hymn to the Sabbath bride: "Come in peace, crown of your husband, with joy and gladness, come bride, come."

The KGB man reappeared. "Come plis."

Behind a big desk sat a fat man with rows of medals on his uniform. He read a statement in Russian, and the KGB man translated: "You have violated Soviet law and goodwill of Soviet people. You must to be punished." He paused.

"However," he continued, "since you are first-time guest in Soviet Union, sentence is canceled and you may join again your tour."

I scanned myself: nothing. No shock, no relief. Depleted. As if the purpose that animated my life was spent.

I was taken to a bus. Everyone was there. We embraced, shouting at once, trying to outdo each other's stories. Two cops had asked Lev for his passport: The first said "pass," the second "port." A cop had held a pistol to Rivkie's temple; Rivkie laughed.

My KGB friend entered the bus. "Be good boys," he said. "Again trouble and you will go for long ride."

We were driven back to the hotel. It was eleven o'clock, eight hours after we had entered OVIR. I was dizzy from hunger and excitement and also a sense of failure. They had, it seemed, outsmarted us. Of all the possibilities we'd imagined — imprisonment, deportation, even getting shot by a jittery guard — we never considered being released back to our tour. Now the Soviets could easily dismiss us to the foreign press as pranksters: How serious could we be if they hadn't bothered to deport us?

We entered the hotel. Men waiting in the lobby turned to follow us: escorts. We walked to the elevator, the door opened, and out stepped Kornbluth. "Comrades!" he said. "We've been expecting you! Everyone's upstairs waiting. You're big heroes."

As we rode up to his room, Kornbluth told us of his day. First he'd phoned the *Times* and the wire services, and they'd all sent reporters. But absurdly, none of them knew where OVIR was; by the time they'd figured out how to get there, we were gone.

Then Kornbluth took a cab to the central post office and wired Krup. Upon receiving the telegram, Krup was to contact the Voice of America, which broadcast into the Soviet Union, so that word of the sit-in would reach Soviet Jews.

Next Kornbluth headed for the American embassy. There he heard that seven U.S. senators had just arrived in Moscow to discuss the Jackson Amendment. "Is there a God in the world, or what?" he said to himself. Just as seven senators were meeting Soviet leaders, seven American Jews were getting arrested at OVIR.

Embassy officials told Kornbluth the senators would be at the Bolshoi that evening but urged him to stay put: Outside the embassy he was on his own. He thanked them and went to the Bolshoi.

He waited at the entrance. A limousine appeared, and a white-haired gentleman stepped out. "Senator?" said Kornbluth, guessing. "Phil Kornbluth, of Brooklyn."

The senator, imagining himself recognized, smiled and shook Kornbluth's hand. Kornbluth informed him that seven American citizens were in a Moscow jail for protesting for Soviet Jewry; the senator fled. Meanwhile, the other senators had already entered the theater. Kornbluth took a cab back to the hotel, sat in his room waiting for the KGB to appear, smoked a cigar, and prayed.

We went upstairs to his room and were greeted by American embassy officials and reporters. We sat on the bed and held a press conference. A new front in the Soviet Jewry struggle has been opened, I announced; American Jews will soon be filling Soviet jails. It was, of course, a lie — but that's the kind of thing one is expected to say on such occasions.

My proclamations were interrupted by the phone: my parents.

They'd just heard about our release on the radio. My father made a speech for the KGB agents monitoring the call: "And let the Russian know that everyone in America are behind you and we won't forget our Jewish brethrens!"

An embassy official asked if we'd be going tomorrow — Shabbos, Passover — to the synagogue. We hadn't bothered planning our itinerary beyond the sit-in; but now that we were released, of course we would go to the synagogue. "We'll have someone there looking out for you," said the official. We weren't just Jews, but *Americans*: protected. "God bless America," I said.

He shook our hands and smiled. "Try to stay out of jail until you leave. Happy Passover."

6.

We were too excited to sleep. Lev, Harvey, and I went down to the lobby, which was filled with KGB agents. We brought newspapers and a camera. We spread the newspapers wide before our faces and tore holes through the middle. Then we walked over to the KGB men and peered at them through the holes, like *Mad* magazine spies trying to be incognito. When they backed away, we took their pictures.

The next morning we walked to the synagogue. A Moscow parade: Jews in yarmulkes up front, KGB men just behind.

The Choral Synagogue, a large pillared building fronted by wide steps, was the last Jewish gathering place left in Moscow, a city of perhaps half a million Jews. As we entered, an old man approached. "OVIR?" he asked. *Da*, we answered. They knew! He ran to tell others. A crowd gathered. People reached out to touch us, as though we were *mezuzahs*, protection from harm. One old man said in Yiddish, "When I heard what you did, I thought the Israeli army was coming to save us." I asked how he'd heard, and he said, "The American radio." Krup had done his job.

A squat man pushed his way through the crowd and said to us brusquely, "Follow me." He was the synagogue informer, whose job was to isolate tourists from the local Jews, in pews reserved for foreigners. He took me by the arm; I pushed him away. We sat in a center pew, among our people.

After services we lingered outside. Old men passed us quickly, afraid even to make eye contact. A police car cruised the narrow street, its loudspeaker warning Jews not to block traffic. In a lot across from the synagogue stood a row of policemen with submachine guns.

The young Jews were waiting for us on the sidewalk. They didn't come to the synagogue to pray but simply to be among Jews. Some wore Israeli flagpins in their lapels, identifying themselves as Zionists in a country where Zionism was treason. They had turned the synagogue into an extraterritorial zone, becoming the only Soviet citizens who dared to publicly fraternize with Western tourists and journalists, even as the KGB and police circulated among them. I envied them for living in a country where identifying with a synagogue was the most radical rebellion possible, where Judaism was so potent, so subversive, it had to be constantly monitored.

The young Jews gathered around us. Someone proposed marriage to Rivkie. People handed me slips with Tel Aviv phone numbers of their relatives. No one seemed to notice the police. We were ten minutes from the Kremlin, laughing together on the street, deliberately casual.

I wandered from circle to circle, trying to memorize every face but unable to see even a single face clearly. One, a poet; another, a rock musician. They knew almost nothing about Judaism, except that they were Jews. In their innocence it seemed to me that Jewish history was beginning again, with our post-Holocaust generation, born after the end. All constraints on the future had been erased with the past; anything was possible now.

A man with thick glasses and a checkered peddler's cap told me he worked in a circus. He dreamed of emigrating to Israel, he said, but was afraid to apply for a visa. "Please," he said, "you must help me." How can I help you, I asked, if you won't even apply to leave? "Please," he said, and rushed off.

I wanted to gather them all to the airport, commandeer an Aeroflot plane, and fly them to Israel. But instead, all I could offer was encouragement. I felt absurd in my pretense as an activist redeemer.

An old man approached. His black fedora, rounded on the top, was several sizes too big and half-covered his eyes. "My name Abraham," he said in tentative English. "Like your American president, Lincoln." Last year, said Abraham, he had applied for a visa to Israel. Since then he'd been threatened with confinement in a mental asylum. " 'Old men don't do such things,' they tell me. 'They die in peace in Russia.'" I took Abraham's name and address, not knowing what else to do.

A young man pulled me away. "He is KGB," he said, pointing to Abraham.

"That old man?" I asked, incredulous.

"They are too smart," he said.

When he left me, another young man approached. "Be careful," he warned me. "That person you were speaking to now — he is KGB."

A taxi stopped before the synagogue, and a young man with long blond hair, elegant in a tailored suit, stepped out. "So I hear our police treated you with the customary Soviet courtesy," he said to me, smiling. He introduced himself: Sasha Levich, son of Professor Benjamin Levich, the most senior Soviet scientist to apply for a visa to Israel.

"Come on," Sasha said, in a nearly accentless English, "everyone is waiting to meet you." I asked Lev to join me and told the others we'd meet back at the hotel.

"I suppose you don't mind that the KGB is following us," I said.

"Don't worry about them," Sasha said, laughing. "They're our friends. We go everywhere together."

We came to a spired building and walked up a dark staircase. A short, balding man greeted us at the door with a hug. "Congratulations!" he said. "A job well done!" This was Genya Dekatov, a journalist who served as the Zionist movement's liaison with the foreign press. Dekatov's wife, Sonya, short and dark, kissed us on both cheeks.

We were at the Dekatovs' apartment. Except for a table and chairs and an old sofa, the apartment had no furniture; trunks and boxes were lined against the walls. "Let me apologize for the less-than-elegant surroundings," said Genya, his speech leisurely, amused. "Whatever furniture we have here is what we couldn't sell. You see, we were given visas a few months ago, and we sold everything quickly, before the government could change its mind. But apparently we didn't do it quickly enough because the government *did* change its mind. Two days before we were to leave." He stroked a large Siberian dog. "Maybe they were afraid the dog knew state secrets."

The leading refuseniks — Jews refused exit visas — were gathered in the empty living room. They had been the Soviet elite: scientists and professors and journalists, barely Jewish; yet they'd thrown everything away for the chance of a visa to Israel, a country they'd never seen and knew almost nothing about.

I knew their names and faces, the texts of their protest letters, and the details of each one's struggle. For years I'd lived with them from a distance; now, for a few hours, we were joined. There was no need for small talk; we felt instant trust among us.

Benjamin Levich approached me. "May I kiss you?" he asked.

Like the others here, Levich was forbidden to work by the government — the country's sole legal employer — and was now being threatened with arrest for "parasitism." I asked him how he was coping, and he said, "We are completely free people, the only free people in the Soviet Union. Only our bodies are not yet free." Having stepped out of the system, he explained, the refuseniks were now immune to the threats and rewards that kept other Soviet citizens docile. The refuseniks' strategy was simple: to act so totally free that the Soviets would have to expel them, as a danger to society. The only question was expulsion to where: Israel or Siberia. And that, said Levich, depended on Western help, especially the Jackson Amendment.

"The regime can do to us anything it pleases," said Genya, joining the conversation. "Perhaps a big Jewish conspiracy trial. Conspiracy for what? Oh, that is not a problem. They can charge us with many things: anti-Soviet defamation, black marketeering, even treason. Why not? Perhaps they have the case already completed and are only waiting for this nasty Jackson Amendment to be disposed of before they can get to business."

The refuseniks had composed a letter to American Jewish leaders demanding that they stay firm on the Jackson Amendment, and they wanted Lev and me to deliver it. An American Jewish activist had just phoned Genya, warning him that Jewish leaders had met with Nixon and might be abandoning Jackson. If that happened, the amendment would collapse. By urging American Jews to support an anti-Soviet amendment in Congress, the refuseniks were risking arrest for treason.

I copied the letter on a scrap of paper, hoping to get it across the border when we left the following day. The letter pleaded with Jewish leaders not to compromise: "Your smallest hesitation may cause irreparable results. Now, as never before, our fate depends on you. Brothers, be strong!"

Here were people living with constant harassment, in expectation of imminent arrest — and they were anxious about the fortitude of American Jews. Our leaders were behaving just as they had during the Holocaust, afraid to confront the White House on a matter of Jewish rescue. "Without the Jackson Amendment," said Levich, "we are finished."

"We're not buying winter clothes," added Genya. "By next year we will be either in a very warm land or a very cold land." Israel or Siberia.

Genya led me to the bathroom and turned on the sink tap and the shower full blast, pointing to invisible presences on the ceiling. "You must hit the bastards very hard," he said quietly. "We like the rough stuff. What they do to us, you do to them. When they cut our phones here, you cut their phones in the Soviet embassy. And so on. You can use your imagination."

We returned to the living room and ate dried salted fish and drank vodka from large glasses. Professor Levich toasted Lev and me: "To our heroes."

Lev replied, "You're the heroes. We're protected by American passports."

"No," insisted Levich, "*you* are the heroes. We have no choice to do what we do."

Lev said, "Neither do we."

It was time to leave. Genya and Sonya walked us downstairs. In the cobblestone courtyard stood a KGB man with a camera. Sonya walked directly in front of him, peered into the lens, and smiled as the camera flashed.

We waited for a cab. Around us were red banners, exhorting. Tomorrow we would board a plane, as though it were an effortless act.

A cab came. We hugged. Genya stroked my arm. "Next year in Jerusalem," I said.

"Not next year," said Genya. "*This* year. This year in Jerusalem."

We would win; we'd already won. No power had prevented us from meeting, and it was just a matter of time and suffering before our reunion would be permanent. This was our generation's messianic mission: to violate sealed borders.

Six

The Whole World
Is Against Us

I.

WE RETURNED to a hero's welcome: cheering supporters at Kennedy Airport, press interviews, a JDL fund-raising dinner ("Come hear a famous comedian! Come meet the brave boys who dared get arrested *inside* Russia! Eat! Drink! Dance!"). In Bernstein's we wore black fedoras with Lenin pins attached to the sides, hoping to create a sensation.

The FBI made no move to arrest us on conspiracy charges. But I began to notice clicks on my phone.

Lev and I crashed a Park Avenue meeting of Jewish leaders convened to debate the Jackson Amendment. I was permitted to read aloud the letter I'd brought from the refuseniks. Then we were asked to leave. We're staying, we insisted. The meeting was adjourned, and Lev and I were left alone in the conference room.

Then, abruptly, the excitement ended; and I returned to routine. I couldn't readjust. At Brooklyn College it was time for term papers, and I wrote one for my psychology class on "The Psychology of the

Moscow Sit-In," another for a Holocaust course on "The Holocaust as Motivation for the Moscow Sit-In."

Two months after my return from Moscow, in early June, Soviet Premier Brezhnev visited the United States. A letter arrived from Genya Dekatov, asking that I help "arrange an appropriate reception for your honored guest." And so, on the day of Brezhnev's arrival, I drove down to Washington with friends, intending to disrupt the visit.

We had hoped that hundreds of JDLers would join us, but no more than a few dozen came. We camped out in a local synagogue, sleeping on the wooden pews. Our plan was to follow Brezhnev's motorcade and leap onto his limousine. The problem was that none of us knew where the motorcade would be at any given time; and even if we had known, there were so many cops protecting it that we'd never get anywhere near Brezhnev himself.

We decided to invade the Soviet embassy instead. The street on which the embassy was located was cordoned off by hundreds of police, many of them positioned on rooftops. We started walking toward the barricades, intending to push our way through. But before we even got close, we were surrounded by cops. Paddy wagons instantly appeared, and we were shoved inside. We hadn't even done anything illegal yet, and we were under arrest.

I didn't join my friends in chanting the usual slogans as we rode through Washington's streets. Instead, I sat silent, slumped in a corner. I felt the same apathetic exhaustion I'd experienced in the Moscow police station as my "sentence" had been read. In OVIR I'd reached my ultimate moment as a protester; everything else seemed anticlimactic, absurd.

I'd just turned twenty, no longer a teenager. Apart from activism, who was I? I constantly set tests for myself, to prove my courage and dedication. I'd hoped that the OVIR sit-in would be my final test and had expected that it would somehow transform me, help me live with myself without pressure. But here I was, back from Moscow, no different than before I'd left.

I had tried to be selfless; but that requires a developed self to surrender. Otherwise, altruism becomes an alibi for an unformed personality. I sensed I'd reached the point where idealists go wrong, begin to turn into politicians. A young person is energized by self-righteousness, but an adult trying to remake the world without confronting his own flaws risks hypocrisy and worse.

I wanted to define myself not by what I did but by who I was, to be as vital privately as publicly. I wanted to be so much an individualist that I wouldn't care whether others perceived me that way or not.

The OVIR sit-in prepared me for self-confrontation by infusing me with a sense of possibility. I knew that fatalism was a lie: We had done the impossible, transformed a fantasy demonstration into reality. The world was elastic and yielded to single-minded will. My self-confidence was enormous: I felt I had only to commit myself to a goal and it would happen. And yet, precisely because of that sense of expansiveness, I now acutely felt my limitations. After OVIR I couldn't revert to a cramped inner life.

I had to get away for a while — from the JDL and the Moscow Eight and my insular Brooklyn existence. When I returned to New York from Washington, I registered for a one-year program at Jerusalem's Hebrew University and prepared to leave that summer.

Krup called. There was a "serious meeting" I had to attend, he said; he'd explain in person. We routinely spoke on the phone with hints, to evade eavesdroppers.

I didn't want to go to any secret meeting, but I couldn't say no to Krup. That was precisely my problem, the reason I had to get away: I still craved acceptance, still needed to prove to the JDL boys that I was worthy of being one of them.

We met in the lobby of the Waldorf-Astoria. Krup asked the receptionist for Max Fisher's suite. "Max Fisher?" I asked, incredulous. Krup smiled. Max Fisher was the unofficial head of the Jewish establishment and President Nixon's confidant. Maybe he'd been sent by Nixon to negotiate with us about the Jackson Amendment. I felt important.

We went to Max Fisher's suite. Krup knocked; the door opened — and there stood twenty-year-old JDL leader Bernie Engle. "Boys!" said Bernie, beaming. "So good of you to come! Regards from the president; we just played golf together on Saturday!"

Bernie, whose tiny yarmulke was lost in his abundant Afro hair, was the JDL's leading comedian. One joke followed another with such rapidity that, even when a routine fell flat, the sheer profusion guaranteed repeated scoring. As soon as he began one of his routines, he would laugh with anticipation, barely getting out the words, his eyes slitted, nostrils flaring. And you had to laugh with him, intimidated by his deep, wild laughter but also delighted that anyone could feel such pleasure, allow a joke to so completely overwhelm him.

"Come in, come in!" he said to Krup and me, still pretending to be Max Fisher. "I hope you'll excuse my modest accommodations. The presidential suite was already booked!"

Then he abruptly switched to his favorite routine, the old Yiddish immigrant, a role he played with such authenticity that his American persona seemed by contrast mere mimickry. "Maybe you youngsters should like a little something to eat?" he asked. He lifted the receiver and shouted, as if speaking to someone hard of hearing, "Hello room soivis! I'd like to order one big herring. With onions. Make sure it's dead. Not the onions, the herring. What do you mean, no herring? Five million dollars a day I pay for a closet in this hotel and you can't get for me a lousy herring?"

Even as I laughed, I waited nervously for Bernie to get to the point. When he summoned you to a meeting, there was a price to pay, some crazy scheme "for Jews" he wanted you to do. And you did what he asked, no matter how outrageous, because you knew that Bernie would do anything for you if you needed him, because he was "doing" more for Jews than you were, because you could never outtalk him, because you were a little afraid of him.

"So what's going on here?" I said to Bernie as Krup and I entered his hotel room.

"What's going on here is serious business, Klein, very serious business. First of all, you're not going to Israel."

"Is that so?"

"Yes, Klein, that is so. We got big plans for you, oooh, do we got plans. Bring out the hookers, Krup! Just a joke, Klein; don't get all excited. What you'll be doing is organizing for a new underground. Hurok was a disaster, I don't have to tell you. Anyone who did anything is either in jail or on the run. So now it's time for those of us who didn't do the crazy stuff to take over.

"So how do you fit in, you no-good Hungarian chicken thief? We need a guy who can recruit promising high-school kids for a 'discussion group.' You know: discuss. Go on trips with them, give them the right books. Brainwash them, Klein. Capish? When you got someone who's ready for more than discussion, you pass him on to us. That's how the Stern Group did its recruiting."

"Why me?"

"You got credentials; you've proven yourself. Kids will listen to you."

"You rented a room in the Waldorf just to psyche me into this?"

"You're an important guy, Klein. A regular Jewish hero."

Becoming a terrorist is the ultimate separatist act, barricading yourself in pain and rage. But I wanted expansiveness, the very opposite of an underground life. I'd already decided that this would be a time for personal growth, not escalating activism. I had a responsibility to make myself an intact person, if only, I thought, to better serve the Jewish people.

"Let someone else do it," I said.

"Klein," insisted Bernie, "you're the *only* guy in the world who can do it. If you don't do it, it won't get done."

"Think about it," urged Krup.

"I thought about it," I replied, "and the answer is no."

"So we're agreed," said Bernie, laughing. "Settled."

"Bernie, I think he's serious," said Krup.

"All right," said Bernie. "Go to Israel. Get laid, have a good time. *Gezunter heit*. When you come back, we'll still be here. Waiting."

I arrived in Israel that July. I rented an apartment in Jerusalem, found a girlfriend for a few weeks who'd been a high-school cheerleader at yeshiva basketball games, and mimicked the life of a normal college student.

Then Meir Kahane called. "You're in the country and don't even look me up?" he asked, sounding like an aggrieved uncle. "So when am I seeing you?"

"You tell me," I said, at once apologetic and wary.

I'd left New York to get away from activism, but I couldn't say no to Meir Kahane. This wasn't Bernie and Krup but the Reb himself.

We met at the JDL office, one large chaotic room that was headquarters for Kahane's election campaign for the Knesset, the Israeli parliament. Kahane said to me, in a deliberately loud voice, "Unless

we want the Shin Bet to join our conversation, we'd better leave."
He seemed to enjoy the idea of being bugged by the Israeli secret
service, as though it enhanced his importance.

Kahane had aged in the two years since he'd left America. There
was gray in his short black hair. He had spent months in an Israeli
jail, charged with gunrunning and sedition. Yet he seemed buoyant,
convinced he was going to win at least one parliament seat; in fact,
polls showed him winning up to three. Much of the public admired
him as a straight-talking rabbi who'd fought for Jewish rights. And
there were now thousands of Soviet immigrants in the country, many
of whom might vote for him in gratitude for his role in the Soviet
Jewry movement.

"The *best* thing the Israeli government did for me was put me in
jail," he said, clicking his tongue against his teeth. Prison had made
him a hero, he explained, and had exposed him to the Sephardi working class, whose sensibility he was appealing to in the campaign. He
showed me a leaflet that was headlined in Hebrew: "Give a *Man* a
Chance." He smiled, pleased with its street tone.

We went to a café. I relished the stares of those around us. I felt
flattered by the camaraderie this famous man offered me — precisely
his intention.

Kahane stuttered and twitched more in conversation than he did
in public speech, and I recognized myself in him: eloquent for the
cause but inadequate in private. He remained essentially a teenager:
passionate, irreverent, uncontrollable. Toughness still excited him;
he enjoyed being one of the boys. But he never forgot that he was
the leader, whose job was to manipulate us into desperate acts. And
we were lured by his youthful recklessness and adult shrewdness.

"I've been interested in you for a long time," he said, with a wry
smile that implied: So what took you so long to find me? The OVIR
sit-in, he said, was "a *thousand* percent." I told him that if Moscow
refuseniks could vote in the Israeli elections, he'd be prime
minister.

"When Jews need help, they're all for Kahane," he said. "But when
I need *them*, nobody's home." He recounted the story about a low-
income housing project that New York's mayor had wanted to build
in the middle-class Jewish neighborhood of Forest Hills. "When I
was trying to protect old Jews in poor neighborhoods, the fat burghers

of Forest Hills denounced me as a vigilante. But when the problem came to *their* neighborhood, suddenly they were more militant than Kahane."

One night, he continued, he'd spoken in a Forest Hills synagogue about the project. Afterward a community leader who'd always opposed the JDL approached him and whispered, "Rabbi, maybe you can blow it up?"

We laughed together. Us versus them: not only Jews against goyim, but good Jews — selfless JDLers — against bad Jews, the JDL's selfish opponents.

Then, having allowed me to share with him an inside joke, he came to the point. He needed intelligent people, he said, to work on his election campaign. "I'm surrounded by n.a.p.s," he said. "You know what's an n.a.p? *Noch a putz*" — Yiddish for "one more jerk."

As low as the intellectual level of many of his supporters in America was, here it was worse. His Israeli followers were mostly Sephardi street kids and maladjusted Russian immigrants, a coalition of losers. Krup's joke was that if a native Israeli who didn't seem psychologically impaired joined Kahane's election campaign, he had to be a Shin Bet agent.

"I've already arranged an interview for you with a reporter from Israel's biggest newspaper," said Kahane. "Tell him *exactly* what the refuseniks said to you about me. It could help the campaign *tremendously.*"

I was surprised, and a little upset, by the fact that he'd scheduled an interview for me without bothering to consult me. But he was the Reb. And so a few days later I met the reporter. The piece was published — but focusing entirely on the OVIR sit-in, without mentioning Kahane.

He called, upset, and blamed me for the journalist's oversight. But don't worry, he said, suddenly conciliatory: He was arranging a press conference for me, where I could emphasize his popularity among the refuseniks. I was being given one more chance to prove myself.

The press conference produced better results for Kahane, and he continued to assign me jobs. He introduced me to Volodya Shlechtman, the Russian Jew who'd gained weight during his hunger strike in a cage in Washington, and who was now running the JDL's election campaign among Soviet immigrants. Kahane wanted me to tour the country with Shlechtman, to woo Russian voters.

Shlechtman had pointed ears, a pointed black goatee, a smile that was sharp and unconvincing; he spoke in a guttural whisper, at once confiding and concealing. He was awaiting trial for an arson attack on a Christian missionary building in Jerusalem — "an *alleged* attack," he said, grinning, a precocious Soviet student of Western judicial norms.

I didn't want to spend time with Volodya. And I didn't want to work for Kahane's campaign. In fact, the more I learned of Kahane's new political agenda, the less I trusted him. I'd followed him because he embodied for me the war to free oppressed Jews; but now he seemed to be moving to Israel's far-right fringe, obsessed with peripheral issues. So far, the JDL's main activities in Israel involved beating up members of Rakah, the Israeli communist party, and Christian missionaries, easy but irrelevant targets. Why was Meir Kahane, symbol of Jewish liberation, acting like a street gang leader settling petty scores?

Kahane was not yet advocating what would soon become his obsession, the forced "transfer" of Arabs from Israel; but he had begun sending letters to Israeli Arabs, offering them money he didn't have to emigrate. I wanted to free Soviet Jews, not uproot Palestinians. I felt the same unease toward Kahane now as I had in the JDL's early days, when he'd spoken of "Nazis in black shirts and black skin." All my suppressed doubts about him over the years, especially his Mafia alliance, intensified. There seemed to be two Meir Kahanes: the liberator and the thug. And I wasn't sure which would prevail.

I disappeared with my cheerleader girlfriend into the desert, without leaving word for Kahane. And when I returned, I didn't contact him again.

2.

The siren sounded at two o'clock on Yom Kippur afternoon, October 6, 1973. The holiday silence of Jerusalem's streets was violated by army jeeps. Civilians-turned-instant-soldiers rushed to assembly points.

Despite rumors that both Egypt and Syria had launched a surprise attack on Israel's holiest day, few people descended into bomb
shelters. The man next to me in the synagogue said, "Who would
believe the Arabs could be so stupid to start with us again?" The war
was probably already over, he added, laughing. "Are you running
home to America?"

There was a rumor that the first wounded would be brought to a
Jerusalem hospital, so I joined the jostling crowds of high-school students in the barbed-wire compound. The wounded hadn't yet arrived;
and the volunteers were taken to a basement, where we spent the
night, waiting. I hoped wounded soldiers would come; I wanted to
touch the war, know death. But in the morning we were sent home;
the wounded were being taken elsewhere.

I spent a week volunteering in a farming community settled by
Iraqi Jews, picking tomatoes beside a Palestinian field hand. We
shared quick, embarrassed smiles. At night I sat with the old farmers, men in berets and square mustaches, and watched the endless
news broadcasts, interspersed with young women singing sad songs
in tremulous voices. Arab POWs appeared and recited their names,
so that their families might know they were alive. "Look how we treat
them," said a farmer. "And what do you think they're doing to *our*
prisoners?"

Slowly we realized that, though the Israeli army had regained the
offensive, something terrible had happened. There were rumors of
high-ranking incompetence, of bases filled with tanks missing tur-
rets. The Syrians could have taken Tiberias, it was said, but stopped
their advance, fearing an Israeli trap. Yet there had been no trap;
the Israeli army wasn't waiting for them. Newspaper photos showed
Israeli POWs, a new sight: young sabras, unshaven, their arms tied
with rope and padlocked over bent heads.

In the last week of the war I returned to Jerusalem. At night the
streets seemed to vanish. Streetlights went dark; buses stopped running; restaurants closed. Old men in ill-fitting uniforms, members
of the civil guard, shouted from the street at a rare lit window. I got
lost walking familiar streets, unable to see even a few steps ahead.
Passing army trucks, their headlights painted blue, deepened the
darkness.

Evenings I hung out at Richie's, the "American" pizza shop that was virtually the only store open past dark, and waited for friends to appear from New York. Thousands of young American Jews were coming to volunteer as agricultural workers, to fill in for farmers called up to the army. And yet, for all our Zionist fervor, we were outsiders; and nothing better proved that than our nightly vigil at Richie's.

I met some JDLers at Richie's who had driven down to Sinai. They'd gotten close to the front and were allowed to pump gas for tanks before being sent back. They seemed pleased with their adventure; they had almost been soldiers. I saw myself in them: consumers of experience, looking for vicarious dangers.

One evening I was sitting on the railing outside Richie's, laughing with some friends, when a soldier on a passing truck shouted, "What are *you* laughing about!" "You": Americans. This was my generation's war, and here I was safe in Jerusalem. To be an American Jew meant being inherently inauthentic, a spectator to Jewish history.

Larry Berger, a JDLer wanted in the United States for the Hurok attack, was hospitalized with machine-gun shrapnel in his chest. Berger had fled to Israel after Hurok and joined the army, hoping to avoid extradition. In fact, the war had saved him: Now that he was a wounded soldier, the government wouldn't dare deport him.

Berger, impossibly thin, lay with his gown unbuttoned, a heaving line of breath visibly moving through protruding ribs. He'd been shot during the last hours of the war, in the army's final attack on a Golan Heights position, which was then returned to the Syrians during the cease-fire negotiations. Berger felt set up. He was bitter against the army for its failures, bitter against the government for having once intended to deport him, but most of all he was bitter against Kahane. "Fucking Kahane," he said hoarsely, forcing the words out through his pain. "Let him get shot up, *then* he can talk."

But what really angered Berger was that Kahane had abandoned him and the other JDLers accused of murder in the Hurok attack. He was too busy saving the Jewish people, said Berger, to worry about saving his own followers.

Krup was writing me similar complaints from New York. Almost all the JDL boys had left Kahane, he wrote; some had even stopped talking to him. Instead of collecting money for the legal needs of the

Hurok defendants, he was fund-raising for his election campaign. Krup even accused him of diverting JDL legal aid funds to the election. "A thief, plain and simple."

I tried to convince myself that the "new" Kahane was different from the old Kahane I'd loved; but the same man who had taught us that any means was justified for a noble end was simply fulfilling his ideology. For if electing Kahane to the Knesset was somehow important, then why let the needs of a few teenage misfits, even if they happened to be his most devoted followers, interfere?

My final disillusionment with Kahane occurred during the war. All political parties had agreed to suspend electioneering — except for the JDL. The shooting hadn't stopped at the front when JDL posters appeared in the streets, warning that only Kahane could save the country. He was trying to exploit Israel's trauma; he was, in every way, shameless.

"I'm finished with Kahane," I said to Berger.

"Good morning," he croaked.

3.

Krup came. He had no plans, no idea how long he would stay or what he'd do — beyond hanging out with me. He simply couldn't bear watching the war from a distance; he came to feel the country's pain, his own helplessness.

We sat in my apartment, getting drunk and talking through the night about "the situation." The Arab oil boycott that followed the war had turned most of the world's governments (Krup and I said simply, "the world") against Israel. Western European leaders surrendered to the boycott and endorsed a PLO state in the Israeli-controlled West Bank — though the PLO openly promised to use any territory it won as a base from which to try to destroy Israel. And despite Israel's aid programs in Africa and Asia, almost the entire Third World severed relations with us — seeming to confirm Kahane's warning that Jews should help only other Jews, because in the end the goyim would betray us.

Only the United States and Holland defied Arab pressure and continued to support Israel. The Arabs retaliated by cutting those countries' oil supplies. Tel Aviv high-school students held a "Thank

You, Holland" rally. "Groveling kikes," Krup sneered. "They should make a banner that says, 'Thank you Holland for not pissing on us.' "

We debated how long it would take before America turned on Israel. "In the end we'll be left only with Holland," I said.

"What makes you so sure about Holland," he replied.

Suddenly much of the world seemed convinced that Israel's very existence was a crime. I was sure another holocaust was coming, that Israel was about to be destroyed. I was hardly alone. Israelis began invoking the Holocaust in political conversations, as if it were the natural context for our predicament. They spoke of "the world" as an enemy, casually repeating the terrible slogan, "The whole world is against us."

Israel's isolation struck at the most tender part of the Jewish psyche: our sense of abandonment, the suspicion that not only the Nazis but the onlookers, too, had wanted us dead, that the killing went on unimpeded for six years because humanity was secretly grateful to Hitler.

Only Israel's existence, our antidote to the Holocaust, had prevented most Jews from rejecting the world in bitter self-ghettoization. But now the pretense of normalcy was over. There could be no crueler irony for Jews than transforming Israel into a ghetto. Inevitably, the suppressed rage from the Holocaust was released; and Israelis began seeing their hope in the grim Revisionist outcasts, in Menachem Begin and his right-wing Likud party.

Israel seemed caught in a cycle: The more it was unfairly quarantined, the more extreme it became — a position that in turn demanded its further isolation. I'd once read a story about children sold to medieval circuses and turned into freaks: Their legs, bound in blocks, remained stunted while their torsos grew to normal size; heads, placed in hourglasses, adapted to the shape of the curves. We too were being transformed into freaks — ghettoized and demonized, until we turned grotesque with rage.

During a hospital visit to Larry Berger, I met my cousin Yossi, who was also visiting a wounded friend. Yossi was stationed across the Suez Canal, at the most advanced Israeli position. His face was brown from the desert sun, his lips were cracked, his boots white with baked mud. On Yom Kippur he'd been sitting at the canal, looking lazily across, when the horizon suddenly filled with tanks.

Yossi fired his machine gun until it emptied. Later he'd been among those who crossed the canal in the Israeli counteroffensive and trapped the Egyptian Third Army — which the Israeli government, conceding to American pressure, had ordered Yossi and his friends to spare.

Everyone in his unit, said Yossi, had become Likudniks. "Begin doesn't give a damn about what the goyim want or don't want. He knows they'll hate us no matter what we do, so we might as well do what's good for us."

I thought of Yossi in the summer of 1967, the boy who laughed at his father's fears and planned to explore distant countries. An Israeli: seeing the world not as a threat but an opportunity for adventure. But now the world had closed up for him, turned him into an angry, bitter Jew.

Israel returned to a numbed routine. Universities reopened, but few young men attended; reservists remained at the front, just in case the war would resume. Our teachers, privately grieving, spoke in monotones. One woman lecturer seemed to glare at the male Diaspora students, young Jews with intact limbs. I couldn't concentrate on Israeli poetry and Arabic grammar and Hasidic philosophy, and stopped going to classes.

Knesset elections were held. The Likud's power grew, and it seemed just a matter of time before the right-wing Revisionists, Israel's permanent opposition, finally displaced the Labor Party.

Kahane didn't get a seat. His slogans and publicity stunts seemed irrelevant, even offensive, to a country withdrawn into grief. Suddenly Kahane was transformed from a leader who could summon the press at will to an ignored crank, despised and ridiculed even by former followers. His political marginalization and the isolation of Israel — the convergence of personal and national ostracism — seemed to have driven him to a nervous breakdown.

Kahane's mental collapse was expressed in the intensification of his hatred. No Jewish leader spoke so incessantly of love for the Jewish people as he did, and none so despised his fellow Jews. He hated entire categories of Jews: Orthodox Jews who refused to follow him weren't religious at all but mere "practitioners of Jewish folklore"; secular Israelis were "Hebrew-speaking Gentiles." And

Israeli leftists were "worse than anti-Semites"; in his *Jewish Press* column, he virtually advocated their murder.

One afternoon Krup returned to the apartment and announced he'd just seen Kahane. Did you speak with him? I asked. Krup snorted. "Klein, I swear to you, he was walking down the street having this whole argument with himself, waving his hands, bumping into lampposts. The guy is so nuts it's unbelievable. I stood there watching him and thinking, 'This is the man I was ready to die for?' "

Apocalyptic images filled my head. Tel Aviv burning, its beaches crowded with refugees fleeing into the sea, while Israeli planes bomb Arab oil fields and plunge the West into a literal dark age. Justice: If the world couldn't find room for a sliver of a Jewish state, then the world didn't deserve to exist.

All my fine resolutions about turning inward and discovering my true being struck me now as absurd, self-indulgent. History had overwhelmed individual needs: The Yom Kippur War, I was convinced, had returned us to an era of Jewish destruction. Just as the Holocaust was preceded by years of Nazi propaganda delegitimizing the Jews as human beings, so too was the world now preparing for Israel's destruction by first rescinding its right to exist. And only the most radical political responses seemed appropriate.

I'd made a decision, which I hadn't yet revealed to Krup: I was ready to join his terrorist group. If the world was returning to the 1940s, then I, like my father, would go "underground" — but this time armed.

Krup and I traveled the country, visiting the sites of Zionist martyrdom. The grave tour, we called it. We stood before the gallows where Irgunists had sung the Zionist anthem, "Hatikva," with nooses around their necks. We stood inside the death-row cell where two Sternists had hugged each other around a grenade smuggled inside an orange and blown themselves up, rather than allow the British to hang them.

In Tiberias we passed a car that flew the UN flag with its symbol of the globe, that hostile place. I ripped the flag off and gave it to Krup, a trophy in our war against the world.

Then we walked the rainy streets, discussing what was to be done. Joining the Israeli army, said Krup, was a waste of time: Rather than being two anonymous recruits in a big machine, we could do far more as independent operatives. We were, after all, among the few of our generation who were ready to sacrifice their careers and even their lives for the Jewish people. Israel didn't need us; but who would protect the Diaspora? The creation of a "serious" underground, concluded Krup, was more urgent than ever — to fight the Soviets and also anti-Semites in America, whom Krup was convinced were about to launch pogroms against Jews in retaliation for the oil shortage.

"Count me in, Krup, yeah?"

"I'd already planned on that, Mr. Klein."

4.

Genya and Sonya Dekatov received exit visas. I went to the airport to greet them and stood at the glass partition near passport control, trying to glimpse the Soviet immigrants gathered on the other side. Their luggage — square, brown suitcases and boxes tied with string — was piled against the glass.

I waited with former Soviet Jews — gold-toothed Georgians and ex-Siberian prisoners with permanently hungry faces — for the immigrants to emerge. A man from Riga told me he'd come to greet a defendant from the Leningrad trial who'd just been released from prison. I asked him his friend's name, and he was surprised when I knew it. Then he told me that he himself had participated in the famous Kremlin sit-in on Purim 1971, the event after which we'd modeled our OVIR sit-in. I wanted to laugh with joy.

The immigrants began emerging, and we followed them outside. The air smelled of gasoline and jasmine, as it did on the night I first came to Israel in 1967. We peered at each passing face. I panicked: I couldn't recall how the Dekatovs looked. Was Genya short or tall, Sonya pale or dark? Their presence eluded me; they weren't faces but emotions.

And then there they were: two tiny people, leading a giant dog. "Genya!" I called.

"Jesus Christ!" he shouted.

We hugged, while Sonya held my arm, weeping. "You, here!" he said finally, laughing, "I had no idea!"

Suddenly anything seemed possible again: History wasn't a fixed series of steps but fluid, full of surprises; and the nightmare of Jewish destruction was temporarily displaced by the vision of an ingathering of exiles, a messianic era without apocalypse.

Alix, the prettiest girl in the JDL, was hiding out in Jerusalem. She was wanted as a witness in a bombing case and had fled to Israel rather than testify against her friends. For the last year she'd been living in a one-room apartment in a working-class housing project, long, flat buildings scattered on the stone hills like abandoned crates. She knew almost no one in the country and had spent days at a time speaking only to her cat.

We were sleeping together. Our relationship wasn't a romance because she didn't let it become one. She had a boyfriend in New York, who was supposed to appear in Israel any week. But he'd repeatedly delayed his arrival, and Alix wasn't sure if he'd ever come. She was cheating on him partly in revenge for leaving her alone. The contagion of intrigue: Fleeing the feds and cheating on your boyfriend were both consequences of an underground life.

Alix had long blond hair and wore a big floppy hat and drove a jeep. Her smile seemed capable of constant expansion. She stretched her words, as if in wonder at sound, a little girl's voice raspy with cigarette smoke.

Alix had gone to a rich kids' yeshiva high school, which she despised as one big fashion show; the other girls there had considered her strange. She preferred boys for friends: "Guys have to put up with much less bullshit, y'know?" She loved hanging out with Krup and me and talking about how Israel was being betrayed. I measured a Jew's intelligence by what he or she understood about the Holocaust: why Auschwitz cut through history like a divide and what it meant for us to live on the other side. Alix understood.

Alix had the best hashish of anyone I knew in Jerusalem. She wanted to be bohemian but also holy. She'd been "adopted" in her Jerusalem exile by an ultra-Orthodox family; and Alix loved the woman of the house, one of those kerchiefed matriarchs who could manage with complete calm a dozen children and still accommodate guests. "She's *so* good," said Alix, "she's *so* pure." Alix wanted to offer herself as this woman had done, to forget her own pain in serving others, to replenish Jewish losses in the Holocaust with babies, populate the Land of Israel with strong, biblical Jews.

Still, Alix was conscious of the privilege she'd renounced as a debutante and wanted to be admired for it. She could claim to be one of the JDL boys precisely because she'd thrown so much away, had sacrificed more than anyone to join us. "I could have had it all," she said, partly boasting, partly with regret. She felt abused: She had sacrificed for the JDL and disrupted her life to protect her friends from prison; but when she needed help, no one had reciprocated. Instead, she'd been given a one-way ticket to Israel and abandoned. Krup called her a victim of the JDL's wars, as if that somehow explained her neglect.

Other JDLers on the run had tried to make lives for themselves, but Alix seemed to be giving up. Self-pity undermined her vibrancy; she was losing the activist's strength to care more for others' suffering than her own.

I spent time with the Dekatovs at their "absorption center," where immigrants were temporarily housed in bungalows near the sea and taught Hebrew.

One day Genya told me his story, in a slightly formal but otherwise flawless English. "I want there to be total trust between us, Yoosi," he began, Russifying my name. "And so I will tell you: When I was a young and foolish man, I was recruited into the KGB."

He watched my face for a reaction and, pleased when I remained impassive, continued his story. Eventually he quit the KGB, he said, and worked as a science reporter for a Soviet newspaper. "I thought that if I concentrated on nonpolitical subjects, I would not be a complete stinker. But, of course, I was kidding myself. Any responsible job in the Soviet Union means you are serving the Lie."

In August 1968 Genya happened to be in Prague, covering a science conference. When the Soviets invaded, he distributed leaflets to the troops, urging them to disobey orders. "Well, they very quickly put me on a plane and I thought, 'All right, so my luck has finally run out.' Instead, they only warned me. But I knew from that moment that I had to get out of the Soviet Union. I contacted the Zionist movement, which was the only emigration game in town, and offered my services. Well, the rest of the story you know."

I reassured myself: It didn't matter that he'd been a KGB agent, because obviously he wasn't one anymore. He was my link with the refuseniks; I wasn't going to jeopardize that intimacy with suspicion or judgmentalness.

I told Krup Genya's story and suggested I consult him on tactics for our underground. Krup appreciated the potential usefulness of a refusenik connection. "Do you trust him?" he asked.

"A thousand percent," I said.

I asked Genya what tactical advice he would give an anti-Soviet underground. He understood that I wasn't speaking theoretically. "I think the attacks have to be done on a new basis," he said, in a slow, bemused voice. "That is to say, the aim is not to get publicity in the newspapers, but to do business directly with the Soviets.

"So let us say there is an African leader whom the Soviets are interested in cultivating. Now, let us say that this leader has a daughter studying in the Sorbonne. Let us say further that the daughter is kidnapped by Zionist extremists, who send a letter to her father: 'If you want to see the girl alive, ask your friends in Moscow to free the following refuseniks.' You see, Yoosi, it can all be done very quietly, very pragmatically. No one even has to know about it, besides the immediate parties concerned."

I was impressed by the originality of his plan. I felt no responsibility for the fate of innocents — perhaps I didn't believe there were any. The terrorist divides humanity into three categories: victims, oppressors, and bystanders. Not innocents: bystanders. The word implies an active watching. I despised even more than Nazis those who could have helped save Europe's Jews but didn't. The spectators' very innocence is their guilt, their comfort and distance an affront to your pain. The transformation of innocent to bystander to complicitor allows terrorists to plant bombs in public places or seize random hostages, and still consider themselves virtuous.

And yet Genya's tone disturbed me. He spoke with an almost mocking detachment — a cynic, not an idealist. His motive for helping us seemed mere revenge against the communists, to "screw the bastards," as he put it, not to save Jews.

Still, I continued to trust him. I was grateful for his offer of help and tried not to think of that African student in the Sorbonne.

*   *   *

Alix loved quaaludes, downers. If you resisted the drug's initial heaviness, you could feel your skin tingle. One quaalude was usually enough for me to get a "buzz," as we put it; but Alix would take several of the fat white pills at once, then drink cheap Israeli brandy and smoke hashish. When we took quaaludes, her speech became flat; instead of drugged vitality, I felt a vague despair.

One night I dropped by her apartment and found the room filled with kerosene fumes from a leaky heater. "What are you trying to do," I shouted, "make your own private gas chamber?"

She laughed and cried. "I just want to be warm," she said, in a quaalude voice. "I just want someone to take care of me."

"Why don't you marry a dentist from Long Island," I said.

"My life is finished. I'm a college dropout. I'm going to be stuck in this room forever. You're not going to save me. Nobody's going to save me."

"What are you talking?"

"I'm talking, I'm talking. I can't take it anymore. My poor parents: their beautiful, smart daughter — and this is the *nachas* I give them."

I tried to reassure her, but she didn't seem to hear me.

"We think we're so good. Big Jewish heroes. But we're just stupid kids playing with fire. It's all an ego game, Klein."

"Saving Jews is a game?"

"The whole thing's turned to shit. The minute the girl died it was over."

"What girl?"

"The girl. From Hurok."

"While you're at it, why don't you blame yourself for the genocide of the Armenians?"

"I'm so tired," she said. "I just want to sleep."

Genya and I discussed assassinating Soviet officials. His job would be to tell us who among them were responsible for anti-Jewish policies, who were the most worthwhile targets. He seemed to know a lot about the inner workings of the Kremlin.

Genya gave me a copy of a report he'd written for the Israeli government about the psychological state of the refuseniks. It was devastating in its nastiness, accusing refuseniks of squabbling over money sent by sympathizers from abroad, and strongly hinting at black marketeering — precisely the accusations the Soviet press made against refuseniks.

I conceded the terrifying thought I'd tried to suppress: that Genya might never have quit the KGB. I reviewed his life story as he'd presented it to me; the details didn't hold. Could one simply quit the KGB and take another job? And that incident in Prague: Soviet dissidents had spent years in prison just for protesting the Czech invasion, yet Genya claimed to have been merely rebuked for distributing seditious leaflets to soldiers.

I recounted the reasons why Genya couldn't possibly be a KGB agent: The Moscow refuseniks trusted him; he'd voluntarily confided his past to me; he'd greeted me with genuine warmth when we met at Lod Airport.

That last point was decisive. I allowed myself to be charmed by his apparent affection for me and berated myself for suspecting such a wonderful man. Still, I couldn't entirely dismiss my doubts and wondered whether I had betrayed the underground and delivered myself to the KGB.

5.

Krup returned to New York, in time for the winter 1974 college semester, and resumed his history studies at Columbia. Despite the imminent holocaust, normal life proceeded.

Krup's letters were alternately desperate and very funny. "We are facing an immediate threat of genocide in America," he wrote. *"This is no joke. The destruction of American Jewry can begin in a matter of months."*

All of America's problems, he wrote, had converged on the Jew: freezing winters and a collapsing economy, an American defeat in Vietnam that would be blamed on antiwar protesters, many of whose leaders happened to be Jews. Krup felt torn between staying in America and fighting pogromists, and fleeing to Israel with as many relatives as he could get to leave. He described a recent family dinner: "When my mother took the roast out of the oven, I screamed, 'Soon they'll be pulling *Jews* out of the oven! Get out while you can! Get out!!' "

*   *   *

I went down to Eilat, where the desert meets the sea, to lie on the beach and consider my life.

I thought of Alix and Larry Berger and Meir Kahane and wondered if their lives held my future. Prison, flight, madness: Those seemed to be the options for anyone who went underground. Almost every JDL terrorist either was wanted or had already been arrested on one charge or another, and Krup and I would almost certainly be next.

My anxiety about Genya had become acute. Even if he didn't turn out to be a KGB agent, my reckless trust in him revealed my naïveté; sooner or later the FBI or the KGB would outsmart me. I recalled what Shabbtai the ex-Irgunist had said when I'd approached him about OVIR: "You Americans have no sense of security." We'd been raised in history's most candid society; we didn't belong underground.

And yet in a few months I'd be returning to New York to become a terrorist — in effect, to destroy my life. Why? Because another holocaust was imminent. Because there are times when individual needs are swept away, and all that remains is a war against evil. Because I wanted to be good.

But was I confusing self-centeredness for selflessness? What, after all, was the difference between Palestinian rage and mine? Between PLO terrorist George Habash's vow to trigger World War III if the Palestinians didn't get a state, and the grim satisfaction with which I imagined a mortally wounded Israel taking with it the rest of the world?

Maybe there was no difference; all peoples with a grudge want to rivet humanity to their pain. But if the JDL was merely the Jewish version of the PLO, so what? I copied down some lines of a W. H. Auden poem into a journal I'd begun keeping:

Those to whom evil is done
do evil in return.

I thought I invoked those words approvingly. But perhaps I meant them as a warning.

That summer, on my way to the United States, I backpacked through Europe. I bought a train pass and crossed borders. I tried to be ironic, to think the kind of thoughts I'd share with Krup: Thirty years ago, a Jew could travel on a train here without even having to buy a ticket . . .

And yet I felt excitement, not irony. I was on my own for a month: free. I didn't *want* to be the Jew in Europe. My collective memories weren't just Jewish but human. I traveled through white seacoast villages in Spain without thinking of the 1492 expulsion of Spanish Jews; in Paris I was drawn more to the city's cafés than to its Holocaust memorials.

I traveled alone. Sometimes I'd pair up for a few days with fellow backpackers, strangers sharing the trust of the road. We looked alike: long hair, tight faded jeans, framed knapsacks and rolled sleeping bags on our backs. I was part of history's first youth internationale, the first generation for whom there were no borders. Europe had been sealed to my father, but it was entirely open to me. No experience revealed more sharply the gap between us: His was history's most traumatized generation of Jews, mine the least.

Only Germany remained off-limits: a hole in the middle of Europe.

Making friends was effortless. You shared a bottle of wine, travel advice, some basic facts of your life. Without an activist persona to shield me, I had to simply be a person among people.

I tested my father's wisdom, instilled into me long ago: At unguarded moments the Goy will reveal his hatred for the Jew. And so I watched peoples' faces when I explained that "Yossi" was a Hebrew name, and when we drank together — that supposedly telltale moment when even the friendliest goy turns ugly — I talked about my year in Israel.

The most intense reaction I got was curiosity. The UN may have been obsessed with Zionism, but most people, it seemed, hardly thought about Jews. That revelation was at once liberating and disturbing: I *wanted* us to be important, central.

On a train in Belgium I met a young woman who invited me to her family's summer home. When she introduced me to her father, he asked, "What kind of name is *that?*"

"A Hebrew name," I said and, just in case he missed the point, added, "a Jewish name."

He laughed. "I thought you said 'Yassir.' We don't like Arafat here."

Small remarks, small kindnesses: But they gave me confidence to continue to explore. Know the world, my father had insisted. But what did I really know of it? I'd looked at reality through an ideological blur; now, slowly, my lense was focusing.

Still, I feared my lack of judgmentalness was betraying a basic trust, dulling my Jewish instincts. I imagined Krup's rebuke: "Very good, Klein. So now you realize the world is complex. But people who appreciate complexity aren't people who *do*; they think, they write books, and they leave the dirty work of making history to those who aren't complex, who aren't as noble as they are. And then they complain about the evil that others do and write beautiful poetry about human suffering.

"And what is this great complexity you've suddenly discovered? That goyim don't have fangs? You meet some friendly goyim and suddenly everything is wonderful. But which do you think represents the world's real relationship to the Jews: a few nice goyim or Auschwitz?"

I went to the Mathausen concentration camp. A train ride from Vienna, into the Austrian countryside.

There was a town near the camp: the town of Mathausen. They hadn't bothered to change the name. Here there was no shame or pretense. Mathausen's people were guilty not because they had lacked courage to resist the Nazis, but because they'd allowed daily life to remain bearable, beside that other Mathausen. Here, hatred of the bystander seemed to me not merely legitimate but essential.

A young man rode by on a bike. I tried to silently curse him; I couldn't find words. I saw elderly people, incriminated by age. But their old faces confused me. What worthy revenge could one extract from these absurdly ordinary people? Suddenly I felt exhausted, depleted even of rage. I fled the town.

The camp was filled with tourists. Speaking in normal voices, even laughing, insane with insensitivity.

I entered the crematorium room. I stood before a brick oven and wrapped myself in phylacteries. Leather strap on my arm like a wire, black box on my head like a transmitter, trying to contact hovering souls.

German-speaking young people entered. I shut my eyes against their words. I felt my presence a rebuke against them, confusing spite for prayer.

I opened my eyes and looked into the oven. There were gum wrappers inside. Unthinking, I reached in to cleanse the desecration. My hand touched something soft, insubstantial: ash. I removed my hand and held it, rigid, at a distance, as if it no longer belonged to me. Perhaps then I realized that one can violate death not only with irreverence but with excessive intimacy.

6.

I returned to New York in fall 1974 to complete my senior year at Brooklyn College.

I had expected to find the JDL boys immersed in plans to save the Jewish people; instead, they were busy devising schemes for making easy money. One spent his time at the racetrack; another opened a furniture store in a black ghetto and boasted about ripping off *"shvartzes"* with long-term credit scams and defective couches whose legs fell off a day after the last payment. There were rumors of extortion, of one friend cheating another in a "serious deal." The same curt street language JDLers once used to describe activism was now effortlessly applied to shady business. They simply diverted their passion for Jewish survival from the collective to the personal.

Krup, honest and austere, was appalled. He was grateful to have me back in New York, if only to have someone to complain to. "This is what the best of our generation is busy with now? Now?! When the oven manufacturers are adding on night shifts to prepare for huge new orders, and the soap manufacturers are putting in bids for Jewish fat? I'm telling you, Klein, the whole fucking world is crazy, crazy! Ahhh!"

Krup found his symbol for the JDL's moral collapse in the gravediggers' strike that was then afflicting New York. When a similar strike had occurred one winter in the late sixties, JDLers voluntarily dug graves in the ice-covered ground, to honor the Jewish practice of burying the body within a day after its death. Now some of the JDL boys were digging graves again — not as volunteers but as scabs. "They're charging rather *stiff* rates," said Krup, cackling, "in fact you might say they're making a *killing.*"

Then there was the Sammy Salowitz Affair. Salowitz, a Borough Park boy and chief JDL bomb maker, was a mechanical genius, ob-

sessed with cars; and a car had been his downfall. After finding un-
licensed guns in its trunk, police had confiscated his Volvo and then
offered to return it — for a price. They also threatened him with
twenty years' imprisonment. Salowitz panicked and told everything,
including the names of four JDLers allegedly involved in the Hurok
death. During the subsequent Hurok trial, police revealed that,
thanks to Salowitz, they'd known the most intimate details of the
JDL underground, even a plan to bomb the Soviet mission using a
remote-control drone airplane.

In the end Salowitz decided he didn't want to betray his best
friends after all and refused to testify. When Salowitz first began
squealing, detectives had assured him that he wouldn't be publicly
exposed as an informer; but they reneged and called him to testify
anyway. In court he revealed that he'd secretly taped his conversations with detectives, including their promise of anonymity; and so
the case was dismissed.

Krup refused to be mollified by the acquittal. He was outraged
that Salowitz was still being treated as one of the boys, despite his
initial betrayal. "This prick was willing to send his friends to jail for
the rest of their lives, for a fucking *Volvo*. Then he changes his
mind — nice guy — and all the boys are beside themselves with gratitude. But it's even worse than that, Klein. They *like* him. They think
he's a good guy, that he's done a lot for Jews." Krup shook his head
and laughed in a hysterical falsetto.

Among the boys, only Krup and I shunned Salowitz, upholding
an absolute standard of friendship and decency. Though Salowitz
had never been friendly to me before, he made a point now of trying to get me to talk; but I turned my back to him. "If we had any
balls," said Krup, "we'd kill him."

In fact, Salowitz had betrayed his friends out of fear, not greed.
And by refusing to ostracize him, the boys were revealing both generosity and wisdom: the less isolated, the less he'd be tempted to
testify.

The new underground, successor to the JDL's Hurok-era terrorist
group, wasn't happening. Krup and Bernie Engel only halfheartedly
tried to raise money and organize cells; they knew that the JDL's
wars were over. Sammy Salowitz, said Krup, had not only destroyed

the old JDL underground but made it impossible for a new one to form. Once an informer had emerged, there could be no more trust among us; even worse, Salowitz had gotten away with it. "Now anybody can turn state's and know that nothing will happen; no one will even be pissed at him. What do you think the Irgun would have done with a Salowitz, let him drink tea in Tel Aviv cafés? We're clowns, Klein. Worse than amateurs. Forget about it. We have no business doing anything."

I felt enormous relief. I was ready to join an underground but didn't trust my endurance under pressure, my capacity for sustained submergence.

Though we couldn't admit it, the JDL had become superfluous. Kahane had insisted that one of the JDL's main goals was to prod the Jewish community, shame the "Nice Irvings" into peaceful but genuine activism; and now that was finally happening. For the first time since the Soviet Jewry movement began exactly ten years earlier in 1964, the Jewish establishment was taking the lead: Like the anti-Vietnam and civil rights protests, their rallies were drawing hundreds of thousands of people. And the Jackson Amendment, linking trade credits for the Soviet Union with emigration, had finally become American law. Anti-Soviet violence was no longer the desperate response of activists trying to promote an obscure cause; the Soviet Jewry movement had gone mainstream.

Still, however futilely, we continued to plan, as though addicted to intensity. One night Krup and I drove around a beachfront neighborhood where Soviet diplomats were said to live, looking for cars with diplomatic license plates; we planned to return later with Molotov cocktails. But we found no suitable target and didn't try again. Another time I joined a stakeout of a Soviet ship docked at a pier along the West Side Highway, to determine where a sniper could fire from without being detected. But no sniper ever appeared.

The JDL split into rival camps. Kahane created a series of front groups that attracted the same handful of followers and folded in a matter of months — groups like SOIL, an acronym for the clumsy title, "Save Our Israel Land," which Krup called "DIRT."

Joey Levy, after serving four months in jail for forging gun permit applications, became a leader of the anti-Kahane faction, which considered Kahane's Knesset ambitions a betrayal of the JDL's original goal of defending Diaspora Jews. Krup and I kept aloof, on the increasingly unlikely pretext that we were "saving ourselves for more serious things."

At a JDL convention, the opposing factions tried to reconcile, but the meeting ended in flying chairs. There were now officially two JDLs, though in reality there was no longer even one. Joey's faction denounced Kahane to the press as an opportunist and an embezzler who'd diverted JDL funds to his Knesset campaign. Kahane called Joey's faction "saboteurs" and ran an ad in the *Jewish Press* with the heading, "Strength with Sanity, Militancy with Normalcy." Krup and I laughed long about that: Meir Kahane, the madman of Jerusalem, was proclaiming himself a paragon of "normal" activism.

In speeches and articles Kahane's brilliant sarcasm lost its perfect timing. He rambled and threatened, strongly hinting that he was a prophet sent by God to warn of the coming destruction: a holocaust in the Diaspora "far worse" than Auschwitz, with an assault against Israel culminating in an international army marching on Jerusalem, just as the biblical prophets had foreseen.

Had Kahane stopped there, Krup and I might have still found his ideas compelling, however repulsed we were by the man himself. Certainly our reading of events was no less apocalyptic. But Kahane went further: He created a theology of Jewish rage and despair.

According to Kahane, the chosen people had to be kept in splendid isolation, consecrated to God and protected from the spiritually polluting goyim. If we ghettoized ourselves, God would protect us from our enemies. But the more we tried to assimilate among the goyim, the more contempt they would show us and the less divine protection we'd receive. Kahane's favorite example was the fate of the German Jews: They had tried to out-German the Germans in their love for the Fatherland, and the result was Hitler.

But we had to do more than just passively accept our ostracism: We had to actively provoke it, by committing outrageous acts that would guarantee our final expulsion from humanity. In using Israel's military might without restraint, we would prove that we feared no one but God; and he would be forced to redeem us. For Kahane, then, Jewish power was no longer meant to improve our political situation but to further isolate us and make us utterly vulnerable: activism in the service of fatalism.

And so Kahane's activism became more extreme, more desperate. To make certain that Israel would be left totally friendless, he urged the "transfer" of all Arabs from its borders — not the voluntary departure he'd been advocating until then, but violent expulsion. He marched with his boys through Arab towns, beer cans in hand, smashing windows; in speeches he called Arabs "dogs." And he demanded prison terms for Jews and Arabs who slept together — a direct if unconscious echo of Nazi Germany's anti-Semitic "Nuremberg laws."

I tried to convince myself that Kahane's hatred was an understandable if crazed response to the Holocaust and the isolation of Israel. And yet Kahane was drawing not only on emotion but on theology. He gathered the anti-Gentile quotes scattered through Jewish religious writings and the rabbinic laws meant to keep Jews and Gentiles apart, and placed those at the heart of Judaism — for Kahane, a religion of Jewish superiority and Gentile subservience. Though hardly mainstream, Kahane's theology was recognizable enough to be, in his words, "authentically Jewish." As always, Kahane was confronting us with an unbearable truth about ourselves.

However tangentially, I felt implicated in the evil that had been released. Once again, Kahane became my teacher, but this time in reverse, warning me against the excesses of rage.

Bernie called.

"Klein? Whatever you're doing Friday, cancel it. I got a big *mitzvah* for you, a very big *mitzvah*. Believe me, for this one you'll thank me."

Bernie was constantly sending me on missions. Just recently he'd called and said, "Pack your bags, you're flying to Kentucky, to give our boys moral support." "Our boys" were two JDLers sitting in a juvenile prison in Louisville; and I was to get into the prison, he'd said, by masquerading as a chaplain. I tried to explain that, at age twenty-two, I couldn't possibly pass as a rabbi, but he laughed and said, "Put on a tie, don't forget to wear pants, and act like you know what you're doing." When I arrived at the prison gate, I was greeted as "Rah-bbi Klein" and taken to our prisoners. Bernie had arranged everything.

Now Bernie had a new assignment for me. He explained that Volodya Shlechtman, the Russian who'd worked for Kahane's Knesset campaign, was in trouble again with the Israeli authorities; he'd come to New York to raise money to cover legal expenses and help his family. "He's going from court case to court case. The Israelis are throwing the book at him; his children are hungry."

"Shlechtman is a lowlife," I said.

"Sure he's a lowlife," said Bernie. "But he's a Jewish hero, and we gotta help him."

I waited with foreboding for Bernie to reveal the plan. "Yos, here's what you're going to do: This Friday, you and Shlechtman will pay our friend Mel Finkle a visit." Mel Finkle was a businessman who'd helped found the Soviet Jewry movement; though marginal ever since, he'd continued to identify himself as one of the movement's leaders, addicted to self-promotion.

Bernie continued: "Go to his office, say around two o'clock, just when he's getting ready to close for Shabbos. Tell him you want a thousand dollars. If he pleads poverty, tell him you and Shlechtman will make Shabbos in his office. And if he threatens to call the cops, tell him you'll call the *Jewish Press* and the story will be all over the city: 'Two Jewish Heroes Arrested by Mel Finkle.' I promise you: He'll sell his children to keep that story out of the paper."

It seemed mad. Someone was going to give us a thousand dollars just because we threatened to write about him in the *Jewish Press?* I wanted to tell Bernie to leave me alone with his crazy schemes. Instead, I said feebly, "If it's such a big *mitzvah,* why don't you do it?"

"Are you kidding me? Do you know how many times I've already pulled this on him? If I show up in his office, he won't call the cops, he'll kill me with his bare hands. They'll have to bury me in pieces: 'Here lies Bernie's arms, over there you can find the head.' "

"What do I do if he insists he doesn't have the money?"

"Give him twenty-four hours. Let him raise the money from his cronies in *shul.* Tell him you expect a call from him five minutes after Shabbos. You don't call him: Never do that. Make him call you. We're yet easy on him. A thousand dollars is *nothing* to a guy like this. He spends that much on one meal, whore what he is. Be tough, Yos. I guarantee you, a thousand percent, this can't fail. And Yos: cash, no checks."

At two o'clock that Friday, Shlechtman and I appeared in Finkle's office. Finkle, a red-faced, heaving man, greeted us warmly, assuming we'd come to pay our respects. He apologized that he couldn't spend time with us because he was closing for Shabbos but urged us to come back for a talk.

"I'll tell you the truth, Mr. Finkle," I said, "we're not here to socialize. We need a thousand dollars for Volodya's family. I think it's a shame that a man who has done so much for Jews has to beg to feed his children."

Volodya looked mournful, a hoodlum saddened by the ways of the world.

"I'd love to help you out, boys, but a thousand dollars — it's the end of the season. Maybe in a few months."

"Mr. Finkle, we're not leaving until we get the money."

"This is outrageous! You will leave immediately!"

"You can call the police. We already have a reporter from the *Jewish Press* waiting to write up the story."

"I don't have the money!"

"We're reasonable people, Mr. Finkle. We'll give you twenty-four hours to raise the money in *shul*. If you don't, we're back here Monday morning with a reporter. Here's my number. Five minutes after Shabbos I'll expect your call. And please, Mr. Finkle, cash. We know we can count on you."

Finkle called immediately after Shabbos. "I got it," he said. "You can pick it up at my office on Monday. And don't ever come to me again."

I felt thrilled, and queasy. I'd pulled it off: one more notch in my career as Jewish militant, one more goof to laugh about with Krup and the boys. And yet I had just extorted a decent, if foolish, man; almost without thinking, I'd slipped into gangsterism.

Soon afterward Volodya walked out on his starving family and moved in with a girlfriend. He got a job representing one of the South African apartheid homelands and appeared on Israeli TV with half-naked tribal women, dancing around him like a pagan god.

7.

The JDL was dead, my activist career finished. Without demonstrations and schemes, I didn't know how to pace my life or give it meaning. I stayed away from the establishment-led Soviet Jewry rallies and no longer even knew the names of the latest Jewish prisoners in Russia.

I graduated in June 1975 from Brooklyn College, with a degree, by default, in Jewish studies. Until my senior year I didn't know what my major would be; when I tallied my credits, Jewish studies won. I didn't bother attending the graduation ceremony and only months later picked up my diploma from the registrar's office. I told my mother she could frame it if she wanted to.

I spent my time with nonactivist friends, getting high — or "wasted," as we more appropriately called it. I earned my money at the unemployment office.

My father and I constantly fought. He insisted that I become a "finished product," which meant getting a Ph.D. The subject didn't concern him, only the degree itself, the "piece paper." A professor, he explained, could earn a living no matter where he found himself stranded. Refugee insurance: the accordionist professor, all angles covered.

I told him I had no intention of wasting more time in school. "So what will you do," he shouted, "become a nothing?"

I moved out of my parents' house, rented an apartment on Manhattan's West Side and began writing an autobiographical novel. Krup's critique of my life was no more flattering than my father's: "You're turning into a cliché, Klein: the Brooklyn boy who moves to 'the city' to become a novelist. Gimme a break."

Krup was wondering if he could still trust me. He feared I was losing my edge, the moral judgmentalness we prided ourselves on sharing. At times, he said, I reminded him of his fellow students at Columbia University, his most damning epithet: philosophers rather than doers, liberals rather than revolutionaries.

I was changing, he said with a concern that moved me. Though I tried to deny it, he was right. Our cynicism no longer energized but depressed me and seemed to me no less a distortion of reality than the naïveté we so despised, a mere pretense of knowing.

For the first time there were misunderstandings between us, awkward pauses in our frenetic conversation, harsh words and clumsy apologies. One day while we were hanging out with Bernie, Krup said something about "niggers." He routinely used ethnic slurs, despising liberal sentimentality. I used them, too — except for "nig-ger." Saying that word, I thought, would turn me into a white man. I was a Jew, temporarily moored in America; I didn't want to take on its guilt.

"Don't use that word," I said abruptly to Krup.

"What word?" he asked, perplexed.

" 'Nigger.' I hate it."

"Oh, I see, Mr. Liberal. *You* try living with them and then talk."

"You got a handkerchief?" Bernie asked Krup. "Klein's heart is bleeding."

We all laughed. But the incident was one more mark against me, additional proof that I was slipping.

I didn't want to jeopardize our friendship, couldn't imagine living without its intensity. I trusted Krup — his intelligence, his decency, most of all his selflessness. He too feared a rupture between us. In an unusual show of affection, he said to me, "Our friendship is a real blessing, and maybe we can turn it into some good for the Jews. Maybe we can even turn a buck off it if we're lucky."

And so we tried to pretend that we could still be funny and out-rageous together, that we were still noble outlaws to whom all was permitted. One night we drove to Yeshiva University, stood outside the dormitory, and shouted anti-Semitic abuses, daring "the kikes" to come down and fight us. No one did. Vintage Krup and Klein: Rubbing the Jews' faces in their own cowardice and reminding them that they lived in a world of enemies.

In honor of the Salute to Israel parade, New York Jewry's annual solidarity march up Fifth Avenue, Krup prepared a surprise for us: two T-shirts imprinted with the words "Gas Me, I'm Jewish." The slogan was Krup's answer to those giant buttons sold at the parade that said, "Kiss Me, I'm Jewish," and his point was: A goy will sooner gas you than kiss you.

We wore the T-shirts to the parade, strolling along Fifth Avenue among the celebratory crowds. As people read our message, their faces turned horrified; some cursed and shouted at us. We were de-lighted: Nothing cheered us more than upsetting American Jews.

Krup announced he was moving to Israel and joining the army. "There's nothing left for us to do here, Klein. Finished. It's time to go."

His decision came as no surprise: We'd been discussing that option ever since the Yom Kippur War. He assumed I would join him. But I told him I wasn't ready, that I didn't want to go until I had some notion of what I would do when I got out of the army.

In fact, I was thinking of becoming a journalist. My plan was to develop contacts in New York and then try my luck as a freelancer in Jerusalem for American magazines. Being a journalist approximated a new idea I had of myself as a post-Holocaust Jew: one who knew the world's darkest corners, whom nothing human could shock. A journalist went everywhere, saw everything. And I still believed, as I did as a boy, in journalism's redemptive power: A reporter could sound alarms and expose hidden suffering.

A journalist is at once participant and observer, and I wanted to live that duality. I'd often brought a pad and pen to demonstrations, standing outside police barricades, removed from other protesters. My need to record was in some way the opposite of the activist impulse, and it was noted among the JDL boys. "Who knows what Klein is writing all the time?" a friend said one night in Bernstein's. "One day he'll write about us in some book and screw us good." Everyone at the table laughed, but the incident reinforced the distance between me and my activist friends.

I told Krup my plan. Journalists, he said, were "a bunch of self-serving, pretentious whoremongers, whose contribution to society may be slightly higher than streetwalkers and numbers runners, but falls far short of any truly productive group, like plumbers and migrant workers."

Krup feared the journalist's objectivity. He understood, better than I did, that my becoming a journalist would conflict with our shared passion. A good journalist empathized with opposing sides of a story; Krup rightly suspected that in knowing many truths, I would abandon our absolute judgments, betray the basis of our friendship.

I went to see him off at the airport.

He gave me a parting gift: his precious copy of *The Deed*, the book about the Stern Group's two young assassins. It was as if he was trying to remind me of the pact of self-sacrifice that bound us. Inside the cover was inscribed, "To my friend and my comrade, Please

take this from me; not in thanks, not as a present, simply because I
want you to have it. All my love, The Krup."

We embraced.

"You're really not coming," he said.

"I *will* come," I promised. "As soon as I get myself together."

I didn't tell him that that process depended on our separation.

I felt aimless. One day I'd meet with friends to plan a documentary
film on the Holocaust or an alternative Jewish magazine, and spend
the next day drugged, listening to the Velvet Underground sing about
heroin.

I reread the Holocaust classics with stunned disbelief, as if only
now discovering the camps. I felt poisoned by the intrusion of my
father's knowledge into my life. I'd grown up with a vocabulary in
which daily life and the demonic commingled: oven, gas, shower,
train. Suddenly the violation of innocent words enraged me.

From the moment my father introduced me to the Holocaust, he
taught me how to confront it: with Jewish resistance and solidarity.
But now, no longer an activist, I faced its enormity without antidotes
and felt, for the first time, inconsolable. I sat in my apartment and
wept; I felt I could go to bed crying, wake up the next morning, and
find myself still weeping.

And yet it wasn't the Holocaust alone that I mourned for, but my
own transience. Not just mass murder, "Jewish" death, but anonymous disappearance.

Ironically, the Holocaust had made death abstract for me. By
equating death with the murder of Jews, I submerged my fear of
mortality into the collective experience of genocide. When death became murder, it was no longer an amorphous, unstoppable force but
a tangible enemy one could resist and even defeat. I could save myself as a Jew, like my father outwitting the Nazis; but as a human
being, confronting a random vanishing, I was helpless.

Death had separated me from the rest of humanity: The unique
way the Jews had died seemed to confirm our distinctiveness. That
wound obscured the universality of death; I'd felt true solidarity only
with other Jews, survivors by proxy of Auschwitz.

But now I walked the streets, watching passersby and thinking,
"They're all going to die, *we're* all going to die." I felt a sudden, dis-

orienting commonality with my fellow human victims, pathetic creatures marked for a mysterious disappearance, unable to resist or even understand.

I dreamed I was in a giant warehouse, filled with Nazis chasing Jews. Every time a Nazi caught a Jew, he would pour instantly drying cement on the Jew's feet. Finally, I was caught: unable to escape, only to shout and wave my arms in helpless rage.

Seven

Emancipation

1.

MY FATHER died of a heart attack on a trip to Israel in the summer of 1978. He was fifty-nine years old.

I flew to Jerusalem for the funeral. A small crowd of our Israeli relatives and friends gathered in the courtyard of the hospital where he'd died, before a stone hut in which his body lay. I watched their weeping as if from a distance. I could almost hear my father's strong, slightly ironic voice, "Here I outlive almost everyone from my town, from my whole generation what was in Europe; I come out from the ground, from my own grave; I survive who knows how many heart attack and raise two children; so where is the tragedy?"

I didn't join the demonstrative mourning. My father would understand: At times of death you don't mourn, you *do*. I was more interested in the details of the funeral, in making sure my mother was all right. The only time my father allowed himself to mourn for his town was at happy occasions, the wedding or bar mitzvah of a survivor's child. At those moments — when joy protected against endless mourning — he would openly weep, recalling the absent guests.

Relatives urged me to enter the hut, to ask my father's forgiveness for whatever I'd done to wrong him. I went inside. The body lay on a stretcher atop a stone slab and was wrapped in a black-and-white-striped prayer shawl.

I didn't ask his forgiveness. We'd fought often, sometimes shouting at each other, but never waited too long before reconciling with apologies and hugs. We'd done our best.

I listened to the weeping outside and thought, "They're mourning for themselves." My father was the first among his friends to die; and who else should have reminded his fellow survivors that death can't be evaded, challenge any wishful thinking that their survival was somehow permanent?

He had seemed to me invincible, capable of eluding any threat, and yet at the same time alive only conditionally, his heart a delicate web waiting to break. When my mother, speaking in a faraway, sedated voice, had phoned from Jerusalem to tell me of his death, I realized I'd been waiting for that news ever since I was a boy, when he'd had his first heart attack.

We went to the cemetery. I rode in the burial society's van, flanked by Hasidic gravediggers, silent in dusty black robes. My father lay on the stretcher at our feet. In Jerusalem bodies are buried without coffins, in prayer shawls or shrouds, close to the holy earth from which they are expected to someday rise.

The cemetery was on a white hill without shade, terraced with flat white gravestones. On a distant hill rose a tall stone finger: a mosque built over the burial place of Samuel the Prophet. My father and I had visited it in the summer of 1967, searching for ancestors who hadn't simply vanished — as his parents had done — but had left behind graves, evidence of existence. Yet only now was our family really reclaiming its link with the Land of Israel.

The Hasidim lowered him into the ground. Then they formed a circle around the grave and did a kind of dance. I said kaddish, the mourner's prayer praising God's eternity. Though disoriented from the flight and the suddenness of my father's death, I repeated the words with a deliberate strength, as if he were speaking through me.

*   *   *

I moved back to my parents' home in Borough Park, to be with my mother and run the candy business. I put on my father's suits and inhabited his life.

Each Shabbos, like a lone funeral procession, I went to say kaddish in another *shtiebl,* or Hasidic synagogue. They were often no more than a small room, though the *shtiebls* of larger sects resembled halls; one even contained stadium-style stands, to grant Hasidim a better view of their rebbe in prayer. But no matter what their size, *shtiebls* were invariably crowded, as though they'd been deliberately built to just barely accommodate their worshippers, to create the illusion of multitudes.

Growing up, I'd resented Hasidim for trying to transform Borough Park into prewar Europe, a society of victims; and I'd escaped into militant Zionism. I'd even seen them as an enemy: opposed to the existence of a secular Jewish state, aloof from our struggle to free Soviet Jewry, they seemed to care only for their shrunken, transplanted sects, not the Jewish people's collective resurrection.

I'd learned to despise them from my father. He couldn't forgive them for blindly following rebbes who opposed Zionism before the war, the single exit to life; he couldn't forgive the rebbes for not being the saviors their followers believed them to be.

Yet I hadn't realized that he'd also loved Hasidim, perhaps as one loves exasperating children. He had, after all, raised me among them, insisted that I learn their songs and prayers. He wanted me to know their innocence and their sarcastic humor; the camaraderie with which they shut out the world like a tight circle of dancers, the petty infighting to which they ascribed cosmic meaning. He loved and despised them for the same reason: their harmlessness.

Now I went among them, trying to share that complicated intimacy. When I entered a *shtiebl,* I felt all eyes merge in a single sidelong glance — that discreet, suspicious look with which Hasidim probe passersby on the street, averting eye contact but alert for hostile outbursts.

I was an intruder. I had no black fedora or sidelocks, none of the Hasidic signs meant to mark Jews apart. My long hair and "modern" clothes came from a world beyond Borough Park — the world that created Auschwitz.

But then I'd rise to say kaddish; and in their loud, deliberate "amens," I sensed an instant acceptance. Afterward someone invariably asked my Hebrew name and the Hebrew name of my father and summoned me to bless the Torah. Then the rebbe waved me over, asked me for whom I was saying kaddish, and blessed me. The Hasidim pressed my hand and urged me to return. Despite my appearance, I belonged among them; for we shared the same Judaism, a loyalty to Europe's dead parents.

Borough Park was thriving. New *shtiebls* and religious schools were going up in every available space. Lots weren't allowed to remain vacant for long: Borough Park's reconstruction tolerated no void, no reminder of emptiness. School buses imprinted with the names of vanished towns filled the streets; little boys with sidelocks and black velvet caps shouted from the windows in Yiddish, unaware that they were speaking a murdered language. Pregnant women wheeled baby carriages holding two and even three small children spaced one year apart, while older siblings trailed behind.

What had incited this profusion of life? My parents' friends had had few children: There was no time for large families; there were health problems from the war. Each child was a miracle. Yet from those eked-out families were emerging dozens of grandchildren. Young Hasidim of my generation were reproducing so generously that it seemed they'd decided to avenge Hitler by substituting one child for each murdered relative.

However improbable, Borough Park's dare had worked. The Hasidic survivors restored prewar Europe, leaping over the abyss and returning to the time of intactness. The ghetto had prevailed — a contagion of separatism that began with a distancing from the gentile world, then from all Jews who weren't ultra-Orthodox, and finally from competing ultra-Orthodox sects and even rivals within one's own group.

Borough Park's victory over the present was confirmed by the survivors' grandchildren. They were growing up unaware that their community was a scale model of a destroyed world; that their own grandparents, stalwarts of Orthodox propriety, had once lived as Jewish outlaws, outside the bounds of Torah.

My father had told me of that time just after the war, when the survivors, a handful of young people, trickled back to Nagy-Károly from death camps and hiding places. Confronting the devastation, it seemed to them that the Nazis had won, had usurped the Jewish vision of an ordered world with the nihilist's vision of an empty cosmos.

They lived without restraint, drinking and gambling and sleeping with whomever was available, whomever had survived. Then, one night, a few months after his return to Nagy-Károly, my father imagined his parents standing before him. Ashamed, he abruptly left the nonstop card game and put aside the whiskey bottle. And he turned his parents' empty home into a shelter for young Jewish women.

For several years, the survivors existed on the margins. Some worked as black marketeers; my father — in later years a scrupulous businessman who despised financial trickery — smuggled cigarettes. They married quickly, almost randomly: One woman was attracted to her future husband because he wore matching socks, a rare sign of intactness. My father married a woman who'd lived through the camps, then divorced her when he discovered she was still sleeping around.

By the time I began to know them in the late 1950s, the survivors had already survived the postwar chaos. Marriage, business, immigration to America — most of all, the arrival of children — helped distance the past. Still, there was a mystery in their ability to not merely survive but thrive, some power expressed by Borough Park's vitality.

My father's restoration to life began with an act of generosity, taking care of Nagy-Károly's lost Jewish girls; other survivors had similar revelations of renewal. It was as if Jewish survival through the centuries had been mere rehearsal for that moment after the war, when those young people returned — tentatively, with irony and bitterness — to purpose.

What was truly essential about the Holocaust, it seemed to me now, wasn't how the Jews were killed but how they survived. Borough Park thrived on *mitzvot*, good deeds. One group specialized in leaving food on the doorsteps of poor people — anonymously, so as not to shame them; another group provided dowries for poor brides; another visited hospital patients. One Hasidic rabbi specialized in contacts with surgeons; his disciples, sick survivors, filled his living room through the night. Borough Park's Hasidim were trying to defeat the

Holocaust by resurrecting the world it had destroyed; they re-created the only alternative to Auschwitz that they knew, a society that valued children, Torah study, charity, life.

I wasn't a practicing Jew. Borough Park's vision of religious intact-ness didn't tempt me: I saw myself as part of a generation for whom the tradition had ruptured and from whose brokenness would emerge new ways of being Jewish.

But I believed in God, believed that behind its veil of chaos existed a purposeful universe. Ironically, I drew my faith in part from the Holocaust. The Final Solution seemed in essence an attempt by nihilism to defeat meaning. Hitler believed that the Jews had invented morality and the soul — both of which enervated man's ability to survive in brute nature. Destroying the Jews, then, would free humanity for its Darwinian war of survival.

But it wasn't enough to destroy the Jews; first they had to be degraded, transformed into living exhibits of the absence of soul. The process began with ghettoization: a controlled experiment meant to turn those who rejected the notion of animal man into animals themselves. Education and prayer became capital crimes; a Jew's entire life would be directed toward competing for gradually diminishing available food.

The Nazis perfected their experiment in the death camps. Transported from the ghettos in cattlecars, branded with numbers, the Jews became laboratory animals. Dr. Mengele's use of Auschwitz inmates as medical guinea pigs wasn't merely another, more intense atrocity, but the philosophical heart of the Final Solution.

And yet Hitler's attempt to prove the absence of soul failed. It was defeated by all those who secretly blessed their food and marked sacred time in the ghettos and camps, who refused to be reduced to matter. Starving inmates fasted on Yom Kippur. A friend of my mother's, imprisoned in Auschwitz, picked out anything resembling meat from her soup, even though Judaism permits eating nonkosher food in life-threatening situations: She wanted to reaffirm humanity over animal need.

The one commandment I still observed was *tefilin*, phylacteries. Every morning I sat cross-legged on the floor, wrapped the black leather strap around my arm, and fastened the black leather box containing the prayer of God's oneness on my head. Whatever the rest of my day would be like, I'd at least begin the morning with a negation of nihilism. I would sit quietly and try to link with the power of all those who ever wore *tefilin*. Often I evoked one particular image, a Holocaust photograph: A tall, bearded Jew stands surrounded by laughing SS men; at his feet are a row of corpses, covered in prayer shawls. The SS men have given him a few moments to say his last prayers; in their mockery is the ancient pagan taunt against the Jews: Where is your invisible God now? He has no time to adjust the strap dangling from his arm, the box crooked on his head. His face is both severe and calm, as though addressing future generations, reminding them of the power of *tefilin*.

The laughter of the SS men belonged to a meaningless cosmos; the Jew's calm, to an ordered world where good ultimately defeats evil. I had no doubt who in that scene was a more trustworthy witness of how reality worked.

For all his bitterness, my father wasn't a bitter man. His last words to my mother in the hospital were "I love you"; and love was the strongest impression he left behind.

When I was a boy he would kiss me fiercely, as if trying to inhale me, leaving wet marks on my cheek. Until he died we kissed each other after any brief parting, as if relieved to be safely reunited. People loved him: Though he claimed little use for friends — "In war you learn that only family you can trust" — many considered him their closest friend, the man to whom they confided their troubles and with whom they most enjoyed laughing. Indeed, my most vivid memory of him was his laughter: mouth wide and voice deep, head thrown back as though from the force of the joke, surrendering to delight.

Our home was intact, even happy. Unlike most of their friends, who'd married spouses because they were the ones who survived, my parents married for love; and they remained, in some way, newlyweds. After dinner my father would abruptly stop washing the dishes and waltz my mother around the kitchen. They didn't quarrel or mock each other's weaknesses; and though he often shouted, especially at me, he never raised his voice to her.

He remained an idealist. He was the only one among his friends who taught his children that group rather than personal survival was the real lesson of the Holocaust: You survived into something larger than yourself. The other survivors were trying to evade Auschwitz, inhabit the corners of a world they couldn't control; whereas he confronted the Holocaust, to negate it. Perhaps that was because he hadn't been in a camp, hadn't been broken like the others. Whatever the reason, he managed to live without illusion or cynicism.

He became a believer. He saw in Jewish survival, in his own persistence, an expression of a power that penetrated and transcended him. He was far less dogmatic in his faith than he'd been in his skepticism. I once asked him, with teenage irony, whether he actually believed that God had handed the Torah to the Jews on a desert mountain, and he'd replied, "What do I know anymore what I believe and don't believe? Only I know one thing: that there is some great mystery with this little Jewish people that no power in the world can destroy."

My father most closely approximated the person I hoped to become. Like him, I wanted to stop fearing the body's death, know that the soul endures and can't be violated except by one's own weakness. Like him, I wanted to know everything the cynic knew, penetrate the most brutal reality, and emerge praising life.

I wanted to be what he almost became: a Jew who related to the world not with the grudges of a victim but with the generosity of a survivor.

2.

The year of mourning ended. I quit the family business and went back to trying to become a journalist. I began writing a story about the JDL's collapse, hoping to interest some New York publication.

I moved to the East Village, a Lower Manhattan neighborhood populated by punk rockers, junkies, and aspiring artists. My apartment — roaches crawling behind wallpaper, a sheet for a bedroom door — was across the street from Hell's Angels headquarters. The janitor of my building, an old Jewish woman, carried a pistol. At night Puerto Ricans lit fires in garbage cans and rolled them in the gutter.

My roommate, Abe Stern, had been born in Poland after the

Holocaust and then moved as a boy with his parents to Los Angeles. Abe had drooping eyes and a thick, brooding mustache, which he stroked slowly and menacingly in response to a perceived insult. Abe's most important biographical fact was that he'd grown up in Poland with a blatantly Jewish name. When his father had gone to register his newborn son, a well-meaning clerk said to him, "You can't do this to your boy. Give him a normal name, like Stanislaw." Abe's father — with courage and self-destructive pride — insisted on a Jewish name for his son. Abe was as proud and stubborn as his father, as though he'd received those traits with his name.

The clerk was right: Abe was marked for a miserable childhood. He was publicly mocked by teachers; when he was six, his violin instructor told him to forget music and think about business, "something you people are good at." Once Abe showed me a photograph of his first-grade class, taken during an outing: The entire class of blond smiling children is grouped together, except for grim, black-haired Abe, who stands at a distance, alone.

Abe identified wholly with the Jews. Every UN vote to ostracize Israel was a personal affront to him, evoked his own isolation as a child in Poland. Like Israel, he too had been attacked and then accused of being the aggressor.

Most of all, Abe wanted to help the Jews, perform some historical act as a love-offering for his people. But he was stymied by circumstance, the only child of clinging parents. He wanted desperately to move to Israel; but his mother, who called from Los Angeles at least three times a day, promised she would die if he left America. "Maybe I'll kill her first," he said.

Abe seemed intent on sacrificing himself; the only question was how. He hung out all night in punk bars and then went to downtown clubs that opened at dawn. He drank in Russian nightclubs in Brighton Beach, where waiters brought a bottle of vodka for each diner and gold-toothed Gypsies danced in the aisles. He was flagrantly generous, as if he were about to die and no longer needed possessions. He drew on his bar mitzvah bank account to subsidize us, and we ate well in restaurants until the account emptied.

Abe was a brilliant political analyst: He had a European Jew's ability to predict long-term trends, especially menacing ones, and a feel for the perverse calculations of totalitarian regimes. But he'd abandoned his political science studies and dropped out of college, contemptuous of his fellow students as self-centered careerists. Yet he also felt inadequate to them, uncertain how to write term papers and too restless to study for exams. Though he spoke a perfect English, he doubted whether he really possessed a language of his own, having learned English as an immigrant while remaining with a child's Polish.

All of Abe's various wounds — the Polish children who abused him, the anti-Zionists trying to destroy Israel, the successful jerks in college, his mother — merged into one undifferentiated rage. If only Abe could avenge the Jews by humiliating their enemies, he would somehow make everything right.

Once, in a restaurant, he found himself sitting beside a group of Polish tourists. He stood and proposed a toast to Poland. The Poles solemnly raised their glasses. "May Russian tanks invade your country and crush it," he said. The outraged Poles hurriedly left.

In the East Village, punk was happening. Abe and I stalked the streets and punk clubs, witnesses to the collapse of the West. Abe insisted that punk culture was inspired by the Final Solution: the leather clothes and Nazi Iron Crosses sold in punk shops, the lines outside clubs presided over by a bouncer wordlessly pointing to those allowed in, like a "selection," and the tattoo they stamped on your hand when you entered. We hung out in punk bars, where teenagers threw up on the bathroom floor and the sound of beer bottles crashing into bins competed with screams from the jukebox; we "interviewed" punks like Anton, who wore his hair in greased strands arching over his forehead like spider legs and who thought that Hitler had been the West's last chance to save itself. I took notes; Abe drank.

It was 1979, and apocalypse had become the fad. Street posters announced performances by punk bands called World War 3, Survival Oblivious, Biological Warfare. On the pavements someone had stenciled the words "Nuclear Target." Punks wore their hair orange as though blowtorched, or like spikes down the center of shaved heads, resembling Hollywood's vision of mutants after a nuclear blast. Women wore black mesh stockings with saddle shoes, long white dinner gloves and children's plastic sunglasses, like survivors of a dead civilization randomly assembling its artifacts.

Suddenly people felt the Bomb hanging over them like a fatal illness, realizing that the big bang of earth's creation could be reversed. There seemed to be no objective reason for why fear of the bomb was spreading now — just a delayed unleashing of dread. For me it was a kind of vindication, as if my childhood fears of another holocaust had infected the world.

Abe and I talked incessantly about the coming apocalypse: Wall Street crashes, California floods, baffling new plagues, street gangs ruling nuclear-devastated cities. For us it was no coincidence that the war which produced Auschwitz had ended in Hiroshima; that a German Jewish scientist, a refugee from Nazism, had invented the Bomb. The murder of European Jewry was humanity's motive for self-annihilation, rationale for the nuclear age. The Bomb was the suicide weapon; Auschwitz, the suicide note.

And it was surely no coincidence that Germany had become nuclear ground zero, frontline for any future Soviet-American war. With a smug knowing, Abe and I watched the TV news reports of marches in Berlin against nuclear extinction. One day Abe brought home a copy of *Time* magazine with a photo of German antinuclear demonstrators on the cover: One of them was wearing a gas mask. "So *nu*, Abe, what does it mean?" I asked, playing straight man.

"*Is du a Gott in der velt*," he said in Yiddish, There is a God in the world.

But something was wrong: I wasn't entirely enjoying seeing the Germans squirm. The universality of fate imposed by the Bomb sabotaged my malicious pleasure. I didn't inhabit a separate Jewish planet; however distasteful to me, Germany's problem was also mine. We shared the same air and, potentially, the same fate.

Growing up, I had naturally assumed that any genocidal threat against me would be "Jewish." But somehow I'd forgotten about the Bomb. Annihilation had become nondiscriminatory; and my father's hole, an intimation of the underground shelters to which surviving humanity might someday flee a poisoned earth.

One day a bum approached Abe and me for a handout. We gave him some money, and he said, "You're Jews, aren't you."

"Is that a problem?" said Abe, slowly stroking his mustache.

"I can tell you're Jews," he said, slurring. "You got good Jewish hearts."

"Are *you* Jewish?" Abe asked.

"Hell no, Irish! But I put in my time fighting for Israel."

"*You* fought for Israel?"

"Damn right. Volunteered in forty-eight."

He rolled up his torn, dirty sleeve: Tattooed onto his forearm was the word "Israel."

"I spent time in the slammer for this. I was working on a boat when some bastard saw the tattoo and called me a kike. You better believe he never called nobody a kike again."

"Why did you fight for Israel?"

"Eightieth Division. Buchenwald," he said and began to weep.

The 80th Division, I explained to Abe, had liberated the Buchenwald concentration camp in 1945.

The bum began shouting, "Never let them put your people in ovens again, do you hear me? Never let nobody do that to you!" And he started to weep again.

We gave him more money. "Never again!" he shouted as we walked away.

I wondered whether the Jews were friendless, whether the "righteous Gentiles," as we condescendingly called our allies, were really rare exceptions.

My father never taught me to hate non-Jews, only to be wary of them; but I had misunderstood him. He never called them, as I did, "goyim," but Gentiles, non-Jewish people, a formal respect. He despised any violation of a person's dignity. Once, as a teenager, I'd shoved off some Italian kids sitting on his van. When we got into the car, he shouted at me, "That's how I teach you to behave? Like animal?"

And yet when it came to intergroup relations, it was precisely the law of the jungle that he taught me. One had to be decent and generous toward fellow human beings; but when individuals became collective, there was no room for mercy, only the hardness of history. Jews like himself had been saved by Gentiles during the war; but "the Jews" had been alone, and always would be.

But I knew otherwise. The Soviet Jewry movement had appealed to the conscience of humanity, and it had won precisely because that conscience had been roused. Western scientists "adopted" refusenik colleagues, and Christian clergymen held prayer vigils; American journalists and diplomats based in the Soviet Union provided publicity and protection for refuseniks. My own experience was the exact opposite of Jews during the Holocaust: The State Department — which had blocked rescue efforts in the 1940s — had protected me and my friends in Moscow.

Non-Jewish backing for Soviet Jewry went far beyond a "few decent goyim." Almost the entire American Congress had supported us. Indeed, the old, bitter line that only Jews would help other Jews had been reversed by the Jackson Amendment — championed by gentile congressmen with minor Jewish constituencies and supported only tepidly by the Jewish lobby.

But what about the global isolation of Israel, the demonization of Zionism, the persistence of anti-Semitism even after Auschwitz — as startling in its way as the survival of the Jews? I struggled with the contradictory evidence, wondering whether a Jew should remain wary or risk being open to the chance of goodwill.

3.

I joined a fiction writing class at the City College of New York. I'd submitted a draft of my JDL story to an editor at the New York weekly, the *Village Voice,* who encouraged me to develop it; and I was looking for direction on how to write characters and scenes. A friend of mine studying in City College's creative writing master's program had recommended a teacher, Mark Mirsky, a young writer of brilliant, excessive novels about Jews and sex and mystical transcendence. I'd phoned Mirsky, and he invited me to audit his class.

In a Harvard English interspersed with obscene Yiddish phrases, Mirsky exhorted his mostly non-Jewish students to read the works of kabbalah scholar Gershom Scholem and write with messianic passion: By creating myth, we could redeem the world. Mirsky hated reticence, concealment, literary stinginess; his enemy was Hemingway. "Wail!" he cried. "Reach for the place where kabbalists saw shattered vessels filled with divine light and flying sparks forming new worlds!"

I tried to write like him, in run-on sentences that groped for revelation. Mirsky urged me not to write cautiously, journalistically, to expand nonfiction into myth: "Don't play it safe, Yossi! Where antinomianism meets the law, where opposites are reconciled in a revelation greater than them both: *that's* the source of Jewish creativity. The only way to bring the Messiah is by taking risks!"

It was in Mirsky's class that I met Lynn Rintoul. She had just graduated from California's Stanford University with a bachelor's degree in marine biology, but then abruptly dropped a career in science and moved to New York to become a writer. She possessed the rare intelligence that could penetrate opposite worlds. She was not Jewish.

Lynn was adorable — her mouth small, her slender nose and strong chin both upturned — though that was hardly the effect she'd hoped to create. She wore a beret, an obvious affectation that only made her appear more delectable, the very opposite of the daring artist she was trying to be. She smoked clove-scented cigarettes, another attempt at sophistication, enveloping herself in sweet smoke. Her fingers, like her backpack, were stained with ink.

Students in Mirsky's seminar had to read aloud their works in progress, and Lynn and I were drawn to each other's blatantly autobiographical stories. Lynn's writing was marked by a watchfulness that seemed to miss no necessary detail. With a single unexpected word she could turn a common sentence into a poem: a waitress "impaling" lemons onto glasses, the white stripe of a boy's sweatpants like a "pendulum driven from the hip." She read in a succulent voice, as though cherishing her words and reluctant to release them, emphasizing key phrases, insisting on the urgency of their insight.

Lynn's stories were about a teenage girl straining against innocence and stumbling into situations of emotional and sexual menace. Those scenes were tempered by lush descriptions of climbing mountains and swimming near-freezing lakes and shooting rapids. In nature, a calm knowing broke through Lynn's childlike facade.

She had grown up in Westport, Connecticut, in one of the town's few nonwealthy homes: Her father had left when she was young and

severed all contact with the family; her mother, a teacher, raised
Lynn and her two brothers.

Lynn imbibed the WASP ethos of achievement and stoical courage from her paternal grandmother, an artist. Lynn loved browsing
with her through a chest filled with family letters dating from the
Revolutionary War, listening to her stories about illustrious ancestors. But however close she felt to her family's past, its intactness
had ended for her when her father walked out. She veered between
a sense of continuity and rupture: almost archaic in her affinity for
calico dresses and harpsichord music and hand-painted porcelain
teapots, yet craving experience — the teenager who tripped at
Grateful Dead concerts and rode boxcars across the Midwest with
an insane boyfriend who spoke in rhymes.

I asked Lynn for a date, and she said, "That's amazing, I was just
going to ask *you* out!" It happened during a break at a reading organized by Mirsky in a downtown Manhattan loft. The readers were
Mirsky's novelist friends, including one man who wrote about a messianic pretender gathering Holocaust survivors to a fortress refuge
on the Lower East Side.

Lynn and I went out a few nights later. I showed her the punk
clubs and bars of my neighborhood, wooing her with a glimpse of
life on the edge.

"I *loved* your JDL story," she said.

"It wasn't too crazy for you?" I asked coyly, knowing that its wild-
ness was precisely what drew her.

"No! I admire your characters' passion and commitment. You'll
laugh: Until you read to the class, I thought you were Scandinavian —
Yoosi of the Laps."

"You never met maybe a Jew?" I said, in an exaggerated Yiddish
accent.

"Not a Jew like you. You know —"

"A Jewish Jew."

"Right. My idea of someone very Jewish was Julius Gold, who
owned the deli in Westport. He had a huge beard, and I used to
think he was a rabbi. On Sundays after church, we'd go to Gold's
and get bagels and lox. He'd give us kids free slivers of halvah."

"What's Westport like?"

"I hate it. The kids are rich and spoiled. All kinds of horrible famous people live there. There's even a gourmet *pet food* shop."

"Sounds like Brooklyn."

"When I was a girl I fantasized about meeting a Brooklyn boy. You know: wearing the kind of hat boys wear in Brooklyn, with the visor and earmuffs."

"I used to wear a hat like that."

"Did you really?"

"I felt like a total jerk. "

"So now I've met my Brooklyn boy."

She was still sleeping when I got out of bed the next morning. I sat on a cushion on the floor, wrapped myself in *tefilin,* closed my eyes, and tried to connect with the Jewish souls protecting me. I heard Lynn stir, felt her watching me. Then I put the *tefilin* back into its velvet bag and kissed her good morning. "Whatever you're curious about, just ask," I said. She nodded.

"It's so spare in here," she said, looking around my room.

"What's missing? I got a desk, typewriter, books."

"I *like* it, it's very pure."

I told her there was a book I wanted to give her. We went to a bookstore, and I bought a copy of Elie Wiesel's Auschwitz memoir, *Night.* "Read," I said. "Then we'll talk."

She went off to a feminist newspaper where she worked as a volunteer editor, the only nonlesbian on staff; and I went to join a radio panel on anti-Zionism that a friend had organized. "I don't want to leave you," I said.

"I want to be with you the *whole* time," she said.

She appeared at my door with daffodils. "Who are those for?" I asked.

"Hasn't anyone ever brought you flowers before?" she said.

Neither of us knew anyone quite like the other; we wanted to see the world through each other's eyes, "inhale each other," as Lynn put it. I gave her books about Jewish history; she gave me poetry books written by women whose struggle between trust and rage reminded me of myself. I made her a Zionist; she made me a feminist.

She taught me to listen to classical music, to cook by simply paying attention to what I was doing, to make love slowly. When we slept together, I forgot to have nightmares.

She taught me how a writer sees. I'd always looked for the broad outlines, the "meaning" behind any experience; she looked for texture. She had that almost quivering sensitivity to detail that I'd known only through drugs. I laughed and called her "a spy" as she'd point out on the street passersby who had no idea she existed but whom she recognized from the bus or the supermarket and whose imagined lives she conjured in intimate detail.

I "reeducated" her politically. Like my father arguing with me during the Vietnam War, I defended America, trying to convince this American child that her country and the Soviet Union weren't morally equivalent, that the silly leftist ideas she'd learned in college had nothing to do with the real world, and that infatuation with totalitarian revolutionaries didn't violate but confirm the innocence of her privileged life. On her shelf of books gathered from women's studies courses was one titled, *Stalin on the Women's Question.* "You ought to read the companion volume," I told her, *"Hitler on the Women's Question."* The Stalin book vanished.

I knew from the start I could "trust" her. My Jewishness was obviously no problem for her: She'd been drawn to me through my JDL story; she couldn't possibly like me without liking me as a Jew. I was amazed that any non-Jew could be so totally ignorant as she was of anti-Semitic stereotypes. "What about Zionists as Nazis," I demanded, "didn't you ever hear *that* from your leftist friends?" Nothing. She'd grown up in a family that didn't notice who among its friends was Jewish, in a town where the Reform temple was just another Protestant denomination. My father had warned me that a gentile woman would betray her Jewish lover in their first fight, calling him a "dirty Jew." Lynn and I sometimes fought, but my father was wrong.

Lynn was a former Episcopalian, a lapsed Christian. I rarely thought of her as a "Gentile" — that imaginary identity invented by Jews. Except for obsessive anti-Semites, there are no "non-Jews," people who define themselves by not being Jewish. Lynn had more authentic identities: writer, marine biologist, feminist, lover of a Borough Park Jew.

I wanted to show her my Jewish world, create a safe place within its intensity where we could be together. I had no American Jewish inferiority complex, but the opposite: I was certain that the Jewish experience was the ultimate human experience and that it could offer Lynn the vitality she craved. If our relationship led to any assimilating, I assumed it would be Lynn assimilating into Judaism. I rejected Borough Park's ghettoization, the notion that Judaism was so fragile it would dissolve in any encounter with "the world" — an unworthy fear for a culture that had passed through annihilation and resurrection.

Lynn asked if we could visit Borough Park. Impossible, I said; I'd cause a neighborhood scandal if I appeared with a non-Jewish woman. "You make it sound like I'm sullied," she said, angry and hurt.

"I can't change Borough Park," I said. "It's hard enough to change myself."

And so, instead, we went one Sunday to the Lower East Side, once center of New York's Jewish immigrant life and now mostly Chinese and Puerto Rican, though it still held traces of Yiddish culture. We ate sour pickles sold from barrels and went to a dairy cafeteria whose customers were old, Yiddish-speaking Jews and whose faucets dispensed seltzer instead of water.

"Look at these wonderful faces," Lynn said.

I told her that I. B. Singer had used this cafeteria as a setting for some of his stories. Lynn said that it was Brett Singer — her writing teacher at Stanford and granddaughter of Singer's brother, I. J., himself a famous Yiddish novelist — who had convinced her to drop science and join City College's writing program.

"So I. J. Singer's granddaughter sends you straight to Mark Mirsky," I said. "You're in deep, Lynnie."

"What do you *mean*," she said, at once rebuffing and urging me to say more.

"Jewish souls are looking out for you. They brought us together."

"Don't go getting any big spiritual ideas about me."

"Big ideas? God forbid."

4.

Abe and I had a plan: to publish a newspaper for fringe Jews like ourselves. The new Jewish ideas, we believed, would come from those misfits who couldn't find their place in the middle-class Judaism of synagogues and the United Jewish Appeal. Our paper would have no recognizable political or religious agenda but rather transcend all existing Jewish categories — "outmoded legacies of the pre-Holocaust world," I proclaimed. We spoke vaguely but passionately about a "post-Holocaust Judaism," expressing our generation's search for its place in Jewish history, in a time of spiritual chaos and apocalyptic dread.

We began with a name: the *New Jewish Times*. The *Village Voice* had recently published my JDL piece, giving us some credibility. We collected a small group of unemployed writers, artists, photographers — fellow "freelancers." Finding a publisher, though, was more difficult. Who, after all, would invest in a newspaper for fringe Jews run by amateur journalists?

The answer was Marv Steinhartz, a young businessman who'd made his money running private hospitals. Steinhartz was what they called in Yiddish a *chazir fresser*, a gluttonous consumer of pork, an expression that described not merely his diet but his being. Marv was always on the make — for quick bucks, quick lays, quick highs. A cigarette dangled from his thick lips, a Humphrey Bogart effect ruined by traces of spittle. His favorite words were "chick" and "chic," and he pronounced them both the same way. "The chicks will be lining up at our door if we put out a chick product," he said, explaining his vision for the newspaper.

Marv was proud of his achievements in the hospital business. "You'd be amazed how easy it is to feed patients on a dollar a day and still meet federal requirements," he'd say when we discussed funding the paper. We realized that Marv was not our ideal publisher, but we also knew that no one would be mad enough to take his place.

Lynn's roommate was a Jewish woman named Sara, a dancer who'd spent time in Israel. In Sara's bookcase Lynn found *The Jewish Catalog*, a how-to guide to Jewish rituals written in a 1960s, countercultural style; cartoons of yarmulked angels telling Jewish jokes appeared in the margins.

Lynn had been raised with an aversion to fervent religion. Her mother, a former Baptist from Alabama, rejected her fundamentalist upbringing and became a liberal Yankee. Lynn's father's father had escaped a fundamentalist Episcopalian sect in which he'd been raised, the Catholic Apostolics, whose members believed the world was about to end and practiced an austere, Pilgrim-style Christianity.

But the Judaism Lynn encountered in *The Jewish Catalog* fascinated her. Judaism's insistence on sanctifying every act appealed to her sense of order and tradition; while the Jews' refusal to abandon the Torah and assimilate appealed to her own stubborn individuality. She began asking me detailed questions about Jewish observance: Why is one kind of fish kosher and not another? Why aren't religious Jews allowed to carry anything on Shabbos outside a fenced area? I told her that the real power of Judaism lay in its history, not its rituals. "I don't have patience for small details," I said. "That's nudnick Judaism."

"But don't you think it's *interesting* that an entire people has devoted itself to these laws for thousands of years?" she asked.

On the anniversary of her father's death, Lynn told me she'd like to light a candle in his memory, the way she'd read in *The Jewish Catalog* that Jews do for their dead. But she wondered whether it was appropriate: marking a tradition that wasn't hers for a father who had abandoned her. "I'm not even religious. I've been trained as a scientist. I'm a rationalist, an atheist."

"What's wrong with bringing a little light into the world?" I asked.

We sat by the candle, and she spoke, weeping, about the father she barely knew, who years later suddenly reappeared one day, by then an alcoholic, and invited her to dinner. "It was so pathetic. He didn't know how to relate to me, so all he could do was flirt."

The previous year he fell into a coma. "I went to see him just before he died. It was fitting in a way that he was in a coma: I wouldn't have known what to say to him. I used to hate him. Now I just feel so sorry for him."

Our fathers had died around the same time. And we were both left, for different reasons, with the paradoxical sense of loss and release: the feeling of being entirely on our own.

"And what would your father say?" my mother demanded, when I told her about Lynn. She meant, How could I risk the future of a Jewish line that had just barely been extracted from the Holocaust?

I could well imagine what my father would say, how difficult it would be to convince him that I wasn't betraying "everything." Yet my mother, though obviously upset, seemed more curious than accusatory. She had always tried to accommodate all my "crazinesses," as she put it. And now she truly wanted to know: How could I rationalize this new, unexpected turn?

"Don't you feel guilty?" she asked, hopeful.

"Sorry."

"What about marriage?"

"Marriage?" I almost shouted. "Who's talking marriage?" Lynn was a twenty-two-year-old graduate student in creative writing; I was a twenty-six-year-old freelance journalist trying to start a newspaper guaranteed to lose money. Neither of us could imagine the future.

I told my mother that in any case I'd never marry a non-Jew. Being Jewish meant too much to me. Either Lynn would convert and share my Jewish commitment, or it wouldn't work; so there was no reason to worry.

In Borough Park interdating was considered treason, allying oneself with the Jew-hating world. But my mother had an innate lack of judgmentalness, a sympathy for the complexity of human relations.

Growing up, I'd mistaken her conciliatory nature for weakness: My father was the survivor; my mother, the potential victim. But since my father's death, she'd proven her strength, even becoming a kind of advisor for fellow Borough Park widows, who sought her help on how to cope with grief.

"Maybe there's something wrong with me," she said, "but I trust you. Anyway, what good would it do to try and stop you? You've always done exactly what you pleased."

I pinched her cheek and told her she was the sanest woman in Borough Park.

And yet, however much I reassured my mother, I *was* anxious. After only a few months of being together, I couldn't imagine life without Lynn. And though I tried to forget the future, I dreaded a choice between Lynn and Jewish loyalty.

I wanted her to convert to Judaism, to share with me the quest of how to be a Jew in this time. But I knew that could work only if she fell in love with the Jewish people. Lynn was too principled to convert for expedience, to assume an identity — especially one so demanding — she couldn't feel was fully hers.

My anxiety was obvious. When we went to see a Jewish film, I'd question her reactions to different scenes, testing the depth of her empathy; when I gave her a book on Israel, I'd point to key parts and offer a running commentary. I wanted her to be passionate and cynical and sentimental about the same Jewish things that I was.

Inevitably, she retreated. "I can't stand you hovering over me," she said one night. "I can't breathe."

"I'm afraid of losing you," I said. She held me, and at that moment it seemed that everything would be resolved, that there would be no contradictions between my various loves.

5.

The premiere issue of the *New Jewish Times* appeared in September 1980. Thirty-two tabloid-size pages, with a cover photo of a mushroom cloud and the words "Next Year in Jerusalem?" We didn't bother writing an accompanying cover story or even an editorial explanation for the shocking but obscure message; Abe and I assumed that apocalypse was self-explanatory.

We were a monthly — when we managed it. Sometimes we appeared in the middle of the month, and one month we forgot to publish at all. Our December issue was late because our art director became depressed on production night, left the office, and was never seen again.

Somehow we managed to sell two or three thousand copies per issue, mostly on Manhattan newsstands. We even got a few subscribers — though we rarely mailed them copies, because no one felt like going to the post office. We avoided the phone, assuming the caller was either an irate subscriber demanding a refund, a photographer who hadn't been paid, or a writer whose piece had been entirely rewritten and published without his consent.

I wrote most of the paper under pseudonyms, together with my coeditor, Jon Mark — a romantic in love with country-and-western music, loser baseball teams, and the Orthodox Jewish life he'd left and couldn't reinhabit. Jon also wrote the classifieds: "Long Island synagogue looking for rabbi with goatee to speak on Saturdays... Sexy yeshiva girl seeks boy to knit yarmulkes for. All colors . . . Young tough from Tulsa, going straight, looking for Jewish babes who are into being sensitive and don't care who knows it."

We amused ourselves by writing letters to the editor that variously denounced us as right-wing, left-wing, self-hating, and ethnically chauvinistic. We wanted the letters' page to be a forum for debate, so we contrived letters that argued with each other. We satirized ourselves: I wrote a letter accusing us of being alarmist for running a story about an anti-Semitic cult; the published editor's note responded, "And what Nazi group are *you* from?"

We looked for Jewish nightmares. We published the paranoid fantasies of a gay Jew imagining a Nazi-style roundup on Christopher Street and a poster by a pair of former Soviet dissident artists of America under Soviet occupation, with Kremlin-style domes and red stars over the Manhattan skyline. When ex-Yippie leader Abbie Hoffman emerged from underground hiding to face a drug charge, we published an interview with him, in which he compared himself to Anne Frank. We didn't care that he was ludicrous and self-indulgent, only that he was Holocaust-obsessed and fringe.

Our few but devoted readers saw us as a community rather than a newspaper. Our office — an expensive, near-empty loft on lower Fifth Avenue; Marv wanted a "chick" address — was a drop-in center for people with obscure obsessions, most of them disaffected Orthodox Jews who kept the passion if not the practice of Orthodoxy. Our regulars included Herschel, an ex-Lubavitcher Hasid who'd spent a year sleeping in subways and who now lived in the homes of young women he met at the Upper West Side café where he held court, charming them with passionate arguments about Jewish schisms resolved decades ago, while spiking their coffee with a flask of whiskey retrieved from his long, shabby coat.

Then there was Jake, a self-hating Jew who wrote us anti-Zionist letters to the editor. Jake had a black girlfriend named Julie, who despite his pleas was determined to convert to Judaism and was studying in a Lubavitcher yeshiva for newly Orthodox Jews. Jake thought Israel was a fascist state, while Julie thought Israel should annex the West Bank. Jake read Trotskyite newspapers; Julie read the *Jewish Press*.

We threw big fund-raising parties. Abe doubled as managing editor and party coordinator: Through word of mouth, he would draw into our loft on a Saturday night hundreds of people, who danced to apocalyptic punk music played on a barely functioning phonograph. Those affairs didn't raise much money — partygoers were either impoverished Russians who got discounts or friends admitted for free — but they helped create the sense of a *New Jewish Times* community.

Lynn loved the outlaw atmosphere at the office, the misfit characters with nowhere else to go. This was the Jewish world I'd wanted her to know: funny, half-mad, alive, the very opposite of suburban Judaism. It had been worth starting the paper, I felt, if only to create a Jewish place in which she could feel at home.

6.

Lynn's apartment in midtown Manhattan was next door to an old brick church. One day as we passed it Lynn asked, deliberately casual, "Did you happen to notice the name of this church?"

Of course I hadn't noticed the name of the church. I still retained my childhood aversion to churches as places of menace, anti-Jewish hostility. And while I no longer crossed the street when I passed churches, I did my best to ignore their presence and certainly didn't read the names on their facades. Churches were all the same to me, part of a single denomination whose defining tenet was "otherness."

"You remember, I told you about my great-grandfather's sect, the Catholic Apostolics? Well, it's a funny thing, but this is a Catholic Apostolic church."

"I thought you said they were defunct," I said.

"I thought they were."

"Lynnie —"

"The answer is no."

"I'm not telling you to convert to them. But you owe it to yourself — as a writer — to check it out."

"They're a horrible group who made my grandfather's life miserable."

"Don't you think it's a pretty amazing coincidence to move next door to one of the last surviving churches of your great-grandfather's sect?"

"You and your coincidences."

"Maybe God does these things just to remind us that we move in invisible patterns."

"I don't believe in God. I believe in what can be seen and measured in a laboratory."

I smiled.

"Don't condescend to me. You think you know me better than I know myself?"

A few days later, while passing the church, she noticed an old man bent over the lock. "Excuse me," she said. He ignored her. She persisted: "I'm looking for information about the Catholic Apostolics. My great-grandfather had something to do with it. His name was Stephen Rich Rintoul."

He abruptly turned and stared at her. "The First Angel," he said finally, in a whisper.

"What?" said Lynn, a little afraid.

"The First Angel. Your great-grandfather built this church."

Lynn was still shaken when she told me the story that night; and she admitted that this was indeed a strange coincidence. "But what does it *mean*?" she asked.

The following Sunday she went to services — which felt, she said, like a group funeral for the handful of elderly worshippers gathered in the cold, gloomy church. Shortly afterward she began writing a novella about the First Angel. She even traveled to the Harvard Divinity School library in Cambridge to research the Catholic Apostolics: When she decided on a project, she committed herself wholly.

One day a packet arrived for her in the mail, from the old man she'd met at the church gate. It contained the Apostolics' prayer book, a small, leather-bound volume perhaps a hundred years old. When I saw her that evening she opened the little book to a specific page and wordlessly handed it to me: It was a prayer asking God's forgiveness for Christian crimes against the Jews.

My mother invited Lynn for Rosh Hashanah dinner. "This is obviously more serious than you said it was," she said to me with a sigh.

"If I accept Lynn into the family, maybe she'll be encouraged to convert."

I'd already met Lynn's mother, Eve, on several occasions. We got on well, partly because Eve was relieved that Lynn now had a boyfriend who, unlike previous ones, wasn't obviously drugged or clinically insane. Eve reminded me of my mother: gracious, sensible, and with a tendency to blurt out anxieties in casual conversation. If we could ever get our mothers together, I told Lynn, they'd actually like each other.

Still, Lynn was nervous about meeting my mother. "She's going to take one look at me and think: goyish."

"She's going to take one look at you and think, 'She's beautiful, what's she doing with my son?' "

"I know I'm going to blow it, Yossi."

"Just don't talk about Christmas in Westport and everything will be fine."

"That's what I mean!"

"I'm teasing, Lynnie. Trust me: She'll love you."

My mother prepared a Hungarian feast. "Welcome to the Hapsburg dynasty," I said to Lynn as we entered the living room, with its chandelier and plastic-covered velvet couches.

"Yossi," Lynn said, trying not to laugh.

"Isn't he impossible?" my mother said.

Aside from my snide remarks, the meal went well: My mother and Lynn liked each other immediately.

Then, in the same chatty voice with which she'd just been discussing her Hungarian cooking, my mother said, "Isn't it funny, Lynn, how Christians can worship a Jew and yet hate the Jewish people? No, really, can you understand it?"

Lynn looked at me, helpless. I rolled my eyes.

"I'm sure you know about the persecution of the Jews, Lynn."

"I know," Lynn said, dutiful.

"Why anyone would want to convert to this people is beyond me. What with all the *tsuris*, the troubles."

"No one is converting to anything," I said.

"And after everything the Jews have done for the world. All the Nobel Prize winners —"

"Come on, Ma, not the Nobel Prize."

"Why not the Nobel Prize? Einstein, Freud, Salk —"

"Jesus."

"Yes, Jesus too. Tell me, Lynn, is he so impossible with you also?"

"Only sometimes," Lynn said, laughing.

"He used to have a terrible temper. Does he lose his temper with you?"

"Well . . ."

"Yosseleh," my mother said to me, "how *could* you, she's such a lovely girl. You know, Lynn, I was married to Yossi's father for twenty-five years, and even though he could be quite volatile, he never once raised his voice to me in all that time. I only hope the two of you can find such happiness."

On Thanksgiving Lynn and I took the train to her grandmother's house in Greenwich, Connecticut, to join the Rintouls' annual gathering. For the Rintouls, Thanksgiving was the ultimate family holiday. They even knew the name of their *Mayflower* ancestor: Noah Phelps.

"Maybe your relatives will appreciate it if I tell them my family also came to America by boat," I said to Lynn on the train.

"Relax, Yossi. It's just my family. Be your charming self and everyone will love you."

"I bet your grandmother is a member of the Daughters of the American Revolution."

"No, her mother was. Grandma thinks they're a bunch of silly old women who take too much pride in other people's accomplishments."

"They don't let Jews in."

"Come on, Yossi, how many Jews were on the *Mayflower*?"

Lynn's grandmother, Mary, lived alone in an old wood-and-glass house surrounded by forest. Among company, she acted like a typical woman of her class and time: She covered her mouth when laughing as though ashamed of gaiety, constantly apologized for nonexistent slights, fretted that the turkey was too dry and the cranberry sauce too watery.

But her true self emerged in solitude. Mary — who'd buried two grown children, including Lynn's father, and was widowed for longer than she'd been married — spent her days in near-meditative quiet, gardening and chain-smoking and painting landscapes, which focused on the varying qualities of light.

Lynn adored her. As a girl, she would help Mary polish the antique silver and listen to family stories: Each initialed spoon was an excuse to invoke the person who'd owned it, and from those sessions Lynn learned her storytelling skills. She and Mary would sip tea from heirloom cups and watch the rain feed the rose garden; and in that stillness feel the concurrence of generations.

Mary's house was the repository of Rintoul family history, a museum of Americana: a pewter chalice from a Colonial-era church, dueling pistols mounted on the walls, a leather chest filled with old letters and diaries and knicknacks like the fan that some relative had held while being presented to Napoleon's court.

In the foyer hung gilt-framed Victorian paintings of Mary's ancestors. There was a portrait of a nineteenth-century young woman in a low-cut red dress, at once self-conscious and also pleased with her beauty; and beside it, a portrait of an old woman with a calm, knowing gaze. Both paintings, Lynn said, were of the same person. Lynn wanted me to understand: In this house she'd learned to penetrate transience and glimpse wisdom.

My knowledge of my own family history extended no further back than to my grandparents; I didn't even know their parents' names. It was as if the Holocaust had retroactively erased the generations. I was the firstborn after the destruction; my family seemed to begin again with me. Yet Lynn had grown up not only with the stories of distant ancestors but with their faces.

Everyone welcomed me. There was little intimidating about these people; they were, in Lynn's words, "middle-brow WASPs," engineers and librarians who spent their summers in slightly shabby Adirondack "camps" hardly more glamorous than Catskills bungalows. I'd come expecting questions about Brooklyn, the Middle East conflict, the meaning of the name "Yossi"; but no one asked anything remotely sensitive. In fact, any subject that risked controversy or emotion seemed taboo.

"Why isn't anyone saying anything?" I whispered to Lynn.

"Shhh," she said, suppressing a smile.

"How can they spend hours discussing the weather?"

"It's good for you: For once you'll talk about something besides politics and Israel."

And yet I liked being there, in the place that had helped form

Lynn. I felt grateful to Mary for filling Lynn with a love for tradition and with the spirit of adventurous ancestors — the very qualities that had attracted Lynn to me.

And I felt something else, unexpected: American. Somehow, I belonged in this house's history. America had created the neutral
ground on which Lynn and I could so effortlessly join, allowed a
Christian girl to bring home a boy named Yossi without creating a
family scandal. America had not only given equality to the Jews but
to Judaism, which Lynn could explore with simple curiosity, ignoring the stigma of centuries. America had let me heal, let me work
out my inherited trauma, and be as angry as I wanted, even at
America itself. And now it had given me a daughter of its elite.

Through most of the afternoon I tried to keep my hands in my
pockets, my voice low-key, avoiding displays of any kind: my first as-
similationist experience. I felt vaguely ashamed of the pleasure I took
in fitting in. But now I understood those American Jews who wanted
nothing more than to be accepted among these decent people and
who resented Jews like me for our demonstrative, subversive otherness.

Toward evening, we went for "the walk." Every Thanksgiving at
sunset, the Rintouls strolled in the woods. We walked in a silence
broken only by a comment about a tree or a bird. I felt the power
of these people's reticence, not a self-impairment but a stilling of
distractions; I felt something of their inner calm, their rootedness in
the shifting seasons and the changing light.

7.

Lynn and I moved in together. We found a sixth-floor walk-up apartment near the West Side piers, an old building that seemed to be
mostly populated by Greek widows. At night, screams and sounds of
breaking glass came from the welfare hotel across the street, followed by sirens.

We perched above the city. We merged our libraries — my books
with titles like *Hanged in Auschwitz: An Autobiography*, her books
with titles like *Mushrooms of North America* — and laid a bamboo
rug in the empty living room and covered the sooty windows with
white paper shades through which the morning light filtered. We

spent our days writing in separate rooms, meeting for tea breaks to share our frustrations and to critique each other's work.

At Lynn's suggestion, we nailed a *mezuzah* — a long, thin wooden casing containing the *Sh'ma,* the prayer proclaiming God's oneness — to our doorpost. Lynn wanted our house to be blessed, she said. The angel of death had passed over the Israelite homes in Egypt because their doorposts were ceremoniously marked with blood, and the *mezuzah* is an invocation of that protection. (Just to be sure, our front door also had double locks and an iron police bar.) I said the Hebrew prayer thanking God for bringing us to this time; Lynn repeated the words in English.

One day she returned from a visit to her mother's house with an antique menorah, bronze petals sprouting from its curling stems. Lynn said that the menorah had been in her family's closet for as long as anyone could remember; no one knew where it came from or how it got there. "It was waiting for our home," she said.

The Catholic Apostolic incident had shaken Lynn's religious skepticism. Her deepening interest in Judaism delighted but also challenged me. If I expected her to love my tradition, I would have to learn to at least respect hers. However distant she felt from it now, Christianity had formed her; Christmas and Easter were her warmest childhood memories. I had to learn to relax around crosses and Christmas trees, if only because they were part of her.

Lynn had written a fine story about a little girl in church, caught between boredom and fantasy, wiping her runny nose on the velvet cushion of the pew and imagining angels soaring from the stained glass. When I thought of her as a girl in church, it no longer seemed such an alien place.

Lynn cherished the New Testament, its imagery and language. I asked her how she'd managed as a child to avoid anti-Semitic associations when reading about the Pharisees. "I just didn't connect the Pharisees with the Jews I knew," she said. One evening I began reading the New Testament she kept as reference for her fiction. I came to a verse about "the Jews"; I quickly shut the book.

Being with Lynn forced me to confront other blocks within myself. Especially anger. Our fights would begin with Lynn complaining about my thoughtlessness — like making notes for some article I was writing while she was trying to speak with me. I reacted to even a mild rebuke with near-hysterical counteraccusations, as if my whole being were challenged. Lynn retreated into weeping. "I can't bear it when you get crazy," she'd say. Her misery instantly sobered me; I would apologize and try to explain the rush of rage that swept away reason and restraint, how my father had been the same way: Any anger drew every anger. But long after I'd recovered my balance, her sense of wound remained.

I had always thought of anger as one of my most essential, vitalizing traits. Lynn herself had initially been drawn to that energy, through the JDL story I'd read in Mirsky's class. I felt torn: afraid I'd lose Lynn if I didn't stifle my anger, afraid of enervating myself if I did.

Marv was getting restless. He'd assumed the *New Jewish Times* would make "big bucks," in his words, but somehow that wasn't happening. He decided that our core audience of disaffected yeshiva boys, sixties burnouts, and Russian alcoholic artists was too narrow, that we needed to appeal to the mainstream.

His solution was to target Borough Park — whose ultra-Orthodox Jews would have been appalled by the *New Jewish Times*. He commissioned someone to write an article about the stylishness of Hasidic women. "You guys better publish this," he said to Abe and me.

"No problem," said Abe. And he set the article in a typeface so small you needed a magnifying glass to read it.

Marv's next inspiration was to appeal to assimilated Yuppies. We were to attract them by including the word "sex" on every cover. And, said Marv, we'd have to print a picture of either Woody Allen or Bob Dylan — "chick Jews" — on every cover as well.

Creditors pursued us. Marv told us to stall them, make promises; and so we stalled and promised.

Finally, Marv stopped paying us too; and in April 1981, eight months after we began publishing, we quit. I felt relief. We'd started the paper with a noble vision and ended with debts and lies. It was the JDL syndrome: All means were allowed to a self-sacrificing elite, operating on an exalted plane beyond conventional morality.

One night I borrowed the van from my family's business, for one last visit to the Fifth Avenue loft. Abe and I filled the van with typewriters and lamps: back pay. And that was the end of the *New Jewish Times*.

Early one April morning, before dawn, Lynn and I joined a small group of Jewish worshipers and ascended the observation deck of the Empire State Building, for the "Blessing of the Sun." The sun had just completed its twenty-eight-year cycle according to the Hebrew calendar, and Jews around the world were waking before sunrise to bless the light.

The group atop the Empire State Building was led by Rabbi Zalman Shachter —"Reb Zalman," as he was affectionately known. Reb Zalman, a large man with a big gray beard, had broken from his Hasidic past and founded the "Jewish renewal" movement that had produced *The Jewish Catalog,* Lynn's guide to Judaism. Reb Zalman had spent time with Sufis and American Indians and taken drugs for spiritual purposes. What elevated him above mere trendiness was his ability to combine ancient wisdom with the most current ideas. He insisted that Jewish law, modified and reinterpreted, could help save the world from the excesses of modernity. He spoke of the Shabbos rest and its prohibition against use of electricity as a way of re-asserting human mastery over technology in the era of Auschwitz and Hiroshima; he extended the concept of kosher to forms of en-ergy (kosher: solar energy; not kosher: nuclear power).

I joined Reb Zalman at the Empire State Building as part partic-ipant, part observer, intending to write about the event for the *Village Voice*; and Lynn, intrigued by the notion of experiencing sunrise sus-pended over New York City, decided to come, too.

We gathered in a corner of the observation deck, which seemed in the fading darkness like a mountain peak. One man wore a rainbow-striped prayer shawl wrapped around his head like a bedouin, another carried a *tefilin* bag on which was stitched the word "Tibet." Some women wore prayer shawls and yarmulkes, flouting the Orthodox custom that restricted those rituals to men. I wrapped myself in the prayer shawl and *tefilin* that had belonged to my fa-ther and in which I routinely prayed. Lynn stood beside me; I ex-tended my prayer shawl over her shoulders, to protect her from the wind.

Below us was a city of gray towers. The distant streets were still, as if some catastrophe had emptied them.

We began the morning chants, offering the prayers that had passed through Auschwitz to bless a wounded planet. "Blessed are you, Lord Our God, who opens the eyes of the blind . . . who spreads the earth over the waters . . . who disperses sleep from my eyes . . ."

Lynn barely glanced down at the fragile-looking city. Instead, she was riveted outward, toward the horizon, spreading open like a multicolored prayer shawl. She looked beautiful, as if the wind had honed her face to its essential features; her gaze at once distant and focused, as though she'd been transformed into the wise old woman in the painting on her grandmother's wall.

The sun appeared, a red half-disc. I felt a gasp within me, as though I'd just seen the moment of creation.

Manhattan turned silver in the first light. Reb Zalman said, "Master of the universe, we pray for forgiveness for what we've done to the earth. Whatever we can fix, please God, show us how. And whatever we can't fix anymore, have *rachmones*, a little pity on us, and fix it yourself."

Where would the planet be in another twenty-eight years? For the first time in history, people no longer could assume the permanence of the natural cycle. I felt despair in our ability to control the menace we'd released, and yet certain that somehow God would save us from extinction.

We read the first chapter of Genesis: "And God saw the light, that it was good; and God divided the light from the darkness."

Lynn stared into the new sun without blinking; her being seemed to extend to the limits of her vision. Afterward I asked her what she'd experienced. She said, "That we were particles of light buoyant on waves, and the waves all came from a single source."

8.

In June 1981 I flew to Israel for the first "World Gathering of Holocaust Survivors." The *Village Voice* and a Boston Jewish magazine, *Moment,* had both agreed to send me as their reporter. Lynn was spending the month with college friends in California. This was our first prolonged separation; and each of us was, in a sense, returning to the life we knew before we'd met, a kind of test of who we had become together and how enduring those changes were.

I went to see Krup straight from the airport. He was working on a doctorate in Holocaust studies and living in a basement apartment in Jerusalem, with leaky pipes forming puddles on the floor and the walls still peeling from last winter's dampness.

We had maintained an ongoing correspondence, despite misunderstandings and threatened ruptures. We had blamed them on the physical distance between us, the awkward approximations of letters. But there were deeper reasons, and we both knew it. I had hurt Krup by indefinitely deferring my emigration to Israel, leaving him to adjust to a new life without his best friend; and he had hurt me by accusing me of betraying our ideals, of caring more for personal fulfillment than Jewish responsibility.

But even our feuds seemed proof that our friendship still mattered to us. We assumed we could grow up together, endure each other's changes, and yet remain linked by common vision — "know" the world together in a way no one else possibly could.

"Nice of you to come on a solidarity mission to your brothers and sisters in the Holy Land," Krup said when I arrived at his apartment, his subtle way of rebuking me for not moving to Israel.

Krup had aged. He was heavier, more sober. His Zionist idealism had been subject to relentless attrition by rude neighbors and deliberately incompetent bureaucrats and would-be Israeli émigrés who couldn't understand why he'd left America, land of their dreams. Krup enthusiastically adopted the stereotypes by which Israelis dealt with their society's overwhelming human diversity: Moroccans were whores; Romanians, thieves; and Israelis generally, lazy and arrogant and provincial.

Politically, he said, things couldn't possibly be worse. Prime Minister Menachem Begin was senile and destroying the country through suicidal territorial concessions to Egypt. Krup was scathing about the recent Camp David summit, in which President Jimmy Carter had arbitrated a deal between Egypt's President Sadat and Begin, who yielded the entire Sinai desert "for a sham treaty," as Krup put it. "They should have put a sign over Camp David that said 'Arbitration *Macht Frei,*' " he said, punning on the slogan that hung over the entrance to Auschwitz, *Arbeit Macht Frei*, Work Liberates.

I wasn't ready for this. I wanted to savor my first moments back in Israel, not indulge in holocaust scenarios. For me, Camp David hadn't been a threat but a hope. Unlike the West Bank, which bordered Israel's major cities, the Sinai desert was far away; and Israel, it seemed to me, had to test the chance of peace with the largest Arab country. During the Camp David summit I'd prayed for a breakthrough, asking God to give the Jews some peace. I didn't see that prayer as a betrayal of Zionism.

But I didn't argue with Krup. I didn't want him to think I'd softened, become a stupid Jew.

Then, with a small smile, he asked, "So how's your *shiksa?*"

He meant Lynn. He was calling Lynn a *shiksa,* a gentile woman, that nasty Yiddish word implying "slut."

I told myself, "He doesn't know Lynn; he doesn't mean to be hurtful. There's even a hint of male Jewish camaraderie in his tone, as though congratulating me on some achievement."

But I didn't feel any male Jewish camaraderie with Krup. Instead, I felt sullied, precisely the way Lynn would have reacted had one of her friends referred to me as her kike. Just as Lynn was leaving old loyalties and moving toward my people, I too had taken on a new loyalty: to her. I would stand with Lynn against any Jew who humiliated or rejected her. In the most tangible sense, Lynn had become "my people."

I didn't rebuke Krup; I didn't see the point. Perhaps that's when I realized we'd never know anything together again.

In a large Jerusalem hall undergoing renovation, with unpainted walls and sloping concrete floor, six thousand survivors gathered for their reunion. They stepped slowly, almost drowsily, seeking lost relatives and friends: peering into each other's heavy old faces for traces of gaunt youths; checking the order of numbers on each other's arms to see if they'd arrived in Auschwitz on the same transport; feeding names into a computer and hoping to reveal missing loved ones wandering in this room, resurrected in Jerusalem. On bulletin boards were tacked messages from survivors who didn't trust technology: "Zicherman, Avram son of David, I heard for the first time this week that someone met you in the Sinai during the 1956 war. Please call . . ."

My father, I thought, would be pleased: After years of silence, survivors were finally facing the past together. Some were compulsive talkers, seeking out journalists; others could only weep. One woman told me, "I survived just to tell the world what happened to us," but fled when I began asking questions.

I asked them not about the war but about 1945, the first moments of reconstruction. How had they made the transition from victim to survivor? My question surprised them. No one seemed able to point to a single incident, a crucial turning toward life. How did we return to the world? We just went on, that's all.

They were driven around the country to candle-lighting and wreath-laying and tree-planting ceremonies. Everything about Israel seemed miraculous to them, and whatever wasn't wonderful was somehow charming and funny. In every Israeli they saw a resurrected Jew from the Holocaust: Children in a kibbutz choir singing Zionist songs from the 1940s were children of the Warsaw Ghetto; obnoxious teenagers shouting on buses were compensating with exuberance for the survivors' own severed youth. No country was ever loved the way the survivors cherished Israel. They loved it not for its landscapes or culture or the quality of its people. They expected nothing of Israel, only for it to exist.

They could have just as well healed themselves without Israel, through family and daily life: private restorations. But only Israel allowed them to dare a public gathering, to face the past together, to speak without irony of God. After the Holocaust mere survival wasn't enough: Only by fulfilling the messianic vision of a return to Zion could we challenge the Nazi apocalyptic vision as the final word on our history.

On the last night of the gathering, the survivors met at the Western Wall. A massive iron menorah on a makeshift stage was lit with kerosene; below were tables covered with glass memorial candles, which survivors had lit for their families. We sang the Yiddish anthem of the anti-Nazi partisans: "Never say 'This is the final road'/ The hour we have waited for is near/Beneath our tread the earth shall tremble, 'We are here.'"

Ten bearded Yemenite Jews, barefoot and in white robes and multicolored prayer shawls, ascended the stage, bearing long and twisting shofars, rams' horns. For more than a minute they blew stampedelike blasts; and that powerful pleading, that cry of animal pain, seemed to link heaven and earth with sound, with intangible physicality. I felt disoriented, no longer in my body. The thousands of souls gathered at the Wall merged with the millions of souls above them: All had passed through death, into life.

Israel was in the midst of its ugliest election campaign ever. I walked the streets of Jerusalem, reading the billboards that offered the Israeli voter dozens of ways to save the country; most of the posters were desecrated by rival party partisans. Supporters of Begin's right-wing Likud disrupted Labor rallies and vandalized Labor campaign offices. Begin had just sent Israeli planes to blow up Saddam Hussein's nuclear reactor; and Labor leader Shimon Peres, himself mixing politics with Israel's security, accused Begin of an election stunt. Apocalypse seemed close.

And yet I felt exhilarated by total engagement with Israel's fate. Everything in Israel mattered to me, pulled me in a way no other place could.

I needed to get back here — soon, and for good. I had told myself that I couldn't move to Israel until I'd reached some professional standing as a journalist. Now that had happened; I had a chance of succeeding as a freelance journalist in Jerusalem.

And I also had my subject: the rise of the "new Israel," that coalition of outcast Israelis — Sephardim, West Bank settlers, ultra-Orthodox Jews, all led by the ultimate Zionist outcast, Menachem Begin — that saw "the world" as hostile to Jewish survival and that had taken over the country from the liberal, secular optimists of Labor. I knew this Israel, its historical grudges and fears; this was the Israel I had to write about and explain.

For the first time, then, I could realistically envision myself living here. And yet, ironically, I could — also for the first time — imagine myself remaining in America. Lynn and I could become Manhattan Jews: seeing the latest films and buying the Sunday *New York Times* on Saturday night and joining one of those sixties-style synagogues where young Jews combined Hasidic fervor with egalitarian practice, trying to create an American Jewish spirituality.

Certainly I had fewer romantic illusions about Israel and my possible place in it than I did as a teenager. I had always assumed I'd feel most at home in Israel, but Krup's difficulties helped me realize that my experience of "homecoming" would be full of small ironies. No matter how many years I'd live here, Israelis would regard me as an American, just as immigrants from Russia and Morocco and a hundred other countries who came expecting to be welcomed as fellow Jews found themselves assuming the very identities their places of birth had denied them. I would always speak with an accent: My Hebrew wouldn't roll but be paved flat by American sounds. As a writer in English, I would be in linguistic exile.

And yet I couldn't bear keeping away from Israel anymore. I had to know its nuances, know how the great Jewish experiment was evolving on the streets and in the army and in the back pages of the newspaper. I had to test the ideal that had animated my life; otherwise, I would remain a Diaspora Jew who vicariously lived his Jewishness through an Israel he didn't understand, as if ignorant of something deep and essential within himself.

Israel's messy life was the testing ground for Jewish myth. For centuries Jews linked the vindication of Judaism to the messianic ingathering of the exiles into Zion. If we failed to make something worthy of Israel, then all the prayers that anticipated our time would be retroactively discredited. If we squandered the return to Jerusalem, we would destroy the sacred history of the Jews.

I had to be a part of this crazy place. Perhaps only now, having made some peace with being an American, could I move here — not as a refugee fleeing an alien identity but as an *oleh,* an ascender to the Land.

And Lynn would come with me.

On the phone I told her that, sometime soon, I'd have to return to Israel, to live. "Don't you think I know that?" she said.

Our phone calls weren't conversations but outbursts. "Yossi, you won't believe it," she said, laughing and breathless, "I'm sitting here reading *Exodus,* and it's so corny; Leon Uris is just the worst writer, but I love it; I weep as I'm reading it because it connects me to you."

"Lynnie, we'll be together in Jerusalem."

"I'll try it," she said. "It will be an adventure."

9.

We planned to leave in August 1982. That would give Lynn a year to complete her master's in writing at City College. I was going to

Israel as an immigrant, Lynn as a tourist, an immigrant's friend. She intended to stay a year — enough time, we agreed, for us to decide our future. Neither of us wanted to think about what would happen if Israel didn't work out for her.

As our departure date came closer, Lynn's anxiety, and resentment, grew.

"It's all on me," she said one night. "I'm the one who has to make the big changes. Fall in love with Judaism, fall in love with Israel. I feel like an appendage to you. It's a setup."

"You're right," I said. "But what's our alternative?"

"There is no alternative. That's what makes me angry."

I got my immigrant papers from the Israeli consulate, "temporary resident" status, which after three years would automatically turn into Israeli citizenship. Lynn began Hebrew lessons in the Manhattan office of a Zionist organization. She filled notebooks with Hebrew letters written in a child's careful script. Hebrew letters had always reminded me of tombstone markings; Holocaust poet Nellie Sachs called them "bones." But Lynn turned each letter into her own personal symbol: The curled pe was a womb, the pillared he a gate. In Lynn's hand those letters took on a new innocence for me, as though I too were learning them for the first time.

In June 1982, two months before we were to leave, Israel invaded Lebanon. I paced the streets of Manhattan, from newsstand to newsstand, looking for the latest editions of dailies that might contain a new detail about the fighting. I couldn't wait to be back in Israel, no longer dependent for my news long-distance. Lynn, too, was undeterred: Her fears about Israel had nothing to do with war.

The invasion was intended to destroy the PLO's terrorist "ministate" in Lebanon. I had no doubt about our right to attack the PLO, whose official goal was Israel's disappearance; PLO terror attacks against Jews were small preenactments of that vision.

Still, this was Israel's first "civilian" war. To defeat a few thousand terrorists, we were laying siege to cities in which they were based, cutting off water supplies, bombing neighborhoods. For the first time, Israelis — and American Jews — were being torn apart rather than united by war. Defense Minister Arik Sharon was destroying the only real edge Israel had: the cohesion of its people and their willingness to fight.

As the siege of Beirut continued through the summer, criticism of Israel became hysterical. Israel wasn't being criticized but demonized. So long as you were careful to say "Zionists" instead of "Jews," you could repeat every classic anti-Semitic slander and still remain progressive, humane.

A college friend of Lynn's was staying in our apartment. "I used to admire Israel," he said to me. "I thought it was good that Israel existed, it would help the Middle East develop. But now . . ." Now that Israel was no longer admirable, or good for Middle East development, its right to exist had been revoked.

The anti-Israel lynch mob made it hard for me to admit my own doubts about the war, and I retreated into a bitter defensiveness. I would scan a newspaper report from Beirut without paying attention, unwilling to confront Arab suffering. The exaggerated reaction against Israel seemed to confirm the cynicism of Israeli hardliners. If the survivors wouldn't be saints, they'd be damned as humanity's worst criminals. The world that created Auschwitz and then demonized its survivors didn't deserve the morally anguished Jew; instead, the Jew it deserved was Arik Sharon.

Anti-Semitic terror attacks began in Europe. One night on TV, I saw a Jewish restaurant in Paris that had just been machine-gunned. A secular French Jew stood before the shattered windows and shouted, "I'm going to put on a *big* yarmulke and grow a *long* beard." He was telling the world: *You* think you can judge *us?* To hell with you; we're returning to the ghetto.

I might well have boarded the plane to Israel with that same despairing rage, slamming the door behind me as I moved to the ultimate Jewish ghetto — had I not been leaving with Lynn. Whatever else Lynn meant to me, she was a reminder that I could no longer slip into the pose of aggrieved Jew against the world. By going with Lynn, I was validating the old Zionist notion that, in ending our exile from the Land, we would also end our exile from the nations; that our return to Israel would open a new — messianic — relationship between Gentiles and Jews.

I thought of Muresán, the man who'd kept my father alive in the hole. Lynn was my spiritual Muresán, keeping me from dying to the world.

The Kennedy Airport terminal of Israel's airline, El Al, felt like a fortress. Israeli security agents scanned the crowds, missing nothing. When I briefly left my suitcases unattended, one of the security men instantly appeared and warned me against careless-ness.

Watching them move among us, I thought of something my father had said after the "Munich Massacre," the murder of eleven Israeli athletes by PLO terrorists at the 1972 Olympics. For me, the massacre had meant simply that Jews were being killed again in Germany, ironic proof of how little had changed for us. But my father, an optimist ever since the Six-Day War, said the massacre showed how much Israel's existence had improved our situation: Thirty years ago, millions of Jews were killed and the papers barely noticed; but now, wary of Israeli retaliation, the whole world was busy with the murder of eleven Jews.

I had laughed then at his peculiarly Jewish optimism. But he was right. If we were still among the most endangered people, we were now also among the most protected. That was progress.

The plane filled with noisy, quarrelsome Jews. Babies screamed; yeshiva girls in denim skirts shouted to friends on the other end of the plane; oblivious Hasidim prayed in the aisles; secularists mim-icked their rapid mumbling. Dour stewardesses dismissed reasonable requests as intrusions, treating passengers like stowaways.

Here we were, the Jews. We regarded one another with the con-tempt of people who've known each other in unbearably intimate places — constantly accusing each other of that worst Jewish crime, betrayal of the ancestral legacy.

"I can't believe what a scene this is," Lynn said. "It's so *alive.*" She kept pointing out absurd details around us. But when we weren't laughing together, I could see the strain on her face, as she won-dered what place she had in my Zionist drama.

We entered Ben-Gurion Airport. An old man speaking American-accented Hebrew called out, "Any immigrants!" He introduced himself as Al, a volunteer from an American immigrants' association that helped fellow immigrants through the airport paperwork. "You've made the right choice," Al said to me. "Nobody's going to call you a Jew-boy here."

"That's true," I said, "but they'll call you everything else."

Lynn and I followed Al upstairs, to the room where immigrants were processed. The room was filled with plastic orange chairs, every one of them empty, reminders of all the Diaspora Jews who weren't coming home. Al urged us to help ourselves to the tea and cookies that were the only sign of welcome. "Where are the immigration officials?" I asked.

"Don't worry," he said. "You'll be taken care of."

It was hours, of course, before any officials appeared. Al meanwhile corralled a few more immigrants. There was a young man from San Francisco with a thin mustache and a thin lavender tie and a rabbi with many children and with diaper boxes for luggage, on which was written their destination: Kiryat Arba, the West Bank. There was a woman, recently divorced, who'd never been to Israel but decided to "try it" — not as a tourist but as an immigrant. Her young son shouted, "I hate this stupid place!" and collapsed, hysterical on the floor. Jews coming to Israel used to kiss the ground; this boy beat it with his fists.

The immigration official read form questions to me without raising his eyes. Then he asked my father's name. Zoltan, I said. For the first time, he looked at me. "Hungarian?" he asked. I nodded. "Me too," he said, smiling. Until then, I'd been just another Jew. But now we had a real connection: We were Hungarians.

I was given a little blue booklet in which to record the tax-free purchases allowed to immigrants and that identified me as an "A-1," a temporary resident. I wanted to mark my arrival with a toast, or at least a congratulatory handshake; but how do you celebrate receiving an "A-1" identity card?

Exhausted, Lynn and I were sent downstairs to another official, whose job was to put immigrants in taxis to their places of destination. The taxi was paid for by the government: the first and last free ride, I told Lynn, that a Jew got in Israel. "I don't want them to pay for me," she said tersely. "I'm not an immigrant."

We waited while the official argued with a cabbie about the price of our trip. The cabbie didn't want to take us; he could fill his taxi with tourists and make real money. The official pleaded my case: He's an immigrant, just off the plane. The cabbie was unmoved. Finally, they settled on a price, and Lynn and I rode through pine-covered hills to Jerusalem.

Epilogue

Nagy-Károly

I.

WE LIVED on the border of Jerusalem. Just beyond our white stone building, the very last in the city, rose the hills of the Judean desert. On a clear winter day you could see the Dead Sea from our porch; at night, lights in Jordan dotted the horizon.

Lynn became a Jew. Shortly after arriving in Jerusalem, we'd befriended an American-born rabbi and his wife, a convert; eventually Lynn moved into their home, partly to learn how to live as a religious Jew, partly to separate from me. She didn't want me hovering over her; she would convert on her terms, not mine. She confided little to me of her conversion process. I respected the intimacy of her transformation and didn't pry. Late at night, when the tourists had gone and only a few solitary Hasidim remained, she would go to the Western Wall and offer her hesitant Hebrew prayers to the God of Israel.

She changed her name to Sarah and asked that I stop calling her Lynn. She chose that name, she said, because, like Sarah, mother of Israel, she too was founding a new Jewish line.

We married. On her insistence we became religious Jews; in a way, I too converted to Judaism.

Observing Judaism with Sarah felt nothing like the practice by rote I'd known as a boy. She performed each ritual with intense concentration, with her customary attention to detail. And through her eyes I saw the power of sanctifying a physical act, saw Judaism in its pristine vitality, stripped of social deadening and historical trauma.

Sometimes, though, I'd laugh at her stubborn exactness. Cleaning the house for Passover took us a month: We scrubbed every corner, shook the pages of every book to ensure that no crumb of forbidden leaven was embedded in the cracks. Sarah explained the symbolism of the search: Leaven, a swelling of the grain, represented ego, an exaggerated sense of self; that is why the Israelites leaving Egypt for the desert took no food with them except for unleavened bread, trusting God's benevolence and surrendering to his will.

I appreciated the imagery and her attempt to explain something of the process that had turned Lynn into Sarah. Still, a month of cleaning seemed to me excessive. When I complained, she said, "This is my Jewish childhood. I have to know what it feels like to live completely inside the tradition, to trust it. Questions can come later."

"All right," I said, "but when you become a Jewish teenager, let me know."

I had long felt that some drastically new form of Judaism, strange and unexpected, must emerge from our experience in this century. Perhaps Sarah and I would experiment together; but that could only come later, once she became fully confident as a Jew. For now, I was back in conventional Judaism.

And yet our Jewish life together did seem to me radically new — as though we were Abraham and Sarah, beginning our own history. What, after all, could be stranger and more unexpected for a Borough Park Jew than to be reconciled with Judaism through a woman who'd once been Christian?

2.

Beginning in the summer of 1989, I was sent on a series of trips to Eastern Europe by several American Jewish weeklies, for whom I wrote from Jerusalem. The Soviet bloc had begun to dissolve, and I followed the collapsing dominoes: in Poland when the Solidarity government took power, in Berlin when the Wall fell, in Prague just after the Velvet Revolution.

Eastern Europe, graveyard of the Holocaust, was the centerpoint of the Jewish-Christian wound. I believed that Eastern Europeans were virtually genetic anti-Semites, whose only complaint against Hitler was that he'd left too many Jews alive. That, at least, was the conventional Jewish wisdom.

I did encounter anti-Semitism in my travels, ugly remarks and graffiti. But I also discovered a different Eastern Europe, and countries that had been nothing more than names on a massive tombstone suddenly came alive for me. Wherever I went I met goodwill. In chance encounters at train stations and meetings in schools, I found young people eager to know Jews, learn something of this people who had been so central to their cultures but who had vanished just before they were born.

Living in Israel and becoming part of a Jewish majority had helped me relax around Christians and Christian symbols. As a journalist, I'd written about monks in Jerusalem who were incorporating Hebrew prayers into their worship, who lit menorahs and fasted on Yom Kippur, searching for the Jewish roots of their faith. Their attempt to undo Christianity's long contempt for Judaism helped me realize that Jews, too, needed a measure of humility, needed to stop denigrating Christianity as an anti-Semitic religion or a second-rate "Judaism for the goyim" and to start acknowledging its spiritual authenticity, its devotion and prayer.

In Kraków I met with several dozen young Dominican monks. Until the Solidarity revolution, such a meeting would have been inconceivable, forbidden by the communists and by mutual suspicion between Poles and Jews. For two hours we discussed Poland's post-communist future and Israel's struggle for survival, monastic contemplation and Hasidic prayer. We felt exhilarated by our encounter, by release from awkwardness and fear. We were religious people, who cherished our respective traditions as well-traveled paths to God but who were trying to sift out the useless resentments we'd inherited with our faith. The Jews had returned to Israel, the Poles had freed Poland, and now we could become acquainted from a distance in a way our ancestors hadn't managed as neighbors.

I was asked to say a prayer in Hebrew. With bowed heads and closed eyes, the young monks listened as I recited the Twenty-third Psalm: "Though I walk through the valley of the shadow of death . . ." We were sitting together, a few hours' drive from Auschwitz, brothers in prayer, transcending borders.

As I traveled through the disintegrating Soviet bloc, I found myself sharing with Eastern Europeans a common victory and joy. My youth had been defined by struggle against the Soviet Union; now that war had been won, thanks largely to the courage of Eastern Europeans. Suddenly I discovered a common language with Hungarian nationalists and Polish priests: We had all in our various ways resisted the Soviet empire, whose depravity had been minimized by Western liberals but which we understood.

With the abrupt collapse of communist power, the gates of the Soviet Union completely opened, and hundreds of thousands of Soviet Jews were converging on Ben-Gurion Airport, bringing with them pianos and poodles. At the same time, the Soviet-led diplomatic siege against Israel lifted. One Eastern European country after another rushed to renew relations with the Jewish state, and Third World countries were following. The thwarted promise of Zionism — to transform the Jews from a pariah people into a respected nation among nations — was finally happening. Suddenly the premises I'd grown up on were becoming obsolete.

In fact, I'd begun feeling the inadequacy of viewing reality through the Holocaust even before my travels in Eastern Europe. When my first child, Moriah, was born in 1985, I'd moved my substantial collection of Holocaust books to higher shelves, to make sure she wouldn't accidentally stumble onto some scene of atrocity. Unnecessarily, I removed even those volumes without photographs, as though I were not only trying to protect Moriah but also making a statement to myself: These books aren't central to your life anymore.

As Moriah got older, I told her stories about her grandfather, how he'd hid in a hole from bad people and how a good person named Muresán risked his life to bring food. But I didn't tell her much more than that. There was time, I thought, for the rest of the story.

But I'd forgotten about Israeli education. One day Moriah returned from kindergarten and said to Sarah and me, "I bet you don't know how Heetler killed the Jews."

"How?" I asked, startled.

"He put them in bathtubs and, instead of water, gas came out," she said, beaming, delighted to know something her parents apparently didn't.

"Not bathtubs, sweetheart," I said. "Showers."

"Of course they were bathtubs," she replied. "You can't have showers without bathtubs."

My father filled me with Holocaust stories because he had no choice. Those were, after all, *his* stories; and he urgently needed to violate the near-total silence surrounding the Holocaust in the early postwar years. But silence was hardly our problem anymore. I wanted my children to be filled with the strength of Jewish history and their family's experience, to know that there was nothing that couldn't be survived. But I had no intention of raising them as I'd been raised, of placing the grim lessons of Nagy-Károly at the center of their lives.

3.

The town of Carei lies on the Transylvanian plain, surrounded by forest. Traffic along the two-lane road leading into town is slowed by bicycles and horse-drawn buggies. The most significant change here in the last fifty years is symbolized by the town's name: Before 1945 Carei was known in Hungarian as Nagy-Károly; but as penalty for Hungary's support for Hitler, Nagy-Károly — and the rest of Transylvania — was given by the Allies to Romania and became Carei.

I arrived in Carei in July 1990 with a three-day visa. I wasn't sure why I'd come "back," what I expected to find in this place that had symbolized for me the abyss between Jews and Gentiles, Jacob and Esau. I certainly had no nostalgia for Nagy-Károly: My father had taught me his own contempt for his town, with its self-deluding Jews denying their approaching doom and their gentile neighbors happily anticipating the Jews' disappearance.

Carei in the summer of 1990 was devastated by neglect. It seemed to exist only formally, its life force gone. Much of the town was covered by squat housing projects whose facades had once been painted

yellow and brown; some apartments were missing windows. Weeds
as tall as sunflowers grew in empty lots. A stone fountain in the park
was filled not with water but with broken glass. The pavement was
cracked; machinery rusted in factory yards. What broke here wasn't
repaired but left exposed, to decay.

The stores offered parodies of commerce. Many didn't bother hanging signs outside or left their display windows empty. In the grocery —
which, despite Transylvania's ample farmland, had no eggs, milk, or
butter — one entire wall was stocked with identical jars of stewed
prunes, another wall lined with opaque bottles missing labels and filled
with murky liquid. The clothing store window displayed a fur hat and
a pair of giant mittens — it was July — and a wedding veil, like random items from a rummage sale. There was a "pot store," which displayed three identical pots. The window of what was presumably a
hardware store held a pair of scales, axes without handles, a hammer
head: artifacts in an exhibit of a dead civilization.

It didn't really matter that there was nothing to buy: Romanian
money was almost worthless, not even convertible across the border
in Hungary — which Romanians longed for the way Hungarians
longed for America. The real currency here was packs of Kent cigarettes, bartered from hand to hand, symbols of a distant prosper-
ity.

Though the Jews were gone, other ethnic enmities lingered among
Carei's 30,000 inhabitants: Romanians against Hungarians,
Romanians and Hungarians against Gypsies. Once Hungarians had
been the majority in Transylvania, but Romanian settlers reduced
them to an intimidated minority. Hungarian was forbidden to be
taught in schools or spoken in offices; parents, forbidden to give their
children Hungarian names. What remained of Nagy-Károly's anti-
Semitism was its essence, random hatred — as if hatred were a living force sustained by schisms, finding substitute grievances to feed
on when old ones became obsolete.

Six months earlier Romania's communist dictator, Nicolae
Ceausescu, had been deposed; but in Carei there was no joy or hope.
People spoke of the new, supposedly democratic leaders in whispers;
some were afraid to denounce them in their own homes. Elsewhere
in Eastern Europe the communists had been replaced by democratic dissidents, but in Romania one group of communists had usurped

another. Here, change was merely another variation of despair; here, the past was never resolved.

I was a guest in the home of Laszlo Gados, a Carei businessman. Laszlo called himself an "importer-exporter." When I asked him what exactly he imported and exported, he answered, "Whatever I can get." He was necessarily vague about details: Business in Romania meant black marketeering, just as in the anarchic days after World War II.

Laszlo was, like me, in his mid-thirties. He was a large, friendly man, with a big laugh and extravagant energy and ambitions. Mostly he wore running suits and moved so vigorously that he seemed constantly about to break into a trot. He lived in an old handsome house with many rooms and high gilt-edged ceilings and drove a new black BMW, which seemed in Carei's gray streets like an apparition from a futuristic world. But in fact his lifestyle only mimicked wealth: Most of the rooms of his home were empty; his BMW usually low on gas.

I had met Laszlo through a friend of my father's, a former Carei Jew named Yidu who lived in Borough Park but returned to Carei every year on pilgrimage, praying at the local Jewish cemetery, in which lay those who'd died before the Holocaust and therefore had burial sites. Whenever Yidu came to Carei, he stayed with Laszlo, though Laszlo was a Christian and Yidu, very Orthodox.

For Laszlo, the Holocaust, and the postwar flight of nearly all the survivors to the West, had been Transylvania's great tragedy — though his reasoning was hardly sentimental. Since the Jews "went away," as he put it, nothing had worked in Transylvania. "When the Jews were here, business was business and shops were shops. Wherever they go, Jews make money; and everyone prospers with them. But we were stupid enough to chase them away."

Laszlo's plan for saving Romania from itself was to lure back the Holocaust survivors and their children, who would help him and the few other "normal people here," as he put it, create a functioning society. "I would put Jewish businessmen at the head of every government department," he said. "And offer them the best salaries."

I had expected Laszlo, a decent man, to feel some pain, if not guilt, about the Jews' disappearance from his town; but all he seemed capable of was an entirely selfish regret. I felt an old maliciousness returning: Laszlo's misery pleased me. Carei's depletion seemed to me just, its missing vitality a punishment for the fate of the Jews. The anti-Semites of my father's generation had a slogan: "The Jews are our misfortune." And now here was Laszlo, longing for the Jews as his lost fortune. What better revenge on Nagy-Károly?

Laszlo told me that his house had been owned, before the war, by Jews. His proof was that, twice a year, during the equinox, at precisely one A.M., the light of the full moon would illumine the old tiles on the living room floor and reveal a Star of David. Laszlo didn't say how he'd discovered this strange fact, but he insisted it was true.

He seemed pleased to be living in a Jewish home, as though it were a good-luck charm, inhabiting the house of plenty. The story pleased me, too: Carei was haunted by its vanished Jews.

4.

I walked Carei's silent streets, watching the grim faces. People's clothes were faded, resembling the facades of Carei's buildings — as if deliberately suppressing brightness, like someone long confined to a dark room who found light painful. In the housing projects, barefoot children with open sores played in pools of mud.

All around town, in the patches of earth along the sidewalk where grass should have grown, were abandoned vegetable gardens, tangles of dried roots and yellowed leaves. Ceausescu had ordered that every strip of earth be used to grow vegetables and increase the harvest. After his overthrow, the hated patches of lettuce and beets were left to wither. And so this town with almost no produce for sale became garlanded with dead vegetables.

That was the kind of detail Laszlo loved telling about Ceausescu and Romania. Laszlo was full of stories about the Great Leader, a latter-day Dracula feeding off the vitality of his people and implicating them, through their fearful submission, in his madness. Laszlo claimed that in the palace Ceausescu built for himself was a toilet that provided computer printouts of the contents of his excrement, that when Ceausescu visited a construction site, workers would be ordered to face the wall so as not to glimpse the leader. Once he phoned the government TV station in the middle of a news broadcast and ordered the anchorman to shave his mustache; the screen went blank, and the newscaster returned fifteen minutes later, without a mustache.

One day it was announced that the Father of the People was coming to visit his happy children in Carei. In the groceries, unimagined delicacies suddenly appeared. On the day of the visit, all the people were ordered out of their homes and into the streets. Word came: In ten minutes, Father's motorcade will be arriving. And so for the next ten minutes, marshals led the people in nonstop applause. Then he appeared; abruptly, the clapping stopped. The Great Leader passed through town in total silence.

I had grown up on Transylvanian horror stories, and now Laszlo offered me updates of the genre. There was, of course, an immeasurable gap between Laszlo's stories and mine: His were about a deranged leader humiliating and impoverishing his people; mine were about gas chambers.

And yet the true difference between us couldn't be determined abstractly, by whose stories were more grotesque, but by our actual lives. My family had escaped its Transylvanian nightmare, which for me existed only in stories of the past; while Laszlo was trapped in his stories.

Had my father stayed in Transylvania, Laszlo's life could have been an approximate model for mine. But my family had moved on, while Laszlo lived in a place where historical change was measured by new miseries displacing old ones. I couldn't resent him for not mourning the destruction that had happened here before he was born; I couldn't even fault his obsession with Jewish businessmen, his attempt to find any exit, however desperate and crass, from his dying town.

I didn't want him to pay for the crimes of the past. That wasn't justice; that only compounded the tragedy of this place.

I searched for traces of my family, but every inquiry ended in disappointment. Yes, said the few old Jews left in town, we remember your grandfather; one man recalled that several Josef Kleins had lived here, and so my grandfather was known as "Klein Soros," Klein Beer, because he dealt in alcohol. But that was the most intimate detail Carei could summon. It was as if my family had passed through here just long enough for its presence to be formally registered — but beyond that, nothing.

The old Conservative synagogue still stood, an empty shell. Oddly, its handsome facade, capped with crowns, had recently been painted, probably by the Jewish community in Bucharest, which managed Romania's abandoned synagogues. Inside, whatever could be removed had long ago been taken. The Torah ark was open and bare. Dust and cobwebs covered the rotting pews.

In the Jewish cemetery I searched among the rows of crooked stones, surrounded by tall grass, for the name of an uncle who'd died before the war; but I couldn't find him. Then I came to a dome upheld by pillars and surrounded by scaffolding, though there was no trace of workers. The dome covered a marble slab that rose high above my head and on which were engraved the names of Nagy-Károly's four thousand Jews killed in the war. I read through the names, which weren't listed alphabetically, as though the survivors who'd built this monument couldn't impose minimal order on their shattered world — and found the name of my grandfather. My name.

For a moment I felt the thrill of recognition, of "belonging"; the same sensation I'd felt when, arriving in town for the first time, I'd seen the sign "Carei" and involuntarily thought: It's real! When I was a boy, I'd doubted this town existed, doubted whether there really was a man named Josef Klein. The details of my father's prewar life seemed mere props for the lessons he was trying to impart; now I wanted to reclaim the family history buried in those stories.

I continued scanning the list of names and found other Josef Kleins. I felt cheated: I didn't know which name was "mine."

Finally, I felt absurd. There was nothing of my past to recover here, nothing in these ruins that would enhance my sense of self. Even mourning was elusive. Despite my best efforts, I'd experienced little grief since arriving in Carei. Guiltily, I'd felt almost as if I were visiting Spain five hundred years after the expulsion of the Jews — more curious than anguished.

Perhaps I would have felt a stronger connection to Carei's Jewish past had I still been an American Jew. Then, I might have longed for Europe's lost Jewish vitality or seen its ruins as an intimation of Diaspora vulnerability, a rebuke to my own sense of security.

But Nagy-Károly's helpless Jewish death posed no threat to me.

I was an Israeli and, like other Israeli men, for one month a year was a soldier. My reality was so far removed from Nagy-Károly that the distance separating me from this place should have been measured in centuries, not decades.

The gift of my father's generation to mine was to have survived so well that I couldn't inhabit its mourning. My Jewish present was too full to accommodate nostalgia for a shattered past. Living in Jerusalem, I didn't need to sift for roots in Transylvania's scorched earth; I'd found a deeper root on which to graft my two children.

Every fall, on the holiday of *Sukkot*, Sarah and I would turn our porch into a *sukkah*, or booth: walls of cloth and a roof of pine branches, from which dangled paper cutouts made by our children. The side of the *sukkah* facing the Judean desert was left exposed, drawing the hills that softened beneath the gathering clouds. In the early morning I would sit on the *sukkah*'s woolen bedouin rug, head covered with a silver-striped white prayer shawl, children on my lap; and together we would hold the holiday's *lulav* and *etrog*, palm frond and citron, fruits of the Land of Israel, and say the blessing thanking God for preserving us for this day. At that moment there was nothing to long for, nothing to regret; everything I wanted was here.

My father's house was on a narrow street just off Carei's main avenue. It was a small, red-roofed stucco building. My father had described the house he'd grown up in as a mansion; but whatever it was before the war, it certainly was no mansion anymore.

A short, stocky man was tending the garden patch just inside the gate. He wore a long nightshirt and high boots and no pants. I explained that my family had once lived there, before the war, and asked whether he'd let me see the house.

He opened the gate and welcomed me in. He said his name was Schneider and that he'd lived here since the late forties. The tiny living room was cluttered with cheap knickknacks; on the walls hung a carpet painting of a harem scene, a drawing of cartoon characters from an old American TV show. The single graceful ornament was a silver crucifix; I felt pleased that religious people still lived there.

I told Schneider I'd expected a bigger house. Yes, he said, it had been larger when he'd moved in after the war but the communists divided the building into three separate little houses. Then he hastily added that my grandparents' house had in fact been demolished twenty years ago, and the three houses that stood in its place were entirely new. His house certainly looked older than twenty years, but for some reason it seemed important to him that I believe that no trace of my grandparents' house remained.

I asked what he thought of Romania's new government. He pretended to laugh and said, "Why talk politics?" as though dissuaded not by fear but by indifference.

Schneider's wife, who avoided eye contact with me, served sour wine and unsweetened, soggy wafers. I asked Schneider how he coped with the food shortage, and he answered with a Romanian joke: "Pork is available in two varieties: Good pork and bad pork. The bad pork is better: It lasts longer."

I asked about his life, and he responded by reciting a list of all the conquerors he'd known: the Romanians, the Hungarians, the Germans, the Russians, and then the Romanians again. His father, of German origin, had been deported to Siberia after the war, along with tens of thousands of Transylvanian Germans. I wondered if he'd been a Nazi collaborator or just a luckless man with a German name.

With his father in the Gulag, he'd moved into this house along with his grandparents. "I remember your father," he said to me. "I remember my grandmother paying him for our home." I didn't know whether Schneider was lying. But his intention was clear: He wanted me to know he wasn't a usurper.

Now I realized why he'd insisted that nothing of the old house remained and why his wife seemed so nervous: They thought I had come to reclaim their home. That wasn't an unreasonable explanation for my sudden appearance at their door: With the fall of communism, old deeds were suddenly resurfacing all over Eastern Europe.

There was something about this scene — the son returning for a glimpse of his lost ancestral home — that echoed uneasily for me as an Israeli. A not uncommon Israeli experience was finding Arab strangers at your door, whose refugee families had once lived in your home and who were now requesting a look around.

I despised the unbearable comparison, sometimes made in the

Western media, between the fate of the Palestinians and of Europe's Jews: The Palestinians were victims of a war that they and their Arab allies initiated and maintained, by treating Israel's existence as a crime. Still, the fact that we hadn't let them destroy us and now occupied them meant that we were no longer entirely innocent. I couldn't return to Nagy-Károly as an accuser; and that, too, marked a crucial difference between being an Israeli and a Diaspora Jew. I wasn't a victim of history anymore, but an active player; I lived, with sadness but no regret, by the rules of the nations.

Just before arriving in Carei, I'd been transferred to an army unit that patrolled the West Bank and Gaza. I hadn't yet served there; but when I'd return to Israel, a call-up notice would be waiting for me for reserve duty in Gaza's refugee camps. For one month a year I would become an occupier: searching bedrooms in the middle of the night, escorting prisoners for interrogation, chasing teenage rock-throwers in alleys where the sewage ran in rivulets.

I would go, because I believed I had no choice. So long as the PLO's "charter" called for Israel's destruction, we were obliged to deny the Palestinians a state. Until they accepted our existence — genuinely, not in mumbled and unfulfilled promises meant for Western audiences — we would continue to enforce their power-lessness and consign ourselves to historical irony.

I thought of my father in this house in the months after the war, tending to his "boarders," the teenage girls just back from the camps: half-mad, hysterical, withdrawn into hardness. What would he have said then, in the midst of that brokenness, had he known that his son's chief burden would be not victimization but power? He would probably have seen my predicament as a kind of Jewish victory.

Schneider escorted me to the gate. I asked, embarrassed, if I could take some earth from his garden as a memento. Not for myself, I quickly added: My father's brother, Uncle Yitzchak, had asked for a vial filled with ancestral ground, intending to place it in his future grave, the way pious Jews in Nagy-Károly had once been buried with a bit of earth from the Land of Israel.

"Go ahead," said Schneider, laughing. "Take all the dirt you want."

It was time to go. I went to Carei's train station and entered the cavernous, shabby waiting room. Then it hit me: This is the place. This is where Nagy-Károly's Jews were brought for deportation. The Nazis hadn't created separate rail routes to Auschwitz, but simply expropriated and implicated the existing system.

I caught the eye of an old man in a railway cap. We stared at each other; he looked momentarily confused, as though something best forgotten had suddenly resurfaced. I turned away.

I tried to envision them here: their suitcases packed with things they wouldn't need, the screaming children, the blows, the desperate reassurances, the anxious faces waiting for the train . . .

But I couldn't see them. Instead, all I saw were the shuffling people around me, in yellow leather jackets and cardboard-colored shoes, bearing old suitcases tied with rope and moving without anticipation from one identical town to the next, where water fountains spouted glass and barefoot children played in mud.

The graceless train heaved into the station. I boarded, without anger or irony. For me, the war was over.

Acknowledgments

Deep gratitude and affection to:

My editor, James H. Silberman, always a gentleman, whose precise and elegant editing made this a much better book;

Pam Bernstein, agent and friend, who believed in this project through its most difficult stages;

Arthur Samuelson, who conceived of this book, convinced me to do it, and understood what it was about long before I did;

Stephen H. Lamont, whose copyediting skills translated my work into proper English;

Sarah, who read too many drafts and whose unerring literary sensibility helped form the final result;

Moriah and Gavriel, for the joy they bring me;

Yoel and Nomi, friends in all ways, who saw me through;

My family — Leo and Breindy, Eve and Tom, Glenn and Chani — on whose generosity I can always depend;

Poet Allen Afterman and journalist Paul Cowan, friends and

mentors who died before the completion of this project, which is in some sense a dialogue with them both;

Hirsh Goodman, editor of *The Jerusalem Report*, who generously accommodated my needs as an author and who made useful suggestions about this work;

My colleagues at *The Report* — Ze'ev Chafets, David Horovitz, Sharon Ashley, Michael Elkins, Calev Ben-David, David Green, Stuart Schoffman, Ya'akov Kirschen — for their literary advice, and to the rest of the staff, for their support and friendship;

Marc Radzyner, for his literary insights over many years;

Jerry and Naomi Lippman, editors of the *Long Island Jewish World*, who gave me a journalistic home and sent me to Eastern Europe in 1989;

William Novak, for his generous friendship; and

Leonard Fein, my patron, a friend in time of need.

And thanks, too, to the following for their sustenance in various ways:

Nina Evtuhov, Becky Michaels, Yeschezkel Landau, Alon Goshen-Gottstein, Sharon and Hananya Goodman, Professor Nathan Winter, Ya'akov Birnbaum, Glenn Richter, Effie Zuroff, Jonathan Mark, Yosef Hacohen, Daniel Ziv, Michael Oren, Mark Mirsky, Steve Brand, Janos Gado, Judit Burg, William Helmreich, Rabbi Rachel Cowan, Sharon Deitch.